DEMOCRACY IN ENGLAND

DEMOCRACY
IN
ENGLAND

BY
DIANA SPEARMAN

THE   MACMILLAN   COMPANY
NEW   YORK

PRINTED IN GREAT BRITAIN BY
A. WHEATON & CO., LTD., EXETER

CONTENTS

ACKNOWLEDGMENTS

A small part of the argument contained in the Introduction appeared in *Time and Tide* and the substance of Chapter I appeared in *History Today* in November 1955. I must thank the editors of both these journals for permission to reproduce them.

I also have to thank Lord Coleraine and Mr. John Wood for their kindness in reading the manuscripts and Miss Chloe Otto and Miss Evelyn Luke for typing them.

NOTE ON REFERENCES

The notes indicated by superior figures throughout the text refer to sources, and these are to be found at the end of the book. All quotations from speeches, after the beginning of the nineteenth century, are from *Hansard*, unless otherwise stated.

INTRODUCTION

EVERYONE in England now agrees that democracy is not merely the best but the only possible form of government for any civilized state. The right of the majority to choose the Government is now so completely accepted that a permanent commission has been set up to keep constituencies arithmetically equal, and the idea that every citizen shall count as one, and none as more than one, has been carried to the extent of abolishing the representation of the Universities in the House of Commons and depriving business men of the right to vote in the constituencies in which they have business premises as well as in those in which they live. The Crown no longer has power, only influence, and the veto of the House of Lords has been reduced to delaying for twelve months any Bill that has passed the House of Commons. The spirit of politics corresponds to the forms; the local influence of great landowners and large employers of labour, which existed up to the 1914 war, has in political matters, vanished. It is difficult if not impossible for a peer to be Prime Minister or Foreign Secretary or indeed to hold any major Cabinet office, except that of Lord President of the Council, an office whose importance is unperceived by the general public. It is one of the chief preoccupations of the constituency associations, particularly in the Conservative party, to make the form and spirit of the associations as democratic as possible. The word 'democratic' in popular usage has become a synonym for admirable or desirable.

But while everyone is agreed that democracy is the best form of government in principle, many people appear to have misgivings about the particular shape which democracy seems to be assuming. While politicians and historians praise the party system as the only effective mechanism for giving effect to the will of the people, the people regard the party organization with suspicion and Members of Parliament are constantly criticized for voting as their leaders decide: in any discussion of politics by people not actively engaged in them, the slavery of the Member to his party is sooner or later certain to be raised. To many people democracy does not seem to have bridged the gap between the Government and the citizen; the expressions 'we' and 'they' are still heard. And, what is more serious, there are some critics who believe that the State has absorbed so much power as to imperil the freedom of the individual, which democracy was originally designed to safeguard.

Criticism is, however, concerned with details. No one challenges the basic assumptions or indeed knows what they are. Democratic theory was formulated for Englishmen by the utilitarian philosophers of the late eighteenth century. We are told that the utilitarian doctrine with its false psychology is dead.[1] Dead in this sense of course means dead in the common-rooms of universities; if the Gallup Poll asked a selected sample of citizens if they agreed that human beings were dominated by a search for happiness and that the aim of government should be the greatest good of the greatest number, ninety-nine out of a hundred would enthusiastically agree. But if these doctrines are wrong, and if each man is not the best judge of his own interests, then there is no basis for believing that majority rule will produce decisions which are either just or adequate, except some form of the theory of the general will. These theories are, however, also generally rejected, having been found more useful to autocratic than to democratic governments.

A lack of interest in theories and an ability to muddle through, are generally regarded as an English trait and as the foundation of English political achievements. A genuine lack of interest in theories, a real conservatism, is a great national asset, but this, the 'stupidity' of which Bagehot boasted, has long since disappeared. Theoretical considerations of a kind are always introduced into even the most pedestrian of election speeches; it is not enough, except in a few instances, simply to offer material or practical advantages, the offer has to be buttressed with arguments showing that they are 'fair' or 'democratic'. The leading articles of even the most popular newspapers are full of theoretical assumptions, such, for example, as that in any dispute between the two Houses the House of Lords must be in the wrong, or that the hereditary constitution of the House of Lords is indefensible. If the writers were asked to defend these assumptions they would no doubt reply that the House of Lords is 'undemocratic', but they would be hard put to it to explain the philosophic basis for universal suffrage. The curious ways in which the word democratic is used are one of the results of this philosophic innocence, but, more important, it confuses people as to which of our modern institutions are essential parts of democracy and which are not. Some of the things about which people complain are indeed the inevitable result of majority rule; but some of them, although essential to democracy as we know it, were never part of democratic theory.

For example, the power of the party machines and the subordination of the Member of Parliament to the party follow from the idea that the party leaders must put a programme before the electorate, which they pledge themselves to carry out if returned. This, however, was no part of the original democratic idea, and it is entirely within the choice of the electorate whether it continues or not. If we were prepared to do without the programme and the pledge, Members of Parliament could be more independent. Most people no doubt would insist on the present form of electioneering, but if they do, it is useless at the same time for them to complain that Members are only rubber stamps.

The liberty of the subject and the rule of law are widely held to be inseparable from political democracy. In England, at any rate, democracy is also, and at the same time, held to be inseparable from the quite contrary doctrine that the majority is sovereign, and that it is either useless or wrong to attempt to place limitations on the power of even a temporary majority. Both these ideas are incorrect. In England democracy was the child of liberty, not liberty of democracy. The rule of law existed in England under Governments which no one would now call democratic. Far from the unlimited sovereignty of the majority being inevitable in a democracy, the most successful of all democracies has a constitution which enshrines fundamental rights and forbids certain actions by the Government even if it should be elected not by a majority but by a unanimous electorate.

If the rule of law and the liberties of the subject are regarded as in some way automatically secured in a democracy, the determination to resist any infringement, which is their only real safeguard, will be relaxed. We have gradually slid from the original conception of a Government with limited powers and of citizens with rights that could not be infringed to the idea of the unlimited sovereignty of the majority. It is true that the unlimited sovereignty of Parliament is an old doctrine, even Blackstone held it in the hey-day of natural rights. But this Parliament was not a single chamber but the King, the House of Lords and the House of Commons together; even the representative House was not elected according to the theory of majority rule, and the sovereignty of Parliament meant something quite different from what it does when the sovereignty is that of a majority in the House of Commons. The idea that a majority, a majority however small or however large, has some kind of sacred right to impose its will on a minority has taken the most extraordinary hold on public opinion. It is constantly said that democracy means that the only possible form of government, even in multi-racial societies, is majority rule based on universal suffrage. For example, during the Cyprus dispute, *The Times* was full of letters claiming that any form of Constitution must entail a permanent majority for the Greeks in the legislature because they were a majority in the country. No theory of democracy ever did say this, some said the exact opposite and it is a conception of democracy which makes it an impossible form of government in any country where there are permanent racial or religious differences.

It may be thought that theories in reality make little difference; for it is now widely held that political ideas are merely leaves floating on the surface of the river, showing which way the water is running, but making no difference to the deep currents beneath. This view completely undermines the foundations of democracy, which is based on a free choice made by reasonable people, reasonable not in any transcendental sense but in the sense of ordinary everyday psychology. It assumes that people will choose what will benefit themselves or their families and that they know roughly what this is. They may be mistaken, but if they are, the mistake arises from an inability to understand all the conditions or to calculate all the consequences, not from ignorance of their own real wishes. Democracy is based on this psychology. It is a theory of choice. Choice may be based on selfish or on altruistic grounds or on a mixture of both. The system will work whether the citizen decides on what he believes to be best for himself or on what he believes to be best for the whole country. It will not work if there is no possibility of free choice, if the choice is already decided by forces of which the individual is unaware and, even worse, which have nothing to do with the issues involved.

The two philosophies which have had most influence on popular ideas—Marxism and psychoanalysis—both maintain that it is not possible for anyone to choose, because the choice is already made, according to Marx by the individual's class interest, according to Freud by his childhood's experience.

The materialist conception of history explains the whole process of history by changes in the methods of production. Different methods demand different social institutions and a different relationship between classes. "Political and social institutions are thus dependent upon and derive their special forms from the underlying economic circumstances of the society in which they exist." The theory, quite apart from whether or not it is an adequate explanation of particular events, suffers from the defect of all theories which attempt to explain history by one factor and one factor only. It accounts for victory and defeat, the growth of a great art and its disappearance, revolution in France and reaction in England, by the same mechanism. Used in this wholesale way it ceases to be an explanation and is reduced to a static background, other and secondary causes have to be elaborated for the actual events.

Technical changes do indeed produce reactions which extend far beyond the actual methods of production, it makes a difference whether people travel by coach, by train or by aeroplane; it also matters what they read while they are travelling, Marx may be as persuasive in an aeroplane as he was in a train, or Burke as he was in a coach. History consists of the interaction of many different factors, not the dominance of one. Marxism is based, moreover, on an old-fashioned scientific determinism; it and all those theories of history variously described as scientific or philosophical were modelled on Newtonian physics. Marx was absorbed by the enormous technical changes that were transforming the world. These had grown out of an application of scientific theories and it is not surprising that Marx adopted the current scientific philosophy as the basis of his work; indeed there was no other for him to accept, and by the middle of the nineteenth century its propositions appeared self-evident to all educated men. There was also a soothing familiarity about the explanation of social phenomena in the terms of physics.

Montesquieu started the first chapter of *L'Esprit des Lois* with the following paragraph: "Law, in its most extended meaning, is the necessary relation which derives from the nature of things, and in this sense all beings have their laws; the Divine mind has its laws, the material universe has its laws . . . man has his laws."

He shows clearly what he means by law by referring to the relations between mass and velocity in Newtonian mechanics. It was not, however, until the nineteenth century that the idea was given its fullest application. It became an axiom that any study was or was not a science according as to whether it was able to make correct predictions, because classical physics was able to do so; indeed this ability to predict was one of its most striking characteristics. Laplace, for example, said that if a mind could exist which was capable of knowing the exact state of the universe at any given moment and also understood the laws which govern all natural phenomena, it would automatically know, not only the past and the present, but also the future. It is this assumption which underlies the idea that deterministic theories of history are somehow more 'scientific' than others. 'As every schoolboy knows' all this is now changed, we are told that even classical physics was not deterministic[2] and modern theories have replaced inflexible laws by statistical probabilities. This conception of the universe, called by Einstein "the God with the dice box",[3] is much more manageable than the laws supposedly revealed by classical physics for anyone trying to deal with social or historical situations, because however upsetting to previously held ideas about 'cause', it is much nearer to the ordinary common-sense approach to history and politics.

Determinism expelled from matter has, however, taken refuge in mind. Some of the theories of modern psychology are exaggerated and some are without valid foundations, but it is not possible to ignore the weight of evidence for an unconscious element in the human mind. This evidence comes from many unrelated sources, the researches of Janet as well as those of Freud and from the investigations into psychic phenomena. Modern psychology magnifies and expands the irrational element in any form of government as much as in the human mind. To this extent it supports Burke's attitude to political problems. Burke must surely be the political philosopher of psychiatrists but he did not go so far as some modern psychologists. He simply distrusted the ability of the conscious mind to construct new forms of society, but although he accepted the doctrine of original sin, he did not suppose that there was in human nature an element of sheer destructiveness or a desire for suffering. If this kind of analysis is accepted a great deal of political theory becomes either superficial or irrelevant and judgments of historical events may also be altered. For example, the unconscious wishes of a population may have created a form of society which suited them. The conscious mind may subsequently reject it under the influence of the success of other forms elsewhere, or foreign ideas, or of the persuasion of individuals with exceptional temperaments. Yet the unconscious part of the mind may prevent a real acceptance of the innovations and ensure the failure of the new forms. The ostensible cause of popular discontent may not be the real cause. Indeed, a theory of society could be constructed on the Freudian hypothesis, which would maintain that everyone occupied in the social hierarchy the position which he in reality wished to occupy, and any resentment consciously felt was caused by a psychological need to feel resentment rather than by any objective social facts.

These theories are more damaging to the accepted idea of democracy than even historic materialism itself. It is not so much that the experiences of early childhood may determine a man's whole political attitude, or that when he believes himself to be defending order or liberty, he is projecting into the external world conflicts which really exist in his own personality. Even more destructive is the view that these forces are not, and cannot be, apprehended by the individual himself, at least unless he undergoes a prolonged and expensive course of treatment, and it is even then uncertain whether he will be free from unconscious motive.

It used to be said that all political theory must start from a theory of human nature. This was all very well when theories of human nature were themselves constructed by political theorists. We are now faced with a more difficult problem. There is a direct contradiction, admitted by nearly all who have made a special study of it, between the psychology of man as known to psychologists and the psychology of man as it is known to political theorists and practical politicians. To politicians, for whom after all accurate diagnosis is essential because it means the difference between success or failure, people seem to pursue their own interests in a perfectly rational way. They may make mistakes, but in the ordinary view these mistakes are due to lack of knowledge or to a tendency to overrate an immediate advantage in comparison with a distant one. For example, weekly wage-earners take a completely rational attitude to wage claims: they would like as high wages as they can get. Other people may think that demands for higher wages in some circumstances are not conducive to the real welfare of the wage-earners themselves. If this is true their persistence is, however, due to a lack of knowledge of the facts of Great Britain's economic position, or to a mistaken belief that everyone else is benefiting at their expense. These may be intellectual failings; they are not irrational in the sense that either Marxist or psychoanalytical theory demands. It is true that books are from time to time published purporting to explain industrial disputes in psychological, even in Freudian, rather than financial terms. It is difficult to accept these views, especially as workers' attitudes to demands for higher pay are influenced by public opinion; during a war, for instance, they will not always be prepared to strike when they would in peacetime. This is strictly speaking the influence of an idea, that of patriotism, of loyalty to the country, or whatever it may be called.

A man's political views may be influenced, or even determined, by the emotional atmosphere of his childhood; but granted this, we know no more about him from the political point of view than we did before. If a man hated his father, he will probably be a rebel. What then? In the nineteenth century he would probably have been a Radical, but by no means certainly. In modern England he might, it is true, join the Communist party. On the other hand, he might refuse to join a trade union, or become a pacifist, or an ardent supporter of the policies of Dr. Malan. It is these secondary choices which are of interest to political theorists.

There is thus a gulf between political and psychological theories. Might it not be possible to cross this gulf by the recognition that politics are concerned with the ideas and wishes which men share? Unconscious motives and wishes are private to the individual, they are rarely expressed in words, and sometimes they are incapable of being so expressed. But if people want other people to take action, they must communicate their wishes, and in the modern world, at any rate, the only way in which wishes can be expressed is in words. Ideas expressed in words are conscious ideas. There is, no doubt, a process called by Freudians rationalization, by which reasons are produced for actions which are really undertaken for quite different motives. We all know politicians in whom the process is obvious. But ideas once formulated have power to canalize desires, both conscious and unconscious, into particular directions. European peasants have been discontented, and sometimes their discontent flared up into rebellion; but it required a framework of theory to mobilize this discontent into a demand for democratic government. The Chartist programme would probably have been economic, not political if it had not been for the activities of the philosophic Radicals. It is the demands, not their underlying content, which are the subject-matter of politics.

If this is granted, more attention must be paid to what people say about their views than has been the custom lately. The class analysis of historical situations tells us less about the real motives than the old-fashioned habit of taking people's professions at their face value. Even the irrational must be communicated in words to other people if it is to have any effect; there were irrational elements in National Socialism and in the Mau Mau, but if the emotions inspired the 'myths' in which they were embodied, the myths also canalized the emotions into a definite direction. The mere fact of putting thoughts or emotions into words changes them even if the words are only symbolic or misleading. The expression of a desire, a want, an intuition may strengthen it, weaken it or even make it vanish. Analytical psychology itself insists on the importance of the process. Once the unconscious wish has been brought to consciousness it may lose its power, once the patient has told the psychiatrist of the forgotten experience it ceases to haunt him.

The formulation of a definite creed, even of one based on the most selfish class interest, may change the original motives even to the extent of transforming them. It is possible to think that the Revolution of 1688 was inspired by the economic interests of large landowners, but it is impossible not to see that the arguments by which it was justified made men behave differently. The most inveterate place-hunter, the stupidest Tory squire, the most arrogant 'grandee' had to act within a pattern in which the theory of the social contract, natural law and natural rights formed a conspicuous part. This made them perceive even their own interests rather differently from the way these appeared to the same kind of person in France or Italy.

There is, however, an even more fundamental reason than the necessity of communication, which makes ideas or theories of supreme political importance. This is the limitation of each man's experience. No one can make any political decisions or indeed any decision at all out of his own experience alone because he has to be able to estimate (whether correctly or not is for the moment irrelevant) his own experience and position in relation to the whole framework in which he lives. He may come in contact with the State in the person of the post office clerk who pays his family allowances or old age pension; but to comprehend the process through which he gets it he has to understand the system of government under which he lives. To judge whether or not he is getting any real benefit he must calculate and set off the sum he pays in taxes against the benefit; if he finds that this leaves him on the debit side, he must calculate the advantages he derives from the knowledge that other people who need it more are getting the same payment, the political value of a contented working class, the economic value of healthy children. All these go on far beyond his own experience.

Scientists when confronted with this type of situation construct a 'model'. Astronomers, for example, cannot know directly what the universe is like, they therefore draw up a blue-print, or a series of blue-prints, which seem to be consistent with the features of the universe as known to them. Economists have lately taken to the same method. The ordinary man, when he thinks about politics, also constructs a 'model' of a world which he cannot know directly. This will be built first out of his own experience, for that will be the most important to him, but since he will not have enough material out of this alone, he will have to incorporate other elements. These will be supplied to him by others through education, political propaganda, literature and innumerable other sources. A great many of these sources will not be contemporary at all. It is one of the main difficulties of politics that the model which everyone has in mind is never up to date, because it takes time to collect and to interpret the materials out of which it is constructed. Words, ideas, theories linger on from one period to another, sometimes forming a criterion by which new developments can be judged, sometimes obscuring the real issues and hiding fundamental changes.

Democratic ideas grew up in the eighteenth century and were the result of the impact of changing conditions on the accepted 'model'. For although the materialist conception of history is wrong in regarding changes in production as the sole, initiatory cause of events, yet they are one cause. Similar changes, however, produced quite different ideas and quite different events in eighteenth-century England and in nineteenth-century Russia, for people saw them in a different light. We know that we do not see the external world as it really is, but as our senses choose to present it to us. Our picture of the contemporary scene is similarly a selection only from a vast amount of data. Which items are selected depends partly on individual temperament, but to an even greater extent on the 'model' of the world which we have inherited. This will make us expect to see certain things and, by doing so, will blind us to others.

The models change from one period to another but they continue to incorporate features which have vanished from the real world and yet still provide part of the framework into which people will fit their own experience. This is why modern democracy cannot be understood without knowing something of the atmosphere out of which it grew and what people thought about it while it was developing. The predominant influence on early democratic ideas both in England and the United States was the eighteenth-century theory of the Constitution.

CHAPTER I

THE OLD CONSTITUTION

I

A PROFOUND belief in the British Constitution and in the virtue of British liberty pervaded every class and opinion in the eighteenth century. The chorus of praise is unanimous from "Rule Britannia" to Cowper's letters, from Horace Walpole, the son of the great Whig Minister, to the Tory Sir Walter Scott, who contrasted "our noble system of masculine freedom" with the unfortunately different arrangements which existed in France.[1]

Today the pre-reform Constitution is generally regarded as a sham or as a joke; as an engine of class domination or as the slightly comic result of our ancestors' lack of political sophistication.

How is it possible to reconcile these two views? Is our idea of liberty so much more penetrating than that of Gibbon and Burke, of Sir Walter Scott and Fielding? We tend to see the old Constitution through the eyes of the nineteenth-century reformers rather than as it appeared to contemporaries before the French Revolution; but there is an even more fundamental divergence; we criticize it in the light of a theory of representative government which nearly every Englishman in the eighteenth century rejected.

Blackstone said: "The political writers of antiquity will not allow more than three regular forms of government."[2] Nor will the political writers of today. But the constitutional theorists of the eighteenth century genuinely believed that they had discovered a form of government which combined the advantages of aristocracy, democracy and monarchy without the disadvantages of any. Blackstone was not a great thinker, nor, it is said, a good lawyer, but he represents better what educated, or even uneducated, people in the eighteenth century believed than more original writers:

> In a democracy, where the right of making laws resides in the people at large, public virtue, or goodness of intentions, is more likely to be found, than either of the other qualities of government. Popular assemblies are frequently foolish in their contrivance, and weak in their execution; but generally mean to do the thing that is right and just, and have always a degree of patriotism or public spirit. In aristocracies there is more wisdom to be found, than in the other frames of government; being composed, or intended to be composed, of the most experienced citizens; but there is less honesty than in a republic, and less strength than in a monarchy. A monarchy is indeed the most powerful of any, all the sinews of government being knit together, and united in the hands of the prince; but then there is imminent danger of his employing that strength to improvident or oppressive purposes.
>
> For, as with us the executive power of the laws is lodged in a single person, they have all the advantages of strength and dispatch, that are to be found in the most absolute monarchy; and, as the legislature of the kingdom is entrusted to three distinct powers, entirely independent of each other; first, the king; secondly, the lords spiritual and temporal, which is an aristocratical assembly of persons selected for their piety, their birth, their wisdom, their valour, or their property; and, thirdly, the House of Commons, freely chosen by the people from among themselves, which makes it a kind of democracy.[3]

The influence of Montesquieu is clear in this passage, but it is probable that Montesquieu himself took his theory of the Constitution from the ideas then current in England. Sir Robert Walpole said in 1734, fourteen years before the publication of *L'Esprit des Lois*: "It is certain that ours is a mixed government, and the perfection of our Constitution consists in this, that the monarchical and the aristocratical and the democratical forms of government are mixed and interwoven so as to give us all the advantages of each without subjecting us to the dangers of either."

And this was the theory of the Constitution until the Reform Bill of 1832.

In accordance with the theory of the separate and independent powers, the Crown and the House of Lords then possessed a position which they have since lost. The Government was supposed to be in more than a conventional sense the King's Government, and organized opposition was considered factious and therefore not really respectable. Not that this prevented opposition; it merely prevented it taking an organized form and contributed to the incoherent nature of parties in the House of Commons. The King's choice of Ministers was, in theory, quite unrestricted; there was, for instance, no obligation on him to choose Ministers from one political party; indeed, until the end of the century opinion was hostile to the whole idea of party; even Chatham never understood the place it would take in representative government. The position of the King was not so strong in practice as in theory; for reasons too well known to repeat, the first two Hanoverian Kings were tied to the Whigs, and George III, even in the early days of his reign, found that he had to choose men who would work together, or at least whose views were not diametrically opposed, and, whatever the theory, it was impossible for the King's influence alone to keep Ministers permanently in power if they were not acceptable to the House of Commons; in moments of political excitement he was forced to take public opinion into account as well. Indeed, there seems to have existed in the old Constitution another balance, not included by Blackstone, a balance between the King and the Cabinet. Independent and powerful men would, when asked to take office, insist on the inclusion of their friends or make other conditions. On the other hand, it was not unknown for members of the Ministry to intrigue with the King against each other.[4]

Besides his strictly constitutional prerogatives, the King had an influence on the House of Commons because, like other great landowners, he had his pocket boroughs, and the patronage at the disposal of the Crown enabled him to 'oblige' Members of Parliament whether they wanted a sinecure for themselves, a commission in the Army or Navy for a son or some humbler position for an old servant. The influence of the Crown was always at the disposal of the Ministry in power and was used to support their majority in the House of Commons. Officers of the Army and Navy still sat in the House of Commons, and promotion was used as an inducement to support the Ministry and dismissal as a punishment for opposing it.

With the one exception that they could not originate financial proposals, the Lords had legislative powers as extensive as those of the Commons, and their legal functions as a Supreme Court of Appeal gave them additional importance; especially as, up to the beginning of the nineteenth century, lay peers as well as the Lords of Appeal still took part in legal business. The majority of the Cabinet Ministers came from the Upper House, the convention about the composition of the Cabinet being almost the exact opposite to what it is today.

Constitutional theory regarded the House of Lords as a check on both the Crown and the House of Commons; its essential function was supposed to be to resist any attempt by the King to increase his powers or any attempt by the House of Commons to encroach either on the prerogatives of the Executive or on the liberties of the people. Lord Shelburne, who was an advanced Whig, almost a Radical, said in 1778: "I shall never submit to the doctrine I have heard this day from the Woolsack, that the other House are the only representative of the people's rights. I boldly maintain the contrary. I say this House are equally representative of the people. They hold the balance; and if they should perceive two of the branches of the legislature unite in oppressing and enslaving the people, it is their duty to interpose to prevent it."

The Peers could point to occasions on which they had fulfilled this duty. In the reign of Anne they had struggled against the imposition of laws against the Dissenters even harsher than those which already existed. And it was the Peers who had intervened in Ashby's case in the same reign to prevent the Tory House of Commons supporting a Tory mayor in preventing a Whig cobbler from voting at a Parliamentary election. On the other hand they were considered to be too susceptible to the blandishments of the King. Peers wished to be appointed to offices about the Court or wanted a step up in the peerage; on more than one occasion hard cash changed hands.

The power of the House of Lords was still further increased by the individual importance of great territorial magnates and by their influence at elections. A proportion of Members of Parliament were always nominees of peers. This did not mean, as it would today, that every vote was decided beforehand; the conditions of eigthteenth-century politics gave a great deal of latitude to the individual Member, even when his patron did not expressly state that his acceptance of the offer of a seat in Parliament involved no obligation. The fifth Duke of Devonshire, the husband of Georgiana, made no stipulation except that his nominees should vote for any proposal for the protection of animals. In most cases it was accepted in a general way that these Members would support a Minister or Ministers that their patron supported and the system was used to build up connections which had the same kind of influence as 'groups' have had within parties at other times. It is now fashionable to consider that these groups were based simply on the furtherance of each other's interest; but at least in a few cases a common attitude to policy also can be discerned, as for example in the Rockingham connection, and even among 'Cobham's Cubs'.

In spite of the power and prestige of the House of Lords and of individual peers, the House of Commons was already in the age of Walpole the most important element in the Constitution; indeed a considerable part of the power both of the King and the House of Lords was derived, not from their own prerogatives, but from the various means through which they could influence the House of Commons. The superior position of the lower House was partly due to its control of finance, which gave it every opportunity of criticizing the Government and which in the last resort would have enabled it to bring the Government down by withholding supplies. Its prestige and therefore its power was, however, further raised because it was directly representative of all classes, but predominantly of the most important, the country gentlemen and the commercial interests. The country gentlemen were not only important because the Government needed their votes, but because all the activities of local government outside the boroughs were either supervised or carried on by country gentlemen. The commercial interests were important partly because of their wealth and partly because even the twentieth century hardly yields to the eighteenth in the importance it places on economic activities.

It is often held that it was the relationship between individual peers and their nominees in the Commons which prevented more friction than actually occurred between the two separate houses, each endowed with such extensive powers. But, as Sir William Holdsworth has pointed out, each branch of the Constitution accepted the position of the other two;[5] the Commons did not claim that because they were the representative House they had some moral right to overrule the Peers. There also seems to be no doubt that it was generally held that there were fundamental laws either of nature or of the British Constitution, which limited the things Parliament could do. Magna Carta was to the eighteenth century what the Koran is to Mohammedans, or *Das Kapital* to the Russians. Horace Walpole had a framed copy hanging on the wall at one side of his bed and a copy of the warrant for the execution of Charles the First on the other. He undoubtedly believed, as did many others, that any laws passed in contradiction of the provisions of the Great Charter would be invalid. If, as all lawyers now say, this was a complete mistake, there was still the law of nature as expressed in the Common Law or simply recognized by common sense. A general recognition that there is a limit to the action of governments tended to reduce arrogance and must have made it easier for the separate and independent powers to get on together.

The concept of the mixed Government was not seen only in the theory of the three powers equal and independent, but also in the franchise arrangements which seem so extraordinary today. The modern theory from which present electoral law derives was described by Dicey as resting upon two principles: "The first, that on the whole each man is the best judge of his own affairs; the second, that citizens should be looked upon primarily as persons, secondly only as members of classes."[6]

The older theory was based on the existence of classes. It was considered in the eighteenth century that every class and interest was entitled to be represented in the House of Commons, and that, while no class should be held to be supreme, property, especially

landed property, deserved special consideration. Before refusing
to take such a view seriously, let the reader consider for a moment
why property was accorded such a position. It was because the
object of the Constitution was to ensure the liberty of the
subject.[7] One of the chief bulwarks against arbitrary government
is the large property owner. Why, it was asked, did England have
the only free Government in the world? Because her aristocracy
was independent of the Court and prepared to defend the rights of
every citizen by maintaining its own. Land was the most important kind of property because it was supposed to give its owner a
particular interest in the stability of the country, but those
fortunes acquired by 'industry' and 'virtue' also had their place.
The one kind of fortune which patriots disliked was the fortunes
made by the 'nabobs' in India, because they were supposed to
have no tendency, as had land and commercial fortunes, to make
their owners the foremost champions of the liberty of the subject.
The property of the poor man was as sacred as the property of
the rich: "The poorest man in his cottage may bid defiance to all
the forces of the Crown. It may be frail—its roof may shake—the
winds may blow through it—the storm may enter—but the
King of England cannot enter. All his forces dare not cross the
threshold of the ruined tenant."[8]

The supremacy of land was protected by the influence of the
landowner over the votes of his tenants, by the rotten boroughs
and by the property qualifications for candidates for Parliament:
in theory no one could stand for a county who did not possess
£600 a year derived from land, or for a borough unless he had
£300 a year from real property. In practice these provisions were
evaded. The Land Tax was the only direct tax, 2s. in the pound
on the annual value was the usual charge in peacetime, during
wars it was always raised to 4s. and although the assessments
are said to have been kept deliberately low, according to the
ideas of the time it was heavy. Property and birth were to be
given their due weight but other interests were not to be excluded.
As Peel said in opposing the Reform Bill in 1832: "There is at
present no class of people, however humble, which is not
entitled to a voice in the election of representatives." The
franchise arrangements had not been shaped in accordance with

this theory; they were the result of a long historical process, the county franchise, for example, dating back to 1430, and the terms of the borough franchise depending on their individual histories. But these historical accidents fitted in with the theory and explains why, before the Napoleonic Wars, they were on the whole accepted.

Everyone knows that in 1793, 154 individuals returned 307 Members, that Cornwall had twenty-one boroughs with two Members each and two county Members, only two less than the whole of Scotland, and that the Members for these boroughs were chosen by 453 electors.[9] It is not so often remembered that thirteen constituencies had what amounted to manhood suffrage, and that in Liverpool and the City of London the ancient peculiarity of their franchise arrangements might exclude the rich, not the poor. In Liverpool, the franchise was primarily confined to journeymen shipwrights, their sons and those who had been apprenticed to them, and excluded, as Oldfield indignantly complained, "all those who paid the taxes and served the public offices".[10] In the City of London the franchise was confined to members of Livery Companies. A small retailer might, therefore, have a vote while a great merchant was without one. In Carlisle in 1780 no banker or manufacturer had a vote, nor any solicitor practising in the town. In other towns, Leicester, for example, anyone could vote who was not receiving public assistance and was not employed by the Government. In Preston all the inhabitants could vote; indeed, not only inhabitants but up till 1782 anyone who had spent the night before the poll in the town. The more solid citizens made several attempts to get the franchise restricted by petition to the House of Commons, maintaining that 'inhabitants' did not legally mean all the inhabitants. The House of Commons, however, decided that it did. In other places the franchise was confined to members of the Corporation, for example, in Bath the franchise was vested in the Mayor and the common councillors, who numbered thirty. In other places the franchise was vested in the freemen. A freeman need not be a resident and could be created, and it was the custom to create them in order to win elections.

It seems to be the general impression today that the eighteenth-century franchise practically excluded the working class, but Gladstone said in the reform debates of 1865, that before 1832 working men formed a majority in sixty-five boroughs which together returned 130 Members. Although these figures were said to be inaccurate by the Liberal opponents of reform, it is interesting that they could be seriously advanced by the Chancellor of the Exchequer. Richard Price, the statistician, complained in 1776 that half the House of Commons were chosen by 5,723 persons of the lowest sort.[11]

The county franchise was also wide because the qualifications dated from Henry VI and, being a property qualification, had become more and more democratic as the value of money fell. The elector in the counties was the forty-shilling freeholder.

The term 'freehold' was not used only to describe a particular kind of land tenure but included anything of which the owner had a permanent occupation. It therefore applied also to offices and to tenancies for life, and was even extended to the occupation of a pew in church. Clergymen had a vote in the counties because their position was for life, whereas Nonconformist ministers did not because they depended on the continued support of their congregation. This definition made the county franchise much wider than it might appear at first sight, for example parish schoolmasters and parish clerks were, according to a book published in 1816, "usually admitted by virtue of their office".[12] "All the inferior officers of the courts of justice in Westminster Hall vote at the county elections for Middlesex; and all the officers of the cathedral churches from the canons down to the choristers have claimed to vote in their respective counties."[13]

Adam Smith said that most of 'the yeomanry' had tenancies for life and that "the whole order becomes respectable to their landlords on account of the political consideration which this gives them."[14]

The average electorate in the counties was larger than the average in a borough and represented, with the exception of the open boroughs, a more varied sample of the population. Yorkshire, in 1751, had an electorate of over 15,000, and was famous for the elevated character of the representatives it sent to

Parliament, culminating in the sainted Wilberforce, whose
enormous election expenses were paid by public subscriptions. In
Scotland the franchise was further complicated because it was
attached to various forms of feudal tenure.

The only kind of borough remembered today, the rotten
borough, in which voters were so few as to be either dominated
completely by the neighbouring landowner, or in the market to
sell their votes to the highest bidder, was an accidental result of
the shift in population which had created new towns and denuded
the original constituencies of their inhabitants, leaving three, two
or even one elector. Many of those most attached to the old
Constitution did not wish to keep the rotten boroughs. In the Bill
which Pitt introduced into the House of Commons in 1784 he put
forward a plan for buying them up and creating new constituencies to replace them. But some people defended them, as
some people defend them even today. Although everyone
admitted that some owners of rotten boroughs simply sold them
to the highest bidder, and where there was no patron, the electors
put themselves up to auction, Sudbury at least on one occasion
going so far as to advertise, others looked about for talented young
men to introduce into Parliament. When, however, the Mayor
and Corporation of Oxford offered to return their existing
Members to Parliament if they would pay the city's debts,
amounting to £7,500, they were severely reprimanded by the
House of Commons and committed to Newgate. Bagehot said
that Canning was taunted with having become a Tory only
because while he was at Oxford the Tories had offered him a seat.[16]
He added that "the Oxford Liberals of our generation are quite
exempt from similar temptations". The remark has an even more
poignant ring today. The rotten boroughs were not only supposed
to give special opportunity to talent, but also to provide a way
for the colonies to be represented, the theory being that men went
to India or the colonies, made a large fortune, came back and
bought rotten boroughs. Shocking as it may be to modern ideas,
the Members who entered the House by buying rotten boroughs
were often among the most independent and public-spirited men
in Parliament.

II

The theory of the franchise was summarized many times in the debates on the Reform Bill in 1832. Lord William Lennox, for example, said: "By the present system, the aristocracy is represented through the counties, the colonies and commercial interests through the close boroughs, the artisans through the votes of the freemen and the labourer through the vote of the pot walloper." The idea of the House of Commons as representative of all interests or classes lasted long after 1832. Sir Hugh Cairns said in 1866: "It is the principle of the English Constitution, that Parliament should be a mirror—a representation of every class not according to heads, not according to numbers, but according to everything which gives weight and importance in the world without; so that the various classes of this country may be heard, and their views expressed clearly in the House of Commons, without the possibility of any one class outnumbering or reducing to silence all the other classes in the kingdom."

This doctrine seems not unreasonable even to modern ears. But theory and practice are not always the same. How far did the Constitution really ensure the liberty of the subject? If liberty means freedom from coercion by the state, the Constitution certainly did protect it to an extraordinary degree, to a degree probably never known to a society ruled by law either before or since. The difference between Great Britain and other countries which most struck contemporaries was the rule of law in Great Britain. This meant that there was a body of law which applied indiscriminately to every citizen, and that the law was administered by courts of justice, which were outside the control of the executive. Laws were enacted by the House of Commons, and interpreted by the courts, no discretion was allowed to the Government, or to any department of State, to make regulations. No one could be arrested unless he was charged with a specific offence and brought before a magistrate.

It has long been the fashion to say that Montesquieu misunderstood the English Constitution, that there was in reality no separation of powers. The Lord Chancellor, the chief judicial officer, was a Cabinet Minister appointed by the executive; the highest court of justice, the House of Lords, was itself a branch of the legislature. Montesquieu may have exaggerated the separation of powers but he was right about the main point; the judiciary was outside the control of the Government, and this was the main distinction between Great Britain and the absolute monarchies, where the judges were officials of the Executive, as they are in modern autocracy, and where the King was not restrained from taking any action against an individual. The example famous in England was the French *lettre de cachet*, the system by which anyone could be arrested and detained without trial by order of the King. Englishmen were never tired of pointing the contrast between England and the rest of the world. Thomas Day, for example, in a speech to the freeholders of Cambridge said:

> In other countries, the causes and pretexts of oppression are those discriminatory powers with which the supreme magistrate is invested; for the use of which he is accountable to Heaven alone. With us no discriminatory power which can affect the life, the property or the liberty of an individual, is permitted to the sovereign himself. We have the right to speak our sentiments with a tempered, but an honest boldness; no restraint can be put on our freedom, unless we have committed crimes which make us unworthy to enjoy it, nor can our property be wrested from us under the plea of State necessity, without at least the appearance of our own consent, and lest the laws themselves, by being too near the influence of the supreme magistrate, should be perverted to our annoyance, it is provided that not the meanest wretch that begs his bread, shall be obnoxious to the public vengeance without the consent of his equals.[16]

Goldsmith described a conversation between a porter "who had stopped to rest his burden" and a soldier and a debtor "through the grate of his prison"; the debtor said the French were nothing but slaves and the porter that they were nothing but beasts of burden.[17] There is no point in the irony unless it represented the attitude of ordinary Englishmen.

In England every citizen had rights: defined by Blackstone as those absolute rights, such as would belong to him in a state of nature, only modified by the necessity of living together in a society.

> Political, therefore, or civil liberty, which is that of a member of society, is no other than natural liberty so far restrained by human laws (and no farther) as is necessary and expedient for the general advantage of the public. Hence we collect that the law, which restrains a man from doing mischief to his fellow citizens, though it diminishes the natural, increases the civil liberty of mankind; but every wanton and causeless restraint on the will of the subject, whether practised by monarchy, nobility or a popular assembly, is a degree of tyranny. Nay, that even laws themselves, whether made with or without our consent, if they regulate or constrain our conduct in matters of mere indifference, without any good in view, are laws destructive of liberty.[18]

These absolute rights are the right of personal security, the right of personal liberty and the right of private property. These, which are derived from the law of nature, include all other rights, because there is "no known method of compulsion ... but by the infringement of one or other of these important rights". Nor is there, especially when it is understood how wide Blackstone's interpretation of these rights was. For example, he included in the right of personal security, the right to the necessities of life which he considered was embodied in the Poor Laws. These absolute rights are accompanied by certain subordinate rights, established to protect them: the rights and constitution of Parliament, the limitation of the King's prerogative, and the right to appeal to the courts of justice for the redress of any injury, the right of any individual to petition either House of Parliament for redress, and the right to bear arms.

The approach to the Constitution which regards Parliament as a 'consequence' of individual rights is very different from the political theory, not only of both modern and eighteenth-century despotisms but even of modern democratic governments.[19]

The one great exception to the right of personal security was the press gang, and it is indeed extraordinary that a country in which the attachment to liberty was so widespread and so sincere should have allowed men to be seized and forcibly put in the Navy. It was realized even then that there was some contradiction between the power of the Government to force men into the Navy and the theory of the constitution. And although only ex-sailors, or those used to the sea, could be pressed; Blackstone, Paley and Gisborne were all uneasy about it.

In spite of this glaring exception the right to personal liberty was on the whole secure. The subject was protected by Habeas Corpus and the right enshrined in Magna Carta to be tried by his peers; which meant for a peer, trial by the House of Lords, for a commoner, trial by jury.

The importance of trial by jury in protecting the citizen from oppression by the Crown or by some more powerful subject is often forgotten today. Juries are regarded by experts as deficient in scientific knowledge, and by those who have to serve on them simply as a nuisance, but they were very important during some periods and nothing like them then existed in any other country in Europe. Juries might of course be intimidated, or bribed or packed. Even the House of Lords might be too willing to oblige a powerful King; but although the Government was accused of packing juries even after the Revolution of 1688, they were unlikely to be intimidated and were generally regarded as a bulwark of liberty. The courts upheld the rights of the citizen even against the Government. After the issue of general warrants had been declared illegal Wilkes secured £4,000 damages against the Secretary of State for trespassing on his property by sending officers to search his house. Juries did not, of course, then any more than they do now, protect anyone against an inflamed and excited public opinion.

A modern reader will miss from the list of Blackstone's rights two which he has been taught to regard as fundamental to political liberty: liberty of speech and the right of public meeting. The law about meetings was uncertain, the most that seemed to be known was that some meetings were lawful while some, those likely to lead to riots for instance, were unlawful. But the law was not important because political meetings for general discussion did not take place; Parliamentary candidates addressed the general public on hustings erected in the street and meetings of electors sometimes occurred, but the technique of the political meeting was not developed until the Anti-Corn Law League organized them in the 'thirties of the next century.

Some people seem to believe that freedom of the Press did not exist although everyone at the time believed that it did. The law, as explained by Lord Mansfield in a famous judgment, was much the same as it is today: "The liberty of the Press consists in printing without previous licence, subject to the consequences of the law."* This meant then, as it does now, that no one may publish statements which are defamatory of individuals, seditious, obscene or blasphemous. Whether a statement is considered to be any of these things depends more on the state of public opinion than on the law; books published in 1750 and in 1950 would have been thought obscene in 1850. As Dicey expresses it: "Freedom of discussion is in England little else than the right to say anything which a jury consisting of twelve shopkeepers think it expedient should be said or written."

The Law of Libel differed from that of today in that until 1792 juries were asked to give a verdict only on whether the statement had been published and whether it was true; it was left to the Judge to say if it was libel or not. The Government has more statutory power to curtail freedom of discussion now than it had then; the Obscene Publications Act of 1857 and the Official Secrets Acts of 1911 and 1920 give wider powers than any which the law allowed the Government of George III. In some ways there was more interference with the expression of political opinion then than now, but an astounding amount of personal comment was allowed and a very wide freedom of criticism, especially as intervention by the Government was capricious and liable to be unsuccessful, as juries were likely to acquit. For example, a bookseller, Irwin, who was charged with publishing a libel on the House of Commons because it committed a man to prison for riotous conduct during an election, was acquitted in spite of the Judge's direction to the contrary. But in 1770 another bookseller was found guilty of selling Junius' letter to the King,

* "This is as true today as it was then," Holdsworth, *History of English Law* (1937).

and Horne Tooke was fined £200 and sent to prison for a year for signing an advertisement asking for contributions for "the relief of our beloved American fellow subjects, who faithful to the characters of Englishmen . . . were, for that reason only, inhumanly murdered by the King's troops at or near Lexington and Concord". In 1758 Dr. Shebbeare was sent to prison and made to stand in the pillory because he published a pamphlet in which he attributed all the public misfortunes to the Hanoverian dynasty. In spite of these instances, however, the chief feeling of the modern reader after glancing at Wilkes's *North Briton* is surprise, not that the Government took proceedings against Wilkes on the publication of issue No. 45, but that it had not taken proceedings before. He had frequently insinuated in no guarded language that the Princess Dowager, the mother of George III, was Lord Bute's mistress, and in one number compared her with Isabel, Edward II's wife, and Lord Bute with Mortimer. The *Morning Post*, in its radical days, chose to inform its readers that it was not true that several ladies had sworn to the Prime Minister's (the Younger Pitt's) parentage of their children.[20]

This sort of thing may be regarded as mere vulgar abuse, but a serious pamphlet advocating armed resistance to the Government could be published. In 1784 Sir William Jones, the distinguished orientalist, published a dialogue between a gentleman and a farmer on the subject of government, in which the gentleman urged the farmer to sign a petition in favour of universal suffrage. Having dealt with the farmer's objections that he knew nothing of politics and that it would be more sensible for him to leave it to the King and Parliament, the gentleman goes on to urge the farmer to prepare for armed resistance:

G. But what if a few great lords or wealthy men were to keep the king himself in subjection, yet exert his force, lavish his treasure, and misuse his name, so as to domineer over the people, and manage the parliament?

F. We must fight for the king and for ourselves.

G. You talk of fighting, as if you were speaking of some rustic engagement at a wake; but your quarterstaffs would avail you little against bayonets.

F. We might easily provide ourselves with better arms.

G. Not so easily; when the moment of resistance came, you would be deprived of all arms; and those who should furnish you with them, or exhort you to take them up, would be called traitors, and probably put to death.

F. We ought always, therefore, to be ready; and keep each of us a strong firelock in the corner of his bedroom.

G. That would be legal as well as rational. Are you, my honest friend, provided with a musket?

F. I will contribute no more to the club, and purchase a firelock with my savings.

G. It is not necessary—I have two and will make you a present of one, with complete accoutrements.

F. I accept it thankfully, and will converse with you at your leisure on other subjects of this kind.

G. In the meanwhile, spend an hour every morning for the next fortnight, in learning to prime and load expeditiously, and to fire and charge with bayonet firmly and regularly. I say, every morning; because if you exercise too late in the evening, you may fall into some of the legal snares which have been spread for you by those gentlemen, who would rather secure game for the table than liberty for the nation.[21]

This pamphlet was the subject of a lawsuit, but not on the initiative of the Government. It had been shown to the Treasury who had refused to prosecute, but when the Dean of St. Asaph republished the pamphlet a private prosecution was instituted which was finally won by the Dean.[22] What makes the Dean's victory so remarkable is that these arguments were not addressed to a law-abiding, passive population but to a people only too ready to take the law into their own hands if they felt that their rights were infringed.

The liberty of the subject was protected not only by law, but by opinion. It was commonly held that 'the people' had a right to resist any infraction of liberty by force; not of course a legal right, the law of treason in itself was quite enough to make it purely theoretical, but a moral right. The Constitution was the result of a revolution and no statement that could reflect on the justice or legality of that revolution could be uttered by consti-tutional theorists or politicians. Blackstone was involved in a series of contradictory arguments in an attempt to reconcile the attitude of the law that the King can do no wrong with the known facts of English history. The theory of the contract between King and people, enshrined for Blackstone in the Coronation Service, goes some way, but he is reduced to going outside the law altogether in the end; after laying down the conditions on which the people might revolt against a King, these conditions being the circumstances in which James II had been deposed, he adds: "It is not for us to say that any one or two of these ingredients would amount to such a situation; for there our precedents fail us. In these, therefore, or other circumstances, which a fertile imagination may furnish, since both law and history are silent, it becomes us to be silent too, leaving it to future generations whenever necessity and the safety of the whole shall require it, the exertion of those inherent (though latent) powers of society, which no climate, no time, no Constitution. can ever destroy or diminish."[23]

The right of resistance was first evoked against the King; but it was soon applied to the 'King in Parliament', in other words the Government. Charles James Fox said in 1793, in the middle of the revolutionary war: "If men should be so resolute on their spirit of destruction . . . as to pass bills in violent opposition to the declared sense of the people . . . if my opinion was asked by the people as to their obedience . . . it would be a case of extremity which would justify resistance. The only question would be whether resistance was prudent."

Many people are now unwilling to believe that ideas have any effect on conduct, but there is no doubt that this view of the relation between the sovereign and the subject had a profound effect on the general attitude to government. Today it is generally considered to be the duty of the citizen to submit to any decision made by a properly elected government; it is doubtful whether a real democrat would regard it as justifiable to resist any action, however bizarre, or even insane, as long as the people were still able to change the government at the next election. The insis-tence on the citizen's right, in the last resort, to resist even a legally constituted Government was partly no doubt because an election did not necessarily mean a change of Government, but it was also derived from the general, if mistaken, conviction that every citizen had fundamental rights which no Government could legally infringe. In the extreme case of actual revolution the right had little practical importance; in the eighteenth century, as today, law and revolution had little to do with each other, but the theory made political obligation conditional, not absolute, and could be adjusted to less desperate situations. For example, Gisborne, no revolutionary writer, says and this in 1794: "The obedience of the subject is immediately due to the existing Government in consequence of its possessing the delegated authority of the State. It is not, however, an obedience without limit; it is not due in any case in which it would be a breach of duty to God." This may sound merely theoretical because, as he himself says, the Government of the day was unlikely to require of anyone the commission of such crimes as had Governments in the past. But in the examples he gives of cases in which dis-obedience was justifiable, one instance is topical both in 1794 and today. "If he were required . . . to serve against a foreign country in a war in which, after adequate inquiry and full deliberation he firmly believes in his conscience to be unjust, he ought to remember that neither the commands of his superiors; not even the unanimous voice of his countrymen, would justify his obedience."[24] This advice was addressed to the higher and middle classes only, but as he gives as his only reason for not including the working classes that they will not read bulky treatises, it is not to be supposed that he would have denied a workman capable of reading his book the same right of deciding for himself. Paley, although he rejects the whole idea of a con-tract as firmly as Bentham, says: "It may be as much a duty, at one time, to resist government, as it is at another to obey it."[25]

The idea of the citizens' rights was both widely spread and deeply engrained in Englishmen. A casual glance at almost any biography of the time will elicit sentiments about the free-born Englishman and his rights; these will be found in the letters of Cowper, a man completely uninterested in politics. That these rights were not equal made them more definite than the rights of an egalitarian society; what everyone has, few people value.

A frequent cause of misunderstanding of the eighteenth-century atmosphere is a confusion between the open and avowed preference given to birth and wealth and the disguised and sinister influence which in Marxist theory capitalists are alleged to have over liberal Governments. When a politician could openly say: "Some decent, regulated, pre-eminence, some preference (not excessive appropriation) given to birth is neither unnatural, nor unjust nor impolitic", it must have meant that a majority of those not distinguished by birth would have agreed. According to the eighteenth century theory, although birth should have preference and property second place, the working man was to have his place, limited but definite also. How valuable were those limited rights to him? In those boroughs where wholesale bribery took place he probably considered them very valuable indeed.* Even from the more strictly political point of view, elections in the popular boroughs were watched by the Government of the day to see which way the wind was blowing.

Some modern writers find it hard to believe that these popular boroughs were of any importance, because even open boroughs were represented by Whig and Tory gentlemen indistinguishable from those who sat for the close and rotten boroughs. But this was because there was no real difference of opinion between the classes until the Napoleonic Wars and the Industrial Revolution had changed everything. No one looked to the Government to change the conditions of his life. There was no theory which explained that poverty and unemployment were due to political institutions and could be abolished or ameliorated by political actions. Working men, whether they had votes or not, were Whigs or Tories, just like everyone else. Where popular opinion was aroused the open boroughs allowed it to be expressed. In Nottingham, in 1776, the framework knitters, who formed the majority of the electorate, chose and elected a candidate to introduce a Bill for fixing wages.[26] In 1832 'Orator' Hunt, standing as an extreme Radical, beat Stanley, the Whig Home

* Lord Shelburne said £700 was offered to a labouring man for his vote.

Secretary, under the unreformed franchise, and Westminster several times returned a Radical candidate against the orthodox parties. Even before the French Revolution an election in a popular borough was not all bribery and personalities, some appeal was made to sentiment if not to argument. In Bristol, for example, in 1754, placards were used with the following words:

Liberty
No Placemen; no general naturalization; no Jews!
No white-washed Protestant!
No French Bottle-makers! No lowering of wages of Labouring men to 4d. a day and Garlic!

Much the same kind of literature is issued today.

It is very easy to make a list of quotations from eighteenth-century writers to the effect that the only function of the people or the lower orders was to obey. What is not so often noticed is that these sentiments were not put forward as a description of the actual state of affairs, but as an ideal, and that these remarks are not recorded as having been made by any practical politician. They come rather from writers more detached from the bustle of the world, especially from clergymen, whether bishops or curates. Contemporary opinion seems to have held that the people had too great rather than too small an influence on politics. Johnson's remark that "the King gave Walpole as a Minister to the people and the people gave Pitt as a Minister to the King" is famous. Pitt's Cabinet colleagues were always complaining that as he knew his chief source of power was popularity, he always played to the mob. Sir George Saville said in a letter to the Rev. Mr. Wyvil "there are, as the world goes, but two practical ways of obtaining a considerable change in great public Regulations; by the means of a Party or by the means of the People. (I do not mean by outward force)".[27]

'The people' did not then mean the working classes, but it certainly included them. Fielding said, in a tone of irony indeed, but at the same time with a considerable amount of sincerity, that "it may seem strange that not one of our political writers in their learned treatises on the English constitution should have taken notice of any more than three estates—kings, lords and commons; all entirely passing by in silence that very large and powerful body that form the fourth estate in this community and have been long dignified and distinguished by the name of mob . . . many things have contributed to raise this fourth estate to that exorbitant degree of power which they at present enjoy."[28] By the name 'mob' it is clear from the context that he was referring not only to the London mob but to the working class in general. Mansfield said in 1770, "I defy him to point out a single instance of my life in which the popular clamour of the times ever had the least influence on my determination. Those . . . who have given up their mind to be the slave of every popular impulse, I sincerely pity. I pity them still more if their vanity leads them to mistake the shouts of a mob for the trumpets of fame." The tone of these remarks seems to show that public opinion, even in its least respectable manifestation, was not without influence.

It was not so much through their votes, however, that the working class made their influence felt, but by actual physical violence. There were serious riots in 1735 over the proposal to allow Jews to become naturalized citizens; in 1768 over Wilkes; and in 1780 under the influence of Lord George Gordon's agitation—apart from minor turmoils and fighting over strikes, of which there were plenty in the eighteenth century. These minor riots were always liable to break out. For example, in May 1765, the silk weavers, incensed by the rejection of a Bill to increase the duty on imports of silk, repaired to the House of Commons with red and black flags, and finally attacked the Duke of Bedford's house. Although people were taken aback by the Gordon Riots, opinion, even respectable opinion, was not unduly shocked by the minor affairs. Politicians professed to regard these riots, when aimed against their opponents, as excusable or even laudable. Chatham said in 1770: "Let me warn the Ministers of their dangers. If by an ignominious compromise they should stain the honour or sacrifice the rights of the people, let them look to the consequences, and consider whether they will be able to walk the streets in safety." It was the real horrors of the French Revolution which caused the lasting preference of the ruling classes for order and discipline. Even after the French Revolution Mr. William

Ward said: "They have an excellent police at Paris, but they pay for it dear enough. I had rather half a dozen throats should be cut on the Radcliffe highway every three or four years than be subjected to domiciliary visits, spies and all the rest of Fouché's contrivances."[29]

The country towns had riots similar to those of London, and an extraordinary series of events took place at Tiverton in 1765. The leading wool merchant of the town having just died, the labourers became worried about prospects of employment. It was known to them that Mr. Baring of Exeter wished to represent the town in Parliament, and if he were elected was prepared to live in the town, and to move his wool business there. The right of election lay with the Corporation, and the first step apparently was to elect Baring as an Alderman. At first the Corporation thought the scheme a good idea, but later they decided that Baring's ambition was too wide-ranging and that his object was to dominate the whole town. A violent conflict then broke out between the Society of Combers and Weavers and the Corporation. The Combers and Weavers combined the eighteenth-century custom of sacking the Mayor's house, pulling his nose and seizing his wig with the more modern method of a boycott of all those tradesmen who did not promise to vote for Baring. The whole episode culminated in the Mayor's country house near Tiverton being wrecked by the angry mob.[30]

There were riots in Nottingham in 1779 after a Bill to fix wages for framework knitting had been thrown out of the House of Commons, and thousands of pounds' worth of damage was done. The house of one of the more unpopular employers was burned to the ground. After all this, the ringleaders at Tiverton were fined 13s. 4d. and sent to prison for six months. At Nottingham the man who had incited the mob to burn the house was fined 6s. 8d. and sent to prison for three weeks.[31]

Quite apart from conceding to force on particular occasions, the English Government was admitted to be susceptible to public opinion. Lord Hardwicke said on the occasion of the Government's capitulation on the Jewish question: "However much the people may be misled, yet in a free country I do not think any unpopular measure should be proceeded with. We should try to treat the people as a skilled and humane physician would treat his patient. If they nauseate the salutary draught we have prescribed, we should think of some other remedy, we should delay administering the prescription until time or change of circumstances removes the nausea." Lord Lyttelton on the same occasion went even further: "Public wisdom must on some occasions give way to popular folly, especially in a free country where the humour of the people must be considered as attentively as the humour of a King in an absolute Monarchy."[32]

The Government's retreat on the Jewish Naturalization Bill was not the only occasion on which an unpopular measure had to be withdrawn. Walpole proposed in 1732 to revive the excise on salt and to reduce the Land Tax. A violent agitation was created and the Bill finally had to be withdrawn. Of course, it could be said that public opinion in those days did not include working-class opinion. Although the opposition to the Excise Bill was no doubt worked up for political purposes, the objection to it was generally shared by the working class, at least by the London working class. Sir Robert Walpole was seized by the collar as he left the House of Commons and was with difficulty extricated from the grasp of a coal-heaver. The agitation against the Excise Bill, strange as it may seem today, was based not so much on economic as on political grounds. The 'mob' were told, not only that they would have to pay more for the goods on which the tax was levied, but that the increase in excisemen would increase the power of the Crown because their votes would be at the disposal of the King.

As there were no police and few soldiers, it is not altogether surprising that the authorities, whether Parliament itself or local Corporations, were chary of provoking the public and liable to retreat before it when provoked. But although politicians did not disregard the 'mob', they did not respect it. Their respect was reserved for the county electorate and the county Members, who were always praised for their independence. Suggestions for reform made by practical men until the end of the century were nearly always for increasing the number of county Members. By this 'independence' was meant independence of the Ministry and the Court. The county franchise was wide and, although the number of voters varied between the counties as they did between the boroughs, even the smallest county electorate was never so small as the close boroughs, and the average of 4,000 was well above the borough average. Voting was, however, open, and the smaller freeholders were liable to be influenced by their landlords, their larger customers and by local magnates of all kinds. A good deal is usually said about intimidation by landlords, but a greater obstacle to independence was probably the general sentiment shared by the tenants themselves that it was their duty to vote for the candidate their landlord favoured. The general technique of 'obliging' those who gave their votes, which we now call corruption, also worked here. It is probable that "Vote for Mr. X and you won't lose by it" was more common than threats.

Until the accession, or, indeed, until the old age of George III, the Crown was not popular, and the kind of emotion now aroused by the Queen was in the remoter country districts given to local magnates like Lord Derby and Sir Watkin Wynn.

Mr. Kitson Clark says: "The landlord tenant relation was by no means a one-way relationship. Probably if he wanted to work his estate, a landlord had to have regard to the opinions of his farming tenants; certainly in many cases he thought it his duty to do so. For instance, when the Duke of Rutland heard what Peel intended to do in 1846, he was at a loss how he should vote in the House of Lords, so he rode round the tenants and labourers on his estate to ask their opinion."[33] Mr. Kitson Clark is, of course, discussing the nineteenth not the eighteenth century, but even in the eighteenth century there were men to whom popularity meant much.

Mr. Forrester says in Northamptonshire it was considered that a farmer should 'compliment' his landlord with one vote and use the other as he chose.[34] Certainly in Northumberland in 1774 the Duke of Northumberland roused the greatest opposition by trying to nominate both Members instead of the one which public opinion seems to have considered him entitled to. A violent contest took place in which all 'aristocratic' influence in elections was attacked. There was a profusion of pamphlets and papers on both sides, the Duke's opponents drew attention "to the glaring impropriety of the nobility interfering AT ALL in elections for Members of Parliament".

"The danger that threatens the political life of this nation, arises from the too great influence of the Crown; and we ought to guard against that, let it approach us in what shape soever, whether with the smooth-fawning leer of a buskined Courtier, or the insolent authority of a MUSHROOM DUKE!"

A bitter poem contains the lines:

> A Percy vouchsafes to accept of your voice,
> Then gratefully grant it, with transport rejoice
> His vassals to kneel, and account it great gain,
> That he honours your dastardly necks with his chain.[35]

After all this excitement Lord Algernon Percy and Sir William Middleton, the anti-Percy candidate, were elected.

We have two glimpses of county elections, one at the beginning of the century and one at the end, and they seem to contain features not unfamiliar even today.

"Lord Wharton was going up and down the town with his friends to secure votes on their side. Entering a shoemaker's shop he asked where Dick was? The good woman said her husband was gone two or three miles with some shoes. His Lordship need not fear for him—she would keep him tight. "I know that," says my Lord, "but I want to see Dick and drink a glass with him. . . ." "Well," says his Lordship, "how does all thy children? Mollie is a brave girl, I warrant, by this time."[36]

In 1784 Cowper was sitting after dinner when "a sharp rap was heard at the door, the boys halloo'd, and the maid announced Mr. Grenville". After some difficulty with a tame hare which happened to be loose at the time,

"Mr. Grenville advanced towards me, shook me by the hand with a degree of cordiality which was extremely seducing. As soon as he and as many more as could find chairs were seated, he began to open the intent of his visit. I told him I had no vote, for which he rightly gave me credit. I assured him I had no influence, which he was not equally inclined to believe. . . . Supposing that I could not be possessed of such a treasure without knowing it, I ventured to confirm my first assertion, saying that if I had any I was utterly at a loss where it could be or wherein it consisted. Thus ended the conference. Mr. Grenville squeezed me by the hand again, kissed the ladies, and withdrew. He kissed likewise the maid in the kitchen, and seemed upon the whole the most loving, kissing, kind-hearted gentleman."[37]

The Duke of Newcastle indeed, in 1829, when his nominee was defeated at Newark, expelled every tenant who had voted against him, and when attacked, in very intemperate language certainly, replied: "Have I not the right to do what I like with my own?"

Sir James Lowther is also said to have behaved with a great want of propriety at Whitehaven in 1780. Mr. Pennington, who wished to represent the borough, says: "Sir James Lowther began *in person* a canvass for plumpers on the Saturday, and meeting with so general, unexpected and *noble a firmness* among men of every class throughout the town and finding himself not able to make any *impression* and from his treatment and language on refusal having brought upon himself the most pointed rebuffs, he was violent beyond all idea. Every species of threat, fear, menace, all the engines of distress and persecution were put into force to shake the integrity of each individual."[38] Pennington, who retired from the contest, said Lowther's conduct was particularly painful to him as he was the nearest relation he had in the world.

Political influence was by no means the automatic result of hereditary position; in really remote counties the local magnate may have been all-powerful, Lowther in Cumberland, Watkin Wynn in Wales, but in more civilized regions constant efforts were required to consolidate and preserve it. Anyone who wishes to see the means, agricultural improvements, hospitality, the breeding of race horses, by which the Rockingham influence was maintained in Yorkshire should consult *The Early Career of Rockingham*, by S. H. Guttridge. Shelburne has left a detailed description of the attention which had to be paid over to a family borough.

"Family boroughs . . . are supposed to cost nothing: but I am sure from my own experience and observation that if examined into, they will be found to cost as much as the purchase of any burgage tenure whatever . . . like public taxes, the amount is not perceived for a great while . . . because it consists in always a little and not commonly a great deal too much being paid on every article, and in every transaction you are confined to a particular set of tradesmen, and often to their connections in town, and can never control their charges. The rents of houses and lands must be governed by the moderation of voters. You must be forthcoming on every occasion, not only of distress but of fancy, to subscribe too largely to roads, as well as every other project which may be started by the idlest of the people; add to this livings, favours of all sorts from government, and stewardship, if there is an intriguing attorney in town, who under the name of your agent will deprive you of all manner of free agency upon your own property . . . without mentioning the charge and domestic disorder attending a great deal of obscure hospitality, and a never ceasing management of men and things, and after all when the crisis comes you are liable to be outbid by any nabob or adventurer."[39]

The great expense of these contested elections, whether in councils or boroughs, meant that the differing 'influences' often made a bargain to share the nomination of Members, either by each nominating one candidate or by nominating the candidates at different elections. It may reasonably be argued that such bargains meant the electors were deprived of their right of election.

We have heard a great deal about 'communication', that is to say, the way in which orders, requests and information are conveyed from one level of administration or from one layer of society to another. Communication in politics is extremely important because the means of communication modify the workings of government, particularly in a democracy. One need only think of the way in which the development of newspapers changed the whole atmosphere in the early nineteenth century. There were newspapers in the eighteenth century and a far larger number of men could read then than it has been customary to suppose;[40] but even in the towns individuals must have played a large part in communicating both information and ideas, and in the country the chief source of political news was probably the local landowner or his agent and this bears a definite relation to the political influence of landlords. Farmers were prepared to vote with their landlord not only out of loyalty but because he was the main purveyor of political knowledge, and the same thing is true of the family borough.

The writers of letters to *The Times* on the subject of modern difficulties in communication between classes have said a great deal about the barrier of accent and phrase; barriers of accent were much less definite in the eighteenth century. The country gentlemen either did or at any rate could speak the local dialect and there was no antagonism towards landowners or employers as a class; rather the contrary, the appearance and voice of a gentleman would recommend him to the town mob or the village labourer. It is almost impossible for us to imagine the atmosphere in which public means of communication, such as the newspaper and the wireless, played so small and the individual so large a part. It is all the more surprising to find how successful the communication was, if success is to be measured by the interest taken in politics. Chesterfield, Goldsmith, Johnson, Arthur Young all comment on the passion with which politics were followed and discussed by the 'labouring classes', both in town and country.

With all this, of course, the Government of Great Britain was unlike that of any modern state; sufficient has been said to show that it was not despotic, it was not democratic either. This is shown not so much by the narrowness of the franchise or even by the superiority of the aristocracy in the State, but because the whole attitude to government was completely unlike that of a modern democracy. While every class had a right to be represented, no class was supposed to give instructions to its representative. While public opinion, or even a section of public opinion, could force the Government to withdraw a proposed measure, no class or section could force it to introduce one. The framework knitters could get a Bill for fixing wages into the House of Commons, but they could not get it passed. The House of Commons was supposed to act as the Great Council of the nation dealing with events as they arose, untrammelled by election pledges or by party ties. The Government was not supposed to act on any 'mandate' from the people, even from the limited electorate of the day. Indeed one of the first duties of a Government was considered to be to carry out necessary measures in the face of a hostile public opinion. Lord Liverpool expressed this view at the end of the century when it was already being attacked:

"The House of Commons, as the democratic part of the Constitution, as the virtual representatives of the people, certainly to a degree, ought to be affected by public opinion in their operations. We must, however, never forget that the first quality of the House of Commons is that of being a deliberative assembly. If public opinion is necessarily to affect their discussions on every occasion, it will cease to be a deliberative assembly, and the members of it would have nothing to do but go to their constituents, and desire to be instructed by them in the votes they are to give on every subject."

III

Parliament is not the only political institution. There is also local government, thought by some political theorists to be, in a democratic state, even more important than the central government; in the eighteenth century it certainly had more influence on the life of the ordinary person. The central government was the work of a revolution, the revolution of 1688; but no revolution had ever occurred in local institutions, at least if by revolution is meant destruction. Nothing in local government had ever been abolished, although there had been a continual process of change, decay and readjustment. The county and hundred went back to the Saxons. The parish had been added by the Church for purely ecclesiastical administration; but secular government had seen its convenience and had made it, first, the authority for the administration of Poor Law relief, and then the authority for the highways. Boroughs were originally merely places which had managed, through obtaining a royal charter or otherwise, to contract out of the authority of the county or the manor.

The counties were ruled by the Justices of the Peace, appointed by the King on the recommendation of the Lord Lieutenant. At first sight this might suggest a system of complete centralization. In reality the Lord Lieutenant consulted the existing Justices before he made any recommendation. The Justices in the eighteenth century, indeed until the Local Government Act of 1888, had functions which they have since lost. Quarter sessions were not then purely judicial institutions. The Justices at the quarter sessions were the public authority and had power to levy a county rate; as the county authority, they were responsible for the constructions and repair of bridges, the county roads and the prisons. As Justices, they were responsible for the supervision of the Poor Law and the licensing of public houses, as well as for the administration of justice.

The government of the towns varied between a very wide local government franchise and a tight oligarchy. "Very few towns are governed by the same laws, and while many of them have whimsical, many more have exceedingly beautiful schemes of government", said the Reverend Mr. Hodgson in 1832.[41] The Common Council was in some places elected by the freemen, while in others it simply made itself eternal by co-opting members. Some Corporations were entirely independent of the magistrates, in some places they exercised their authority jointly, while in others the Council was the only judicial authority. The Common Council could, but need not, provide for the policing of the borough, the regulation of the market, the maintenance of the gaol and of the harbour, if there was one. Their chief function was often to manage the property of the Corporation, and this property was absolutely their own. It was laid down by Lord Eldon that "over such property the corporation exercised the same rights as individuals did over their own property. . . ." What the Corporations actually did varied as much as the character of the towns. In one town the Council were accused by the Royal Commission on Municipal Corporations in 1835, of "having borrowed money excessively in order to divide it amongst themselves". Others had already started on the way to sanitary reform, and paved and lighted their streets and provided water supplies.[42]

 It was not only the general tolerance of eighteenth-century England or its reverence for existing institutions that prevented any attempt at reforming the Corporations, but the memory of James II. One of the ways in which he had tried to extend the royal prerogative was by demanding the surrender of municipal charters, and any attempt on the part of the central government to interfere with local authorities would certainly have been resented.

Below the Justices and below the Corporation was the parish, organized on a wholly different basis. Every householder in the parish was obliged to act in turn as overseer of the poor, surveyor of highways and churchwarden. These offices were highly unpopular; they consumed a large amount of time, and no payment or compensation of any kind was ever made. They were so unpopular that no religious test of any kind was ever imposed, and even Roman Catholics had to shoulder their share of the parish burden. The churchwardens could levy a church rate for certain purposes, which had to be paid, of course, by Nonconformists and Roman Catholics as well as by Churchmen. The surveyor of the highways could call on farmers to provide teams of horses and men to repair the highway, and the overseer of the poor was responsible for the support of the aged, the sick, the orphan children and the unemployed, as well as for the men whose wages were not sufficient to keep their families. As the paupers could appeal to the Justices, it is not surprising that the overseer of the poor was a peculiarly unpopular office. Those who were able to, bought themselves out of these onerous duties by paying a substitute. In the country parishes everyone could turn up, if he wished, at the meetings at which these officials were appointed, although no doubt in reality the parish was run by the squire, the parson and the big farmers. In some towns all the residents were entitled to attend the parish meetings, in others they had surrendered their powers to what was known as a select vestry. The corruption, extravagance and incompetence of the open vestries was one of the main sources of argument against universal suffrage.

All the local authorities, the Justices, the parish and the Corporation, were completely independent of each other and of the central government. Within their jurisdiction they could do exactly as they pleased. "The eighteenth century was an era of almost complete autonomy for the local institutions of the country. Their duty was to carry out the law and not to obey the commands of the central executive."[43] The only way in which the Government could coerce them was to bring an action against them in the courts.

IV

Life for the ordinary man in the eighteenth century, unless he was a village labourer tied to his parish by the Law of Settlement, or a Member of Parliament anxious to "sway the listening Senate to command", was not greatly affected by the governing institutions of the country. Never was there a society less planned or one in which the individual was left more to his own resources. While he might fall into great misery, he might also rise to great heights. There was a great difference between classes, but very little difficulty in moving from one class to another. Social mobility, in current jargon, was high. Everyone believed in inequality, but it was an inequality quite different from that which existed in every other European country, where the aristocracy was a class apart and separate from the rest of the population. England did indeed respect her ancient aristocracy,* but it was a respect influenced by the peculiar English regard for

* The institution at least was ancient and no one in England has ever been very particular about the age of the pedigree of individual peers.

wealth. It was Burke who wanted "some decent regulated pre-eminence" given to birth, but it was also Burke who blamed the French for not giving sufficient weight in their Constitution to wealth. Everyone in England believed in a man rising by his own efforts. It was Burke again who said: "There is no qualification for government but virtue and wisdom, actual or presumptive. Wherever they are actually found, they have, in whatever state, condition, profession, or trade, the passport of heaven to human place and honour. Woe to the country who would madly and imperiously reject the services of the talents and virtues, civil, military, or religious that are given to grace and serve it; and would condemn to obscurity everything formed to diffuse lustre and glory round a state."[44] He added that it was important not to make it too easy: "I do not hesitate to say that the road to eminence and power from obscure condition, ought not to be made too easy, nor a thing too much of course. If rare merit be the rarest of all rare things, it ought to pass through some sort of probation."

Something approaching equality of opportunity did exist. Except in politics and the Army there was no barrier and not even exceptional difficulty in anyone rising to any height. Even in politics the difficulties of the ordinary man are often exaggerated. At the beginning of the century, Craggs, who was popularly believed to have been the Duchess of Marlborough's footman, became Postmaster-General, and his son Secretary of State for War. It used to be said that Burke was not included in Rockingham's Cabinet because of his birth, but the more that is known about Burke the more apparent it becomes that it was his character that debarred him from really high office. The law offices were held by lawyers, and the law was one of the great avenues by which men rose from any rank. The awe-inspiring Eldon was the son of a coal merchant. Leslie Stephen said: "There is probably no period of English history at which a greater number of poor men have risen to distinction."[45] Porson, the famous scholar, was the son of a hand-loom weaver in a Norfolk village. His schoolmaster was so impressed with his abilities that he told the curate of his marvellous pupil. The curate in his turn was so impressed that he offered to educate the child with his own sons. Porson lived with him till he was thirteen, going home to his parents on Sunday; the eighteenth century was particular about parental rights. When he was thirteen the curate suggested to a neighbouring landowner that he should be sent to a public school. The landowner said he would send him to Eton if three Cambridge dons were consulted and advised it, and to Eton he went.[46]

White, the Professor of Arabic at Oxford, had a somewhat similar history, except that he had left school and started to weave with his father when some of the local gentry heard of his talents and subscribed to send him to a university. Although there are parts of his career which might not be considered too creditable (he apparently got someone else to write his more important sermons), he not only became a Professor but married the sister of a Norfolk landowner.[47]

Intellect seems to have flourished in the weaving industry. Dalton, the chemist, also started life as a weaver, although he had no patrons and was entirely self-educated. James Mill himself was the son of a small farmer and was educated by Sir John Stuart, the father of Louisa Stuart, Sir Walter Scott's first love. James Mill and Louisa were deeply attached to each other. After her death he wrote to Francis Place: "She was in point of intellect and disposition one of the most perfect human beings I have ever known. We grew up together . . . and were about the best friends that either of us ever had. . . . She spoke about me with almost her last breath."[48] It may have been the memory of Louisa Stuart which made him so contemptuous of poor Mrs. Mill. James Lee, another Professor of Arabic, had started as a 'mechanic' and was actually married with two children before he embarked on his education.

Of course, luck and chance entered into such careers much more than they do today. The story of Chatterton and of Clare are reminders of what might happen; but the literary career of a poor man was probably smoother than it would be today. The modern educational net would have caught Burns, but, if by chance it had missed him, a farm servant would have greater difficulty in getting his poems published now, and it is unlikely that their reception would be so immediate or so generous.

There is another factor which is often forgotten. Every step towards the increase of equality of income means that competition for the prizes in the professions is also increased. The restriction of gentlemen to the Church, the Army and the Law, though never so absolute as is now often believed, may have blocked those professions to people without birth or interest, but it left other professions and business free to all comers. Eighteenth-century England was a fiercely competitive world in which a man might easily fall to ruin but in which he might also secure great prizes.

Although it is hidden from us by the formality of eighteenth-century manners, the classes mixed together much as they do to-day. Every period in English history has thought itself a great deal more socially democratic than the one before it. Dr. Johnson said that "it was wonderful that (Izaak) Walton, who was in a very low situation in life, should have been familiarly received by so many great men, and that at a time when the ranks of society were kept more separate than they are now."[49]

This mixing of the classes was one of the things which people noted as being different in France. Arthur Young, when he went to stay with a French Duke, complained with annoyance that no farmers had been asked to meet him: "At an English nobleman's, there would have been three or four farmers asked to meet me, who would have dined with the family among the ladies of the first rank. I do not exaggerate when I say that I had this at least a hundred times among the first houses of these islands."[50] To anyone familiar with the society of these islands even today, it is not necessary to add that the great were treated with deference, and that a Lord was a Lord. Even Priestley, the democrat, who thought that the upper classes were demoralized by not having enough to do, added: "When the mind is not hurt in such a situation, when a person born to affluence can lose sight of himself, and truly feel and act for others, the character is so godlike, as shows that the inequality of condition is not without its use."[51]

CHAPTER II

DUKES, DEMOCRATS AND DEMAGOGUES

I

EVERY society has a dominant psychological pattern, although it does not control every individual talent or temperament these must work within it. There was nothing to prevent anyone in eighteenth-century England from dreaming of a totalitarian reformer; but to approve of a despot in England, as apart from less fortunately constituted realms, required an originality verging on eccentricity. On the other hand, the social and political atmosphere encouraged democratic ideas. Thus Professor Ogilvie, who produced a theory of agrarian socialism and some proposals for land reform which he thought might justify 'a conquering despot',[1] was an isolated thinker, who not only had no influence but seems to have attracted little attention. Proposals for universal suffrage, however, were made from the middle of the century and at times received considerable support.

The atmosphere of the period encouraged democratic ideas because the psychological basis of democracy is a feeling of self-reliance and self-confidence, exactly the mood which the prevailing conditions were likely to produce: everyone had to be much more capable of looking after himself than is necessary in the modern world. The bulk of the population lived in the country, households of any size produced a large part of their food themselves, all households produced some of it. Before the development of coaches at the end of the century, people had to depend on their own efforts to get from place to place. Even in illness, that emergency in which we are most dependent on outside help, there was little to be had. There were no nurses, and doctors knew so little more than their patients that their treatment was very different from the mysterious miracles of modern science. If anyone was robbed, assaulted or otherwise injured, except in London and Scotland, he himself had to find the criminal and take him before a magistrate. The necessity of exerting oneself was much more obvious than any dependence on the collective whole. Yet men were not helpless before the forces of nature, as they had been in the Middle Ages. Plague and famine had disappeared and agricultural improvements were visibly increasing human control over the environment.

The dominant ideas were easy to understand. Science, literature and even philosophy were democratic in that most important sense that they could be understood by any educated person and even by intelligent people without much formal education; this was the age of common sense, or, in its own words, of triumphant reason. Reason had discovered the laws which ruled the universe and the human mind. It was the singular good fortune of the Englishman or the inscrutable dispensation of Providence that both these discoveries had been made by Englishmen, and Mr. Locke had put his compatriots under further obligations by going on to reveal the rules of ultimate political wisdom. The almost universal acceptance of the ideas of Newton and Locke might have led to the imposition of a scientific and political orthodoxy which would have strangled political as well as scientific speculation. It did not do so partly because on the political side Locke's writings themselves contained some contradictions, but essentially because the successes of the Glorious Revolution as well as those of Newton were regarded as triumphs of the human intellect. Englishmen did not then pride themselves on 'muddling through' but on discovering the fundamental laws of nature, and in those days even political speculation was concerned with these laws. In cosmology it might be thought that the ultimate discoveries had been made. Indeed it was so thought for over two hundred years; but this was because of the remoteness of even the nearer stars, the universe did not thrust its problems on human attention. But in mundane affairs no one, even if he thought the best form of government had been discovered, could suppose that all political and social problems had been solved. Newton's achievements, however, seemed to show that all problems were in principle soluble; it was only necessary to elucidate the laws which governed the phenomena and these laws once discovered would be easily comprehensible.

The attitude thus engendered was a great contrast to that of previous centuries as well as to that of today. In the periods dominated by theology all fundamental problems were already solved. Today ordinary people think that the forces that control our destiny are too big for them to influence, and various mythologies have been devised which personify these forces as historical trends. Even those who still consider that all questions can eventually be given an answer of some kind are by no means certain that we shall like the results. Not only were Newton's discoveries exhilarating because they were a triumph of the human intellect, but his universe was, as long as God was retained at its centre, profoundly satisfying. The universe which had once seemed a chaos of unrelated phenomena was revealed as ruled by laws majestic in their simplicity, and its Creator as a being deeply sympathetic to English ideas, who preferred to govern through these laws rather than to reign as an arbitrary despot.

> The spacious firmament on high,
> With all the blue ethereal sky,
> And spangled heav'ns, a shining frame,
> Their great Original proclaim.
>
> .   .   .
>
> Soon as the evening shades prevail
> The moon takes up the wondrous tale,
> And nightly to the list'ning earth
> Repeats the story of her birth;
> Whilst all the stars that round her burn,
> And all the planets in their turn,
> Confirm the tidings, as they roll,
> And spread the truth from pole to pole.
>
> .   .   .
>
> What though nor real voice nor sound
> Amid their radiant orbs be found;
> In reason's ear they all rejoice
> And utter forth a glorious voice.[2]

The revolutionary effect of the philosophy of reason on France is well known; its effect is not so apparent in England because it did not conflict so dramatically with existing institutions. Its importance is also obscured because it is often thought that the democratic movement in England rose out of the impact of the French Revolution. Demands for Parliamentary reform, even going as far as manhood suffrage, were made in England long before the French Revolution. It is true that these demands were only for electoral reform; their advocates did not wish to destroy either the monarchy or the House of Lords, only to confine them to their proper spheres. The French Revolution had a profound effect on the democratic movement but it was not the idea of democracy that it introduced but the idea of political salvation, of a total transformation of society. These Messianic visions never occurred to the early English Radicals, except perhaps to Priestley. They did not look forward to infinite vistas of progress but back to the original Constitution of the Anglo-Saxons and to the county franchise before Henry II. They stood, as even Thomas Day, one of the more extreme reformers said, "not for the destruction of the Constitution nor even a new modelling of it but only its restoration".[3] It was this attitude which was finally successful in 1832, although by that time some, though not the majority of the advocates of reform, hoped that the extension of the franchise would produce far-reaching change.

This period is the most individualistic in English history. It was individual liberty and not the liberty of associations or parties which the English Constitution was designed to safeguard. Individual liberty means also individual responsibility. Today it is considered not only inevitable but meritorious that the individual should merge his conscience and opinions with others in associations of various kinds. The ideal is the team and the team spirit; the political party and the trade union are considered among its most respectable manifestations. In the eighteenth century any association was somewhat suspect, including the political parties; most serious opinion regarded them as hardly respectable, and associations either of workers or employers were under the ban of the common law. It was not even thought that a man should surrender his conscience to his country; officers of the Army and

Navy frequently resigned their commission rather than fight in wars of which they disapproved.

Prevailing opinion gave everyone encouragement to exercise his reason on any opinion that came before him, and the inequalities of wealth and power encouraged criticism. It is not surprising that every aspect of the social and political structure was freely criticized. The problem of the relief of poverty, for example, exercised many minds all through the century, the existing system appearing to combine great expense to property owners with failure to do much for the poor.

The conflict between the teachings of the Christian religion and the manners and morals of all classes gave the religious a strong desire to improve and reform; which itself involved criticism. In this atmosphere it was unlikely that political institutions alone would be immune. The attitude towards the Government created by the revolution of 1688, the theory of the Constitution itself, the growth of humanitarianism, the ease with which men moved from class to class, all created an atmosphere in which it was bound to occur to some people that liberty could be defined in other ways than it was by Locke and Blackstone, and that it was not only kings who held a position that could not be justified by reason. We forget how radical much eighteenth-century sentiment was. "Some village Hampden, that with dauntless breast, The little tyrant of his fields withstood" is now so worn with use as to be meaningless to us. But the little tyrant of his fields was presumably the local landlord. Akenside, in his 'Ode to Lord Huntingdon', published in 1747, compared him with his ancestors:

> From rich domains, and subject farms,
> They led the rustic youth to arms;
> And kings their stern achievements feared;
> While private strife their banners reared.

> But loftier scenes to thee are shown
> Where empire's wide established throne
> No private master fills:
> Where, long foretold, the People reigns:
> Where each a vassal's humble heart disdains,
> And judgeth what he sees; and as he judgeth, wills.

> Here be it thine to calm and guide
> The swelling democratic tide;
> To watch the State's uncertain frame,
> And baffle Faction's partial aim.

These words might almost be addressed to the present Lord Derby. Thompson seems even to have anticipated the Welfare State:

> . . . I see the stores profuse
> Which British bounty has to these assign'd,
> No more the sacrilegious riot swell
> Of Cannibal devourers! Right apply'd,
> No starving wretch the land of Freedom stains;
> If poor, employment finds: if old, demands,
> If sick, if maim'd, his miserable due;
> And will, if young, repay the fondest care.[4]

Nor was this kind of thing confined to intellectuals. Chatham at times referred to the people in terms which might almost have been used by Winston Churchill: "My Lords, I myself am one of the people. I esteem that security and independence, which is the original birthright of an Englishman, far beyond privileges, however splendid, which are annexed to the peerage. I am myself an English elector and join with the freeholders of England in this common cause."[5] Horace Walpole said: "A superior power cannot bestow superior wisdom or strength, nor destroy the real equality between man."[6] Lord Chesterfield, in his will, spoke of his servants as "my equals in nature and my inferiors only by the difference in our fortunes", and in his letters poured scorn on the conventional ideas about birth: "Are you better born, as silly people call it, than the servant who wipes your shoes? Not in the least. He had a father and mother and they had fathers and mothers and grandfathers and grandmothers and so on up to the first creation of the human species, and is consequently of as ancient a family as yours. It is true that your family has been more lucky than his, but not a jot better."[7]

These ideas were, of course, somewhat theoretical; no one, as we know, was more apt to resent a liberty than his Lordship. The general insistence on the virtues of 'subordination' may seem to conflict with this almost equalitarian sentiment, but it was, owing to the doctrine of the balanced Constitution, quite possible to combine belief in subordination and in the virtues of an hereditary governing class with belief in manhood or even in universal suffrage. Gladstone long after cited the respect shown by the average working man for 'superiors' as a sign that they were well qualified to exercise the franchise. Proposals for reform in the eighteenth century were, moreover, concerned only with the method of electing the Members of the House of Commons and did not even usually include suggestions for the abolition of the property qualifications for candidates for Parliament. Reformers merely wished the people's choice to be free and Members rather more responsible to those who elected them.

Suggestions for Parliamentary reform were made from the beginning of the century and were continually revived. Lord John Russell says that Lord Shaftesbury, in 1689, brought up the comparison, afterwards so famous, between the representation of Cornwall and Scotland.[8] Locke himself has a famous passage on the rotten boroughs:

Things of this world are in so constant a flux that nothing remains long in the same state. Thus people, riches, trade, power, change their stations, flourishing mighty cities come to ruin, and prove in time neglected, desolate corners, whilst other unfrequented places grow into populous countries, filled with wealth and inhabitants. But things do not always change equally, and private interest often keeping up customs and privileges when the reasons of them are ceased, it often comes to pass that in governments where part of the legislative consists of representatives chosen by the people, that in tract of time this representation becomes very unequal and disproportionate to the reasons it was first established upon. To what gross absurdities the following of custom when reason has left it may lead we may be satisfied, when we see the bare name of a town, of which there remains not so much as the ruins, where scarce so much housing as a sheepcot, or more inhabitants than a shepherd is to be found, sends as many representatives to the grand assembly of law-makers as a whole county numerous in people and powerful in riches. This strangers stand amazed at, and every one must confess needs a remedy; though most think it hard to find one, because the constitution of the legislative being the original and supreme act of the society, antecedent to all positive laws in it, and depending wholly on the people, no inferior power can alter it. And therefore the people, when the legislative is once constituted, having in such a government as we have been speaking of no power to act as long as the government stands, this inconvenience is thought incapable of a remedy.[9]

Sir Francis Dashwood, still remembered for very different activities, proposed Parliamentary reform during the Jacobite Rebellion of 1745, for exactly the same reasons as Socialists proposed Socialist measures during the Second World War, to give the people something to defend. In Burgh's *Disquisition on Politics*, published in 1775, can be found all the arguments used in 1832, including, of course, the comparison between Cornwall and Scotland, the dislike of the "ignorant and venal voters" in the open boroughs, and the argument that the Corn Laws were a charge on the rest of the country imposed by a Parliament of landowners. The Rev. William Mason wrote to Horace Walpole in 1780 that as long as he could remember he had been uneasy about the state of the representation.[10]

The orthodox theories of the Constitution themselves provided arguments for universal suffrage. Constitutional theories were based on the philosophy of Locke. Locke's political ideas were derived from the view that every human being was endowed by nature with certain inalienable rights and that government originated in a contract between the individual and the State, by which the individual surrendered a part of his rights to the State in return for the performance of certain limited and specific functions. It may seem unlikely that these somewhat academic propositions should have had any effect on the ideas which ordinary people held about government; but Locke stood to the Whig party in something like the relation in which Marx stands to the Communist party. The parallel is not, of course, exact. Locke's *Treatise on Government* was the justification for a revolution that had already taken place, not the inspiration for one about to begin. But 'Mr. Locke' was constantly invoked in pamphlets and newspapers, and allusion made to the theory of contract in everyday political propaganda, as in the *Craftsman's* list of ideas associated with the Whigs: "The power and majesty of the people, an original contract, the authority and independency of Parliament." Indeed, the doctrine that there was an original contract between the English people and their sovereign rests on an authority higher than that of any philosopher, the House of Lords having decided in 1689 by 55 votes to 46 that such a contract existed.

The theorists of the Constitution went in some cases very near to admitting manhood suffrage in principle. Blackstone is not usually considered a democrat but he said that "if it were probable that every man would give his vote freely and without influence of any kind, then, upon the true theory of liberty, every member of the community, however poor, should have a vote in electing those delegates to whose charge is committed the disposal of his property, his liberty and his life. But since that can hardly be expected in persons of dependent fortunes or such as are under the immediate domination of others, all popular states have been obliged to establish certain qualifications whereby some, who are expected to have no will of their own, are excluded from voting, in order to allow other individuals, whose will may be supposed independent, more thoroughly on a level with each other."[11] The people excluded were more likely to seize on the first sentence than to accept the reason for their exclusion. Men who were anxious for the vote would be certain that they themselves would exercise it independently, and they might come to think that the inequalities which prevented a man giving an independent vote might be decreased or removed. The passage was quoted by Norgate, a member of the Society for Constitutional Information, in his notes to the edition of Sir William Jones' pamphlet on government issued in 1797; indeed Blackstone was constantly invoked by the democratic writers.

Even before the political excitement over Wilkes in which English Radicalism is often said to have originated, there were local manifestations of something like a demand for the extension

of the franchise. In Tiverton in 1754, about two months "before
the general election for burgesses to Parliament, the members of
the several societies of the labourers in the woollen manufacture
and most others of the common people having been taught to
believe that they had an equal claim with the members of the
corporation to elect the Burgesses to Parliament for this borough,
proposed their claim, by letter, to Sir Dudley Ryder, one of the
present Representatives, whose assistance they solicited, and
endeavoured to convince him of the reasonableness of it. They
also informed him of their resolution to support their claim, for
that no improper conduct of their fathers and predecessors could
justly deprive them of their rights."[12] It will be noticed that this
claim was not founded on any idea of inherent natural or
political rights, but on historic rights once possessed before they
were resigned to the Corporation. Dunsford says that there had
been trouble at every election since the new charter of 1724 had
confirmed the Corporation in their sole right of election.

It is not certain, of course, how the citizens of Tiverton regarded
their 'rights', whether as a right to representation or as saleable
commodities for which there would be a brisk demand. But the
incident shows that once there was a widespread feeling against
Government policy there would be demands for reform in the
whole basis of representation. The American war and the increased taxation it necessitated roused this opposition; but even
before this the Middlesex elections had involved the House of
Commons in the greatest unpopularity. Wilkes, already a
hero with the 'mob', was four times elected Member for Middlesex,
a 'popular' constituency and one moreover in which there was no
predominant 'influence'. The House of Commons refused to
recognize his election as valid on the ground that having once
been expelled from the House he was no longer eligible as a
candidate. After the last election the House declared Colonel
Luttrell, Wilkes' opponent, to be the Member. The current idea
of representation might be limited, but as far as it went it was
genuine, and these proceedings caused violent indignation. How
intense and widespread may be seen in the attitude of George
Grenville, who had been a member of the Government which
prosecuted Wilkes for the publication of No. 45 of the *North*

Briton, and yet spoke against the Government on the Middlesex election and published his speech as a pamphlet. Whether his opinions were sincere or inspired, as Horace Walpole said, by "a wish to gather some popularity", they are a tribute to the strength of public opinion.

It was in these debates that Chatham expressed sentiments which, taken literally, probably went far beyond his real opinions. When he said: "The Constitution intended there should be a permanent relation between the constituent and the representative body of the people. Will any man affirm, that as the House of Commons is now formed, that relation is in any degree preserved?" he seemed to be making a criticism of the whole basis of representation.

Petitions poured into the House of Commons from towns and counties deploring its actions; these were, however, not only inspired by what we should now call democratic sentiments but also by the prevailing constitutional theories. The House of Commons, one branch of the Constitution, was accused of usurping the rights of Parliament. The Buckinghamshire petition, for example, begins by declaring the right of electors to choose their own representatives, but goes on: "The claim of either House of Parliament to make ordinances which shall have the force of laws hath once already been fatal to the Crown and the Constitution and will, we fear, if the exercise of it be encouraged, prove again destructive to both." It is true that this petition is said to have been written by Lord Grenville but it must have received the approval of the other freeholders.

It was at this time that Chatham was playing with the idea of a reform of Parliament which would take the form of annual elections and an increase in the number of county Members. He did not find much support for those views. People disliked, as well they might, more frequent elections; "as to additional knights of the shire, I collect little encouragement, at best the thing in theory is not quite disapproved, but the execution not much desired by any".[13]

The quarrel between the House of Commons and the City of London over the printing of debates is often treated as if it was the outcome of democratic ideas. It is, however, doubtful whether

such ideas were involved at all. It is clear that everyone wanted to
read every word of every debate in both Houses, but it is by no
means clear that this desire, so markedly unshared by the democracy of today, had anything to do with any wish to change or
even reform the Constitution. The struggle finally resolved itself
into a contest about a special right, the right of the City Corporation to uphold its own privileges against the right of the House of
Commons, as undoubted then as now, to arrest anyone who
committed a breach of theirs. The mob, it is true, supported the
City, but Wilkes, as an Alderman, was concerned in the matter
and the Corporation were anyhow highly popular for their
Protestant and 'popular' principles. The newspapers who printed
those debates were committing a breach of privilege, but it
almost appears as if those Members who raised the question in the
House of Commons had seized on this as an excuse to stop the
abuse and misrepresentation to which they had been subjected.
Colonel Osborne, the Member who first brought the matter
before the House, certainly had grounds for complaint as he had
been called 'little cocking George', 'the little scoundrel', and 'that
paltry, insignificant insect'. Even the Annual Register which
deplored the measures taken against the Press, deplored also
the language newspapers had used.[14]

II

The American War had profound results on this nascent
democratic movement because it roused strong opposition to the
activities of George III and because many people sympathized
with the revolt in the colonies. "No taxation without representation" was certain of a cordial response on this side of the Atlantic.
There was also a feeling that the defeat of the colonists would have
encouraged the King in his suspected designs on the Constitution.
"The British spirit still flourished unbroken and unimpaired in
the American provinces. They disdained to yield to an usurpation
unknown to the Constitution of their ancestors or to brook
encroachments on their rights, against which their ancestors had
risen in arms. They resisted; and to that resistance, however you

may have suffered in a diminution of wealth, commerce and external consequences, you are indebted for all the liberty that is left you." Burke returned to this idea even in 1791 when he was fulminating against another revolution, and said that he had never wished the colonists to be defeated because he believed that "armies, first victorious over Englishmen, in a conflict for English constitutional rights and privileges, and afterwards habituated . . . to keep an English people in state of abject subjection, would prove fatal in the end to the liberties of England itself."

Those who sympathized with the colonists were furious at the war itself; those who were hostile to them were exasperated by defeat and to this was added revolt against a constantly growing burden of taxation.

The agitation was directed primarily against the King himself or against his 'influence', which was said to be growing through the increased number of excisemen and others employed by the Government, whose votes were at the disposal of the Crown, and through pensions and sinecures of all kinds. The agitation extended from the House of Lords, the City and the House of Commons all through the country where it often developed into demands for Parliamentary reform. In Parliament it was concerned with reducing taxation and curtailing the King's influence. Outside Parliament it started with those two objects but in many places it developed into a demand for a reform of the franchise.

The popular movement which expressed itself by petitioning the House of Commons started in Yorkshire. Christopher Wyvil, who possessed the double respectability of being both a clergyman and a landowner, convened a meeting of the freeholders in York to discuss the lamentable situation of the country. The meeting was widely advertised because the Reverend Leonard Smelt, who had been connected with the royal household, made a long speech defending the King and the position of the Crown. This speech was published and occasioned various replies, counter-attacks and comments.

The Yorkshire committee approached other boroughs and counties and the petitioning movement spread through the country; nearly every county in England held a meeting and prepared a petition. Some of these dealt only with the waste of public money but many also went on to demand Parliamentary reform. The Principles and Resolution of the Constitutional Society at Cambridge said: "Every individual of mankind is born with a natural right to life, liberty and property . . . the consent of the People is the true origin and the happiness of all, the only worthy end of civil government . . . our ancestors, in very remote times, used to make their own laws, and elect their own officers; and that in later times every free man voted for representation in Parliament, for it was only in the reign of Henry VI, that voting was restricted to Freeholders of 40s. a year." In *A Declaration of Rights*, a pamphlet distributed free by the Society for Constitutional Information in 1780, it was said: "An Englishman's liberty or freedom consists in having an actual share either in legislation itself or in appointing those who are to frame the laws."[15] And added that there must be an annual election otherwise thousands of those who have come to man's estate since the last elections would be unjustly denied their rights. Lord Carysfort thought that "it is highly probable that the Government of this country was in origin a pure democracy."[16] This was a reference to the constitution of the Anglo-Saxons; the evidence of Tacitus was also adduced in support. Nor were those ideas confined to those outside politics; the Westminster Election Committee of 1780 presided over by Charles James Fox issued a report recommending equal electoral districts, annual election, manhood suffrage, vote by ballot, the payment of Members and the abolition of the property qualification for candidates for Parliament.

The boroughs returned a variety of answers. The Constitutional Society of Nottingham in 1780 declared that "an equal representation is the Right of the People and essential to the very idea of a Representative body." Meetings of citizens at Edinburgh and at Aberdeen were strongly in favour of reform. Glasgow, however, replied: "The Corporation do not hesitate in declaring that they would be sorry to see too extensive a system of Reformation rashly obtruded on Parliament." The Constables of Manchester, who said they had consulted many prominent citizens, were also against Parliamentary reform and so was the Corporation of

Doncaster. Ninety-nine electors, out of the 130 said to comprise the electorate of Portree and Penryn, signed a letter vigorously defending their rights, beginning: "We trust you will not permit the idle and groundless censures on Cornish Boroughs in general, to prevent your giving us a fair and impartial hearing".[17] Some of the Corporations were repudiated by those unrepresented in them, as for example Poole, and we hear again from Tiverton that "its inhabitants . . . have been excluded from the privilege of Voting for their Representatives in Parliament by a Corporation of twenty-five men only (chose by themselves)". But this time it is not the combers and weavers but "the most opulent and considerable part of the inhabitants". The letter is signed by three merchants and a lawyer.

Even those who wanted Parliamentary reform were divided. The Duke of Richmond, the Westminster Committee and Dr. Jebb wanted universal suffrage. Wyvil himself and probably the majority of the county committees wanted the abolition of fifty of the small boroughs with compensation to their owners; a hundred more members for the counties; and triennial, if not annual, Parliaments. The Yorkshire peers, who had been at first not unsympathetic, were not at all taken with the idea of abolishing their boroughs, and the City democrats had no wish for the landed interest to send a hundred more Members to Parliament. Charles James Fox himself later repudiated manhood suffrage.

Whatever the exact shade of reform they advocated, all the reformers used phrases which, if employed after 1790, would have been regarded as seditious. When Hardy and other members of the London Corresponding Society were prosecuted for high treason in 1794, part of the argument for the defence was that the opinions ascribed to them and alleged to be imitated from France had been widely held by the most respectable people in England long before 1789, and the author most quoted in justification of this view was Burke.

Certainly Burke's speeches, one would think, must have contributed to the birth of the democratic sentiment he so much disliked, and not only by the famous phrase so often quoted against its author: "I am not one of those who think that the people are never in the wrong . . . but I do say that in all disputes between them and their rulers, the presumption is at least upon a par in favour of the people." He constantly alluded to the power of the people, to the original contract and to the trustees of power. In his speech on the economical reforms in 1780 he said they were "necessary from the demands of the people which, when they did not militate with the stable and eternal rules of justice and reason (rules which are above us and above them), should be as a law to the House of Commons". And this is by no means an extreme example of Whig oratory. These phrases sound more radical now than they did then, and even then they were more radical in phrase than in intention. 'The People' in the eighteenth century did not mean the proletariat but everyone represented in the House of Commons against those represented in the House of Lords.[18]

The reformers, even those who were regarded at the time as the most extreme, were intensely conservative; they were intent on a reform of the representation in the House of Commons. There was no attack on the House of Lords or on the monarchy as an institution. Although it was widely held that George III had greatly exceeded his constitutional powers, all the petitions, even when they go on to demand universal suffrage, begin by protesting their faith in the British Constitution and government by King, Lords and Commons. In reading early democratic or reforming writers the limits of their experience must be remembered. They sound more revolutionary than they really were because they did not know, any more than anyone else at the time, what we now mean by revolution. Revolution meant to them either 1688 or 1640. The civil wars had been revolutionary in the modern sense, but no one could have supposed that a second civil war was imminent. Difficult as it may be to believe, there was neither a theory nor a sentiment of class antagonism. There was no demand for equality, even political equality. A demand for universal suffrage did not then involve political equality. Electoral reform did not and was not meant to touch the powers of the House of Lords. Expressions found in the letters of Jebb and other reformers about "aristocratic lust for power" referred to the influence of individual peers on elections. Still less was there anything like 'levelling' doctrines of economic equality or even of social reform. The idea of the seizure of power, so prominent in modern political movements, was completely absent. Nor were the reformers trying to form a political party in the modern sense. The whole idea of a party with a definite set of measures which it submits to the electorate was far in the future.

In some of the pamphlets on the American War more radical doctrines are to be found, although it is not certain how far these authors really meant what they said. For example Priestley, in his *Essay on Government*, published in 1769, put forward two quite incompatible theories. He starts with the current philosophy of natural rights, but goes on to say that the test of a Government is whether it favours progress, by which he seems to mean material progress. If this is the criterion, circumstances might arise in which it would be justifiable to ignore natural rights, indeed Priestley says that "all claims of the individual, inconsistent with the peoples' good, are absolutely null and void". On this view the power of Government is unlimited, whereas the believer in natural rights would surely say with Junius, "if we are sincere in the political creed we profess, there are many things we ought to confirm cannot be done by King, Lords and Commons". Priestley, however, was never happy with theories. A devout Christian, he taught a form of materialism which would be bound to undermine any belief in a future life. An experimental genius, he isolated oxygen but clung to a theory of the nature of air which was disproved by his discovery. Both his views and his history are curiously like those of some of the natural scientists of our own day. He believed, rightly as it turned out, in the possibility of science transforming the material environment, and also, wrongly as it turned out, that as the environment improved, so would human nature.

"Nature, including both its materials and its laws, will be more at our command; men will make their situation in this world abundantly more easy and comfortable; they will probably prolong their existence in it, and will daily grow more happy, each in himself, and more able (and, I believe, more disposed) to communicate happiness to others. Thus, whatever was the beginning of the world, its end will be glorious and paradisaical beyond

what our imaginations and nature conceive." With these views
he naturally did not altogether approve of the Government of
England in the eighteenth century. But his practical criticisms in
the *Essay on Government* seem to echo the ordinary Whig accusations against the King and the Ministry. The French Revolution,
however, opened to him a more glorious prospect, as the Russian
Revolution has done to some of our contemporaries.

It is recorded that later reformers were bored by Major Cartwright, and no doubt we might have been also had we met him
in person; to those who know him only through his books, he has
a certain charm. The son of a small landowner, he had been a
naval not a military officer; he was a major only in the militia.
He had been through all the experiences of an enlightened gentleman of the period. He refused to take part in the American War,
once dismissed a servant for going to see a man hanged, and, in a
more modern manner, organized a restriction scheme in a
commodity, the commodity being woad. He was one of those
people who believe that a letter explaining the real facts and the
true theory will immediately convert anybody. He wrote to,
amongst others, George III, the President of the French States
General and to Burke. He remarks in the letter to Burke: "To
one . . . whose liberality of sentiment and integrity of character
ensure him being open to conviction . . . it is no useless attempt
to point out errors."[19] He therefore enclosed his pamphlet
advocating manhood suffrage, apparently believing that Burke,
whose convictions were well known and who at that time was
Rockingham's private secretary, would recognize the truth,
renounce his previous ideas, and presumably his connection with
Rockingham. Cartwright's support of universal suffrage was
not only due to the view he shared with so many of his contemporaries that taxation was too high (he said that with universal
suffrage "not a blade of grass would be taxed without the consent
of its owner"); he also wanted humanitarian reforms. In his
pamphlet, *Take Your Choice*, published in 1776, he attributed the
harshness of the penal laws, the distress of the poor, as well as
Government extravagance to the lack of political democracy.

Richard Price, the statistician, also believed in progress, but
in the manner of a Victorian clergyman rather than a French

philosopher. In his defence of the American colonists, which is the real theme of *The Observations on Civil Liberty*, he relies on the current Whig doctrines of natural right and the contract between the sovereign and the people. In his next political work, however, *Observations on the Importance of the American Revolution*, which he published in 1785, he set forth some very advanced ideas, even going so far as to suggest that Governments might try to prevent the growth of inequality of wealth, though not to reduce such inequality if it already existed. There is in the Essay an evident dislike of the aristocracy and an obsession with bishops, understandable enough in a Dissenting minister at that date. Price's views are drawn more from books than life, he quotes Plato, Sir Thomas More and Mr. Wallace; and, though he does not mention him, the influence of Rousseau is also visible. It is clear that his real complaint against the Constitution of England is the position of Dissenters. He has no sympathy with the poor, his ideas on inequality were confined to preventing anyone from becoming rich; he seems to have had little or no interest in improving the lot of the working man.

Dr. John Jebb was the only reformer who was a consistent democrat, at least as to the representation. He was the son of an archdeacon and had himself been a clergyman but resigned his living when he developed Unitarian opinions. He then became a doctor and, it appears, a successful doctor. He was already known to the enlightened world through his pamphlets on religious subjects, and when the petitioning movement began, he threw himself into it. He was from the first quite clear as to his objectives. "An English House of Commons," he said, "should be a representation of persons, not of property; of men, not of things." Jebb made the only really revolutionary suggestion advanced in the whole course of the petitioning movement. "Is there any absolute necessity for having recourse to the House of Commons in order to re-establish the inhabitants of this country in their undoubted right to an equal, annual and universal representation of themselves in Parliament? And would not an act of delegates freely chosen by the people assisted by the King and the hereditary nobility be sufficient for the purpose?"[20] But if the first part of the proposal is sufficiently startling, the inclusion of the King and the hereditary nobility shows how conservative, even in its most 'radical' members, the movement really was. Jebb died before the French Revolution, and although it might have turned him into a more enthusiastic democrat as it did Price and Priestley, it might equally have produced, in his clear though limited mind, a violent revulsion against democracy.

The agitation of 1779-80 was partly checked by the Gordon Riots and partly satisfied by the accession to power of Rockingham. This seemed to show that George III had given up his more sinister designs, as Rockingham was known to be most distasteful to the King, both from his opinions and connections. Some measure of 'economical reform' was introduced and the more advanced Whigs, being supporters of Rockingham, were for the moment less ready to encourage popular discontent. The interests of the Scottish burghs seems to have moved from Parliamentary to local affairs.[21] 'The people' also seem to have disappointed the reformers by their apathy. Wyvil himself later said, with a candour very unlike that of modern reformers, that the movement had collapsed for lack of popular support. The Yorkshire committee itself struggled on until 1786 and then dissolved.

The more enthusiastic reformers were, however, neither satisfied nor discouraged, and a society for propagating democratic ideas which had been formed was continued. Known as the Society for Constitutional Information, among its members were Cartwright, the Duke of Richmond, Charles Howard of Greystoke afterwards Duke of Norfolk, Lord Derby, Lord Effingham, several other peers and thirteen Members of Parliament, including Charles James Fox and Sheridan, as well, of course, as well-known Radicals, such as Horne Tooke and Richard Price. The Society professed the most democratic views and demanded manhood suffrage, equal electoral districts, the ballot and payment of Members.

It is not usually considered that this propaganda had much influence, but it is striking that all the demands made in the Chartist programme were first put forward in 1780. It is still more striking when it is remembered that the grievances of the Chartists were economic and that these demands were purely political; neither the French Revolution nor Paine's writings, supposedly so popular, seem to have had any effect in altering or obliterating this Radical tradition. The Duke of Richmond actually introduced a Bill into the House of Lords "for declaring and restoring the natural and inalienable and equal rights of all the commoners of Great Britain (infants, persons of insane mind and criminals incapacitated by law only excepted) to vote in the election for their representatives in Parliament." The Bill was not received with enthusiasm by their Lordships and was rejected without a division. But the Duke was certainly trying. The Duke of Norfolk* was even more enthusiastic; he caused great scandal at a public dinner in 1796 by proposing the health "of Our Sovereign—the majesty of the people". The Government was so angry that he was removed from all his offices.

The Younger Pitt was at one time connected with the Society for Constitutional Information, and it was in consultation with its leaders that he framed the motion that he moved in the House of Commons in 1782 proposing a committee to inquire into the state of the representation of the people in Parliament. In this speech he expressly disavowed any belief in manhood suffrage. He said: "My idea of representation is this, that the Members, once chosen and returned to Parliament, are in effect the representatives of the people at large as well as those who do not vote at all." The motion was rejected by only twenty-two votes.

The Society for Constitutional Information did not end its life in the atmosphere of respectability in which it had been born. In 1794 the Government in which Pitt was Prime Minister and the Duke of Richmond Master of the Ordinance, instituted a prosecution against seven persons, including Hardy, Horne Tooke and William Godwin, and their membership of the Society was part of the evidence against them. The prosecution maintained that the object of the society must have been to undermine the respect for the British Constitution in the minds of its citizens, because the principle of 'active citizenship' involved universal suffrage which, if introduced in England, would destroy the

*His activities were not confined to politics. It is recorded that on one occasion, on arriving at Greystoke, he found the house full of children. Somewhat taken aback, he asked the butler: "Whose are these children?" and received the reply: "Those, Your Grace, that are not yours, are mine."

Constitution. This argument turned out to be the basis of a most powerful defence. The Prime Minister and the Duke of Richmond were called as witnesses for the defence, and the defence counsel was able to say in his opening speech: "If the Crown's evidence had been carried as far back as it might have been . . . you would have found that the Constitutional Society owed its earliest credit, if not its very birth, to the labour of the present Minister and its principles to the Duke of Richmond."[22] And he went on to say that these proposals had been urged by the Duke of Richmond "with a boldness which, when the comparison comes to be made, will leave in the background the strongest figures in the writings of the accused". He was careful to say that "I do not say this sarcastically. I mean to speak with the greatest respect for His Grace." When he got the Duke into the witness box he handed him a copy of the House of Lords Journals and said: "Will Your Grace have the goodness to cast your eye on this journal of 8th February, 1780?" which, of course, contained His Grace's speech on the motion for introducing universal suffrage. The accused were acquitted.

Even the most conservative and responsible reformers were in the habit of using the most extraordinary violence of expression, which was perhaps a reflection of the stability of English society. Horne Tooke, a clergyman, if a clergyman of a somewhat peculiar kind, who did not even believe in universal suffrage, said: "In such a cause [the cause of reform] I would willingly dye my black coat red." Wilkes, when he was presented with a silver cup for supporting the City Corporation in their row with the House of Commons over the printing of debates, chose for a subject the death of Julius Caesar and for an inscription: "May every tyrant feel the keen deep searchings of a patriot's steel." Even Sir George Saville, when he presented the petition from his Yorkshire constituents to the House of Commons, said: "I make no threats, this petition is not presented by men with swords and muskets. But if it should be refused—here I leave a blank, that blank let the feelings, let the reasons of Ministers, supply." No one really wanted to search the heart of poor George III with "a keen deep steel", any more than Fox, whatever he may have said, really meant that the people should rise against the Government. The horror with which the French Revolution was received by nearly everyone in England shows how superficial these ideas were.

III

In the prevailing atmosphere anyone wanting changes which the Government did not carry out was likely to advocate a change in the basis of government because he would think that an extended franchise must increase support for his own ideas. Until the end of the century there seem to have been few ordinary men who wanted drastic changes or, indeed, changes at all. But there are always extraordinary men who are not content with things as they are. The individualism of the eighteenth century inevitably led to the recognition of evils which had not been seen before; it requires some theory of the overriding importance of an idea, like the State, Church or party, to justify the infliction of suffering. The habit of regarding men as individuals taught people to see the slave trade, the penal code, the prisons and the conditions of the poor in a new light.

Humanitarianism did not necessarily lead to a belief in democracy. Both Wilberforce, and Shaftesbury in the next century, were opposed to the extension of the franchise, but many who, like Cartwright, wanted social reforms must have thought they might be produced more quickly after a political change.

Another motive was the wish for legal reform. The criminal law was appallingly harsh, and, although the penalties were often not in reality imposed, the harshness was not even that of a consistent theory of retribution or prevention. The criminal code had grown up piecemeal, and the death penalty had been introduced from time to time for a variety of offences and for a variety of reasons. Apart from the severity of its punishments, the law, especially the law of property was, and for long remained, in a condition of complicated obscurity which made it as easy for the ordinary person to understand as the higher physics of today. Bentham's interest in government started with a desire to reform the law; it was only when he found the Government indifferent and lawyers hostile that he became an advocate of political reform.

There were also people who, to use a nineteenth-century phrase, were not "within the pale of the Constitution". These outcasts were not social or economic classes; no one prevented a man voting because he was poor, although a poor man did not have a vote in every constituency. Nor was anyone prevented from going to Oxford or Cambridge if he could pay for it. But there was a class debarred from taking part in municipal government, or becoming officers in the Army or Navy, or from entering a University; these were the Dissenters from the established Church. Everyone who aspired to any office, and anyone wishing to go to Oxford or Cambridge was required to take the Oath of Supremacy, to sign a declaration against transubstantiation and to take Communion according to the rites of the Church of England once a year. This did not apply to the Parliamentary vote, which could be exercised even by Catholics, and was never applied to Protestant Members of Parliament, although Catholics were not allowed to stand for Parliament. These provisions, which were known as the Test and Corporation Acts, completely excluded Roman Catholics from local Corporations and, in the days of acute religious controversy, would have excluded Protestant Dissenters. In fact Dissenters became members of municipal Corporations and were in some cases even in a majority. Every year after 1729 Parliament solemnly passed an Act of Indemnity to exempt from prosecution those who had not been properly qualified. In any case, as the century went on and reason extended her reign, fewer and fewer Dissenters objected to the oaths, and annual Communion might in time have been regarded simply as an act of courtesy to the State Church. Indeed, as long as there was a possibility of a Stuart restoration, the Dissenters were among the most fervent supporters of the Constitution; and even after 1745 nowhere, except in Great Britain and her colonies, and in Holland, did religious toleration exist at all.

But two things happened to disrupt the harmony between the Dissenters and the Whigs: the American colonies revolted and some Dissenting ministers became intellectuals. The Dissenters sympathized with the colonists, as did nearly all enlightened opinion, but the Dissenters' sympathy was quickened because the majority of colonists would have been Dissenters in England, and

after the establishment of the United States there was a country
in which their position compared very favourably with their
position in England.

The original Dissenters had been religious fanatics, and until
the middle of the century were usually quite uninterested in
intellectual pursuits. But owing to their exclusion from Oxford
and Cambridge, they developed academies of their own to
educate their sons. From these academies developed an entirely
new type of Nonconformist minister, as unlike the ministers of
the first half of the century as they were unlike the ministers
of the nineteenth. The best known of these were Priestley and
Richard Price. Until the days of the trained minister the Dissenters had objected to the disabilities they suffered chiefly for
practical reasons, but the new type of Nonconformist minister
objected to them on a basis of theory, as a modern intellectual
might object to the suppression of indecent novels, although he
himself might wish neither to read nor write them. To the
Cabinet Minister who paid the accustomed dues to the established
Church, although he himself might be a deist or an agnostic,
these men were quite incomprehensible. The attitude of the
majority of educated people was probably that of Blackstone.
"The Roman Catholics divide from us upon material, though
erroneous, reasons; but many of the Dissenters upon matters of
indifference or in other words for no reason at all." Price's
remark that the tests were "a qualification of rakes and atheists
for public posts" shows the Dissenters' attitude. The Dissenters
had few of the reasons for clinging to the established order,
which animated most other classes and they were obviously
likely to be attracted by proposals for reform. Wyvil said that the
more advanced committees in his movement, such as that of
Nottingham, were largely composed of Dissenters.

There was a small but enthusiastic body of men drawn from all
classes and all occupations who advocated manhood suffrage.
These, however, tended to be 'Radicals' and outside the circle of
power. But inside that circle there were, even apart from Fox,
more conventional figures who supported the abolition of the
rotten boroughs and the transfer of their franchise to the new
towns. The Younger Pitt was one of these and his interest in

Parliamentary reform did not evaporate when he became Prime Minister. In 1785 he introduced a Bill which proposed that thirty-six boroughs returning two members each should be abolished, and their representatives transferred to the counties and to four new towns. This was not to be done without the consent of the boroughs themselves, and as they were 'property' with the same claims as other property, he would have provided a fund to compensate their owners. He was, however, in spite of all his 'public' and 'private' efforts, unable to get the Bill through the House and was defeated by 248 votes to 174. He is said to have been 'mortified' by this reception but it is some index of the differences between government then and today that neither he nor anyone else thought that he should resign.

In spite of the attitude of the Commons on this occasion, there is little doubt but that if it had not been for the French Revolution, some reform would have taken place before the end of the century. But the Revolution caused a revulsion against any kind of constitutional change, even the most carefully regulated, still more against any playing with democratic fires. Sir Samuel Romily, himself a Radical, said that the Revolution had had two effects: "among the higher orders it has produced a horror of any kind of innovation; among the lower, a desire to try the boldest political experiments, and a distrust of and contempt of all moderate reform".[23] These two attitudes reinforced each other, the wilder the talk of the left wing, the more determined were the ruling classes not to yield; the more unyielding their attitude, the wilder and more threatening became the speeches in working men's clubs and corresponding societies. For now for the first time appear societies which are specifically working-class in origin and composition. We do not know exactly what attitude the 'labouring classes' had taken towards earlier proposals for universal suffrage. They had strongly supported Wilkes, but this seems to have been more sympathy for someone done out of his just 'rights', then and long after a characteristic of working-class opinion, though now it has vanished, than any belief in democracy.

It must be confessed that the Constitution of the Anglo-Saxons and the county franchise before Henry VI are not slogans likely to have had any wide popular appeal. But the 'rights of man' were very different, and although the revolutionary Governments were not Socialist in the modern sense, the division of large estates among the peasants threatened not only the interests of the governing class, but the whole basis of English society and government and were thus as fundamentally revolutionary as Socialist doctrine.

All English institutions were assailed. Doctrines of class-hatred particularly upsetting to the English aristocracy, who had always believed themselves to be extremely popular, were preached in books and pamphlets. "The tyrannies of the world, whatever the appellation of the government under which they are exercised are all aristocratical tyrannies".[24] The same pamphlet went on to attack "these Draconian codes of criminal jurisprudence which enshrine the idol property in a bloody sanctuary and teach the modern European that his life is of less value than the shoes on his feet."

One of the numerous addresses of the revolutionary societies to the French Convention, that of the Friends of the People in Newington, referred to "that destructive aristocracy by which our bosom is torn, an aristocracy which has hitherto been the bane of all the countries of the earth". It is difficult now to realize how fearful this sort of thing sounded to those whose whole philosophy of social life was based on the ties which bound all classes in reciprocal duties and obligations. Nor was the monarchy spared. George III was assailed in language which might have fitted Caligula or Hitler. Paine in his *Rights of Man*, which is said to have sold 200,000 copies, in two years, attacked the monarchy, the House of Lords, the electoral system and the established Church, indeed every aspect of the cherished system of English liberty. Nor was the attack confined to the Church of England; many French sympathizers assailed Christianity itself as well as particular Churches.

Perhaps even more threatening was the changed attitude of men like Priestley and Richard Price who, before the Revolution, had been less democratic than the Duke of Richmond or Wyvil. Price had complained in 1780: "I cannot help thinking it hard, after repeated declarations of my preference for such a Constitution as our own, to be considered an advocate for pure democracy", and yet in 1790 Price welcomed the Revolution with unstinted praise.

After the great disillusion these ideas were held by a small minority only. The first riots were directed against, not for, revolutionary principles; in Birmingham, Priestley's house and laboratory were destroyed by a Church and King mob. Talleyrand, who was ambassador in London, warned the French Government in 1792, that there was no real support for revolutionary ideas in England. Francis Place is a witness to the genuine support the Government enjoyed during the war, and although himself a leading member of one of the corresponding societies at which the Treason and Sedition Act of 1795 was aimed, said: "Infamous as these laws were, they were popular measures. The people, ay, the mass of shopkeepers and working people, may be said to have approved them."[25]

The horror with which the whole country regarded the latter proceedings of the French was all the greater because of the enthusiasm they had first aroused. Nearly everyone welcomed the fall of the Bastille, most people because they thought France was about to have a revolution on the pattern of 1688, the more cynical because they thought France would be so occupied with her domestic affairs as to lose her dominant position in Europe. The great Conservative writers, Wordsworth and Coleridge, were democrats when they were young. We know that to be alive was bliss in that dawn, and in the intoxication of the moment Southey wrote a play on Wat Tyler which afterwards became a grave embarrassment, for when he was preaching against Parliamentary reform, unscrupulous opponents used to quote from this document. Huskisson, Canning and Lyndhurst had been 'Jacobins', or nearly Jacobins, in their youth. Even Pitt once gave the Revolution a temperate and qualified approval. Only Burke saw from the first that the French politicians were not Whigs.

The cruelty of the French Revolution was one of the worst shocks ever received by the civilized world. People in 1790 were as convinced as they were in 1913 that the worst form of political oppression, the more violent manifestations of popular fury were dead. The horror roused by incidents like the September Massacres was all the greater because England was used to popular tumults. In 1780 the mob had terrorized London, burnt the prisons and many private houses, and although a bishop was dragged from his coach and Lord Sandwich's face was cut and as usual a number of peers had their wigs snatched, no lives were lost except those of the rioters themselves. There was no attempt to injure, far less kill individuals. Aristocrats who were used to being pelted with dead cats and rotten eggs and to having their wigs tweaked off by excited citizens must have been all the more outraged by riots that did not end in such incidents but in wholesale murder. The reaction against the theories which led to such horrors was all but universal. Writers of that age were not so tough as some of our more progressive contemporaries. Large-scale executions horrified them and they did not find any comfort in the thought that the guillotine was a small price to pay for the inauguration of a form of government so successful as French democracy has turned out to be.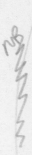

This emotional recoil was increased by reflection on the course of events. The English attitude is sometimes discussed as if it were democracy itself which aroused much distaste. But the lesson of the French Revolution seemed to be that democracy inevitably led to dictatorship. The lesson was easier to learn because all education was then based on the classics, and Plato had said that democracy was always followed by tyranny. It is not always remembered that if Napoleon had won the battle of Waterloo the history of France would have been another illustration of this thesis.

It is not altogether surprising that the majority of Englishmen should have concurred with the sentiments of the Bishop of Winchester, the friend and biographer of Pitt. "The French Revolution holds out an awful warning to governments; how they allow, and to all men of fair intentions and of weight in a country, how they encourage the slightest tendency to resist the constitutional authorities, or the first attempt to unsettle and change what has been long established under the specious attempt of correcting abuses, bringing things to their supposed primitive purity, or attaining an imaginary standard of purification."[27] It was not until fifteen years after the final defeat of the Corsican tyrant that Parliamentary reform again became respectable.

CHAPTER III

THE FIRST REFORM BILL

I

THE Reform Bill of 1832 was the result of an almost unanimous desire for Parliamentary reform, which united the most extreme Tories with the most extreme Radicals. Landowners, manufacturers, industrial workers and agricultural labourers were all dissatisfied and nearly all of them had come to believe that a 'change in the representation' was necessary. But although nearly everyone wanted reform, most of its supporters, with the exception of the philosophic Radicals and some of the working men politicians, were vague about its details; they were only agreed that the existing system was intolerable.

Opinion had completely changed since Talleyrand had written that the English were attached to the Constitution "by ancient prejudices, by habit, by continual comparison of its lot with that of the people of other states, and finally by its prosperity". All these supports had one by one failed. Habit and ancient prejudices were dissipated by war and economic change. The comparison with other states no longer seemed so favourable to Great Britain. Prosperity had been exchanged for depression, which hit farmers, manufacturers, landowners and working men alike. The impact of total war is so devastating that people now find it hard to believe that earlier wars had any impact at all. But the effect of the struggle with Napoleon, though not to be compared with that of modern wars, was nevertheless enormous. The interest in politics in the towns was already lively, the war extended it to the remotest parts of the country. The coaches wreathed with laurel linked small English villages to the battle-fields of Spain and the fleets in the Mediterranean and the Atlantic. For many years England expected to be invaded.

War produced inflation, as it always does. Prices rose roughly as much as they did in the last war, that is to say, they doubled. Income tax was an invention of the period, and indirect taxation was heavily increased. The war and taxation had a disastrous effect on housing. Bricks were taxed and so were windows, and it is to war and taxation rather than to the beginning of industrialism that bad housing in the early nineteenth century must be attributed.[1]

This picture cannot be refuted by Jane Austen. It is clear from her letters that the limitations of the life depicted in her novels are the limitations of art. If she had wanted to paint a 'picture of the age', she could have brought in some scene in which a family waited for news of a soldier or sailor, as the Austens waited for news of her brother Charles when they heard of the battle of Trafalgar. She could have described the feelings of her first cousin when she heard that her husband had been guillotined. Scott, who even in his contemporary novels related his characters to their historic settings, described the alarm of invasion and the turn-out of the Volunteers.

The war fell on a country already in the throes of economic change; that process which we are no longer allowed to call the Industrial Revolution, was by now at least two generations old. The rate of economic development and with it the disturbing effects of change were quickening. The introduction of machinery meant the end of many old trades. The textile industry was the first to feel its effects, hand-loom weavers and the framework knitters could not compete with machine-made products, so as prices rose, their earnings fell. Although machinery cannot permanently reduce the demand for labour—indeed it increases it—it may at first displace labour. Even in those days men and women were not anxious to change their jobs and when to changing techniques was added a trade depression, it was not easy to find other work.

The new industries were mostly located in the north, and some towns were affected by the decay of their old industries or by their migration. Rapid change would have caused dislocation and hardship anyhow, but everything was complicated by the war and still more by its aftermath. No one now alive needs to be told that the end of any major war involves difficult and painful readjustments. Large numbers of men were disbanded from the Army and Navy. Orders from the Admiralty and the War Office abruptly stopped. Agriculture, after years of isolation from Europe, had again to meet foreign competition. This was the age of economists, but only Malthus suggested that the Government and private landowners ought in these circumstances to increase their expenditure, and his *Principles of Political Economy* was not published until 1820, when recovery from the first post-war depression had already begun. The sharp fall in prices that followed the sudden ending of the war produced not only wide-spread unemployment but also the ruin of business men and farmers. Bankrupt manufacturers and ruined farmers naturally lent a ready ear to those who told them that their misfortunes were due to the stupidity and selfishness of a Parliament domin-ated by landowners and that their sufferings would never be cured until the basis of the representation was altered.

Englishmen no longer congratulated themselves on the superiority of their institutions to those of all other countries. The French Revolution was so spectacular that the similarly disturbing example of the United States is now forgotten, but it was very important. As early as 1804 Paine could say: "The American Revolution began on untried ground. The representa-tive system of government was hardly seen in practice and but little thought of in theory. The idea that man must be governed by effigy and show, and that superstitious reverence was necessary to establish authority, had so benumbed the reasoning faculties of men, that some bold experiment was necessary to shock them into reflection. The practice of almost thirty years . . . has proved the excellence of the representative system and the new world is now the preceptor of the old."[2] Every year that democratic government existed in the United States it became a more damaging contrast to the Government of England. Many manufacturers had business contacts with the United States, as for example Cobden and the Radical manufacturers of Leicester. Cobbett, whose books and pamphlets were best-sellers, especially among the working class, published a *Journal of a Year in the United States*, in which he painted that country as an earthly paradise. Everyone who was dissatisfied, the middle class, the working men, the Dissenters, naturally asked why a system which worked in one country would not work in another.

Respect for the Crown was undermined by the character of George IV and his brothers. The morals of the Royal Family perhaps chiefly affected the middle classes and others under the influence of the Evangelical revival, until the position of George IV's wife captured the imagination of the working class, who saw in her a victim of the same injustice which they themselves suffered and "a stainless and unfortunate female" into the bargain. The passion of enthusiasm roused by this somewhat unattractive lady was inexplicable; although the spectacle of a queen turned away from the door of the Abbey at her husband's coronation was not likely to encourage any sentimental attachment-to the Crown.

Even the ideas of the infidel French proved more attractive in the long run than they had at first appeared, or to speak more accurately, one of these ideas, equality. Liberty held no attraction, although the word was freely used to denote Parliamentary reform; Englishmen were free already. Nor did anyone bother much about fraternity. Equality did not then mean what it means now; there was no suggestion of economic equality, and even Paine said there would always be differences of wealth. There was Socialist talk among working men in the towns, especially in London, but Francis Place, the most important of the working-class leaders, was a strong Liberal in economic matters and had no words bad enough for the Socialists. Equality meant social and political equality and appealed as much if not more to the middle class than to the working class. The urban middle class were excluded from political power, not as individuals, but as a class. This exclusion was ceasing to be justifiable even on the old theory of representation. One of the changes in the scene which most struck contemporary observers was the growth in wealth and education of the middle classes of society. This was true of the old middle classes—the provincial lawyers, bankers and shopkeepers. On the old theory of the franchise these were supposedly represented in the boroughs, but in many places even they, especially the less well-to-do, had no voice in political affairs.

There was also a new middle class: the manufacturers, who used machinery and carried on their business in factories. They had avoided the old towns because industry was enmeshed in numerous regulations about wages, apprentices and such matters, and had gone to the remote, harsh but unregulated districts in the north and midlands. The new towns, Manchester, Leeds and Birmingham, were continually growing; by now they had not only large populations which on the old theory need not have been represented, but a new kind of property which was entitled to its voice in the House of Commons. Some of the inhabitants voted for the county Member but they were outnumbered by the agricultural vote; and, as they complained, the county Members, even where they were anxious to do their duty by their constituents, "have not the knowledge requisite to study the grievances and wants of manufacturers". This new property was doubly excluded, by class and by geography. Until the end of the eighteenth century the south of England had always been the most populous part of the country, and therefore the bulk of the constituencies, the rotten boroughs as well as the old but still living towns, were in the south. At first sight it may look as if it would have been simple to remedy at least the geographical anomalies of distribution, but any redistribution would have shifted the balance of power; it was the great employers of labour who wielded in the new towns the influence which was elsewhere exerted by landowners, and to give any representation to new towns raised at once the whole problem of the franchise.

The new capitalists, even on their first appearance, aroused a good deal of hostility. They were rich men, and rich men, moreover, not on the eighteenth-century pattern. Many writers, many City merchants, provincial lawyers and bankers, had made money in the last century, but they had been brought into close contact with gentlemen and had adopted the habits and manners of London or county society. The new manufacturers were self-made men on a new pattern, without the ties which bound all classes together in the old provincial life. Some of them, of course, like the father of Sir Robert Peel, bought land and became country gentlemen on the old pattern. But many did not, and those who still lived in the towns where they worked were the most determined and influential opponents of the old system.

The gentry in the north, especially in Lancashire and Yorkshire, were usually poor, for the land was barren, and isolated from the main currents of eighteenth-century life, nearly always Tories, often Catholics. They regarded the new men with jealousy on account of their wealth, contempt for their manners and had not the faintest idea of the importance of what they were doing. These sentiments of dislike were often increased by pity for the workers in their factories or by a pious horror of the workers' habits which they ascribed to the nature of their employment. Manufacturers seemed to be just the kind of people who had made the French Revolution. The country gentleman's sympathy for the industrial worker, then as now, was often regarded as hypocritical. In some agricultural areas the agricultural labourers were worse off, but probably not in the north where the competition of industry kept wages up and where part of wages by immemorial custom was, and still is, paid in food, thus affording protection from the worst effects of rising prices. Poverty, at least to the spectator, is more tolerable in the country than in the town. The people who are usually, except for political purposes, most distressed by poverty, are the people born to comfort, who feel, when they see a man hungry or unemployed, that but for chance the man might be themselves. The self-made man, however, knows that there is no chance about it. His reaction is often: "I have worked when I could have idled. I have saved when I would rather have spent. I have exercised common sense in the conduct of my life. And so could other people. The complaints of the poor are excuses for laziness and extravagance." Independent themselves, the manufacturers hated the structure of country life and the patronizing charity of squire and parson, and they thought the obvious way to help the industrial workers was to reduce the price of bread by abolishing the duties which protected English agriculture.

The industrialists had also what the eighteenth-century reformers had lacked—policies that they wished to promote. The ideas of the earlier reformers had been limited to reducing taxation and diminishing the influence of the Crown. Although

high taxation and wasteful Government expenditure were one of
their main grievances, the manufacturers had other and more far-
reaching aims. Manchester was already dominated by the
doctrines of free trade, and Birmingham, under the influence of
Attwood, by a theory that the return to the gold standard had
been a mistake, and that it was possible so to manage a paper
currency as to cure trade depression and unemployment. This
may sound like an anticipation of the Keynesian theory; in
reality, however, it was more like those social-credit doctrines
which were developed by a number of writers between the wars.
In order to get a Parliament to listen to plans for a change in
economic policy, it seemed as if it would have to be a Parliament
elected by different voters.

The workers too were as anxious for reform as their employers.
Modern historians have modified the picture of working-class
misery in the towns painted by some writers.[3] The distress was
partial, not universal. The early factory was not so bad as it was
believed, or at least said to be by its contemporary opponents and
its modern critics. But it was nevertheless a period of working-
class unrest. Nor is this surprising. It is usually a period of improving standards rather than of stable poverty in which discontent
and criticism are most apparent. Change, even if it is unwelcome,
teaches the poor that change is possible, and once convinced of
this, they naturally begin to think of changes which might
improve their lot. And, apart from poverty itself, the working
man had experienced inflation in war and unemployment in
peace. Although it appears that the standard of living was actually
rising, this chiefly showed itself in the command over new commodities, such as cotton and tea. Of all forms of improvement
this is the least likely to be consciously recognized; indeed it was
taken by contemporary observers as a sign of increasing poverty.
Although the man who moved from the village to the factory
may have been better paid, most workers disliked the discipline
of factory life and they must have felt completely lost in illness
or misfortune. They may have disliked the squire or the parson
or even all squires or parsons, but in the country some kind of
help or advice could be had from one or other. In the new
towns there was usually neither, and this was not due to brutality

on the part of the employers; it was due at least in part to a respect for the workers' independence and to a belief that solicitude about their welfare was an intrusion on their independence and an imitation of the condescending and patronizing charity of the landowner.

The gloom and terror in which the fortunes of the agricultural labourer have been enveloped have also been lightened by modern research. The effect of the Enclosure movement in driving the small farmer or yeoman off his land and reducing him to a landless labourer has been found to have been exaggerated.[4] The census of 1831 shows that for every household occupying land there were only two and a half households which had no land and which were working entirely for others; for every household employing labour there were five which did not.[5] When the numbers employed on large farms and estates are remembered it is clear that there were still many peasant farmers. But the enclosures had in some counties led to the smallholders being bought or forced out, and in others had had possibly the more serious effect of depriving agricultural labourers of pasture for a cow or a few geese. If these had been held by 'rights' they were recognized and compensation given, although it was probably inadequate and some of it, as contemporary observers complained, quickly found its way to the pockets of the innkeeper. But where the labourer had used the common simply from custom, he was not always given anything, although in some counties he was. This, together with a harsh and rigid interpretation of the law, had produced a number of ruined and embittered men.

The chief misfortunes, however, of the agricultural labourer were caused by misguided attempts to help him. In the middle of the war the magistrates in Berkshire had tried to alleviate the sufferings caused by rising prices by making up wages, out of the poor rates, to a certain level based on the price of bread. Their motives were similar to the motives which induced the Government to introduce food subsidies during the last war. The Speenhamland plan, as it was called from the village where the magistrates had first propounded it, rapidly spread over the whole country with disastrous effects; as wages were in fact subsidized the farmers were enabled to pay very little, knowing that the parish would make up the difference, and as the subsidy was paid out of rates, contributions were sometimes levied on men almost as poor as the recipients. No one who owned property was allowed to receive poor relief and as no farmer would employ a man whose wages were not subsidized, the ownership of a house in some counties became far too expensive for the labourer. After the fall in prices in 1820 food became cheaper, but the agricultural depression which the fall brought with it lessened the chances of employment and made farmers more anxious than ever that the parish should pay as much of their men's wages as could be extorted from it. This raised the rates to the most alarming heights; at Great Shelford in Cambridgeshire, they were 10s. an acre, at Kettering in Northamptonshire, in 1807 they were 28s. in the £.

Rates, however, are levied on houses, and though some of the poorest householders were excused paying, many people must have paid who found their incomes barely enough to cover necessities. Miserable as the condition of agricultural labourers in some counties was, it was well above that of the Irish peasant and after the end of the war wages were still further depressed by a large immigration from Ireland. The picture is, however, not unrelieved black. Most of the distress was in the southern counties; in the north the competition from industry kept wages up, and relief was used rather to provide for unemployment than to subsidize wages. In some counties in which a proportion of wages was paid in kind, as it was and still is in Scotland, or where the unmarried labourers were fed by the farmer, things were different. But there existed sufficient agricultural distress to make many farm labourers among the most radical of the population.

Nor were farmers or indeed landlords much more satisfied. Agriculture during the war had been extended to more and more marginal land and carried on in a more and more extravagant and inefficient manner. Farmers had become used to a standard of living they had never known before. The depression ruined many farmers and many small landowners. Those farmers who were able to hang on pressed for reductions in rent. This was at the time almost obligatory on a landlord when his tenants were in difficulties; in any case it paid no one to have his farms unlet; so that the landlords, the main support of the Tory party, were also embarrassed.

There were few people in England satisfied with their condition. At other periods or in other countries there might have been a demand for dictatorship rather than for democracy or for changes in economic policy rather than political reform. In England the prevailing discontent resulted in a demand for electoral reform because it was an idea which had long been familiar and because the old system was not easy to defend in theory. It had always previously been possible to point out to critics that however odd in theory, in practice it worked, but now in the eyes of many people it had ceased to work. All the desire for change, all the discontent was concentrated on Parliamentary reform; as Melbourne put it, "on every occasion of public calamity and distress, from whatever cause arising, the people call for an alteration in the representation".

Distress and the spread of revolutionary doctrines made agricultural labourers less willing to listen to landowners and aristocrats, while at the same time the growth of large towns made many working men inaccessible to their influence. Large employers in many places exercised the same influence as did the landowner in the country and they were among the most determined enemies of the existing political system. The prominent individual, whether landowner or manufacturer, was, however, becoming less important as a channel of communication and a source of information and opinion, for at this period the Press first begins to appear as an independent force. Nothing disturbed the governing classes more than the growth of its influence. There had been newspapers in the eighteenth century, in 1780 there were eight morning newspapers in London alone. But it was then as now impossible to make a profit or even to pay expenses out of the sale of the paper alone. Editors had been subsidized by the Government or the Opposition and even paid by private individuals to insert attacks or 'puffs'. The trade of journalist was one of the most despised of occupations. But in the opening years of the nineteenth century newspapers found a source of revenue in advertisements and gradually emancipated themselves from complete dependence on outside support. The Government still paid both editors and writers and continued to do so after the Reform Bill; but some even of the daily papers were more or less independent; *The Times* now entered on its career of respectability and the periodicals, the *Edinburgh*, the *Quarterly* and later the *Westminster Review*, were completely independent and extremely powerful. Writers, whose names were household words and who would have been insulted if asked to write an article for *The Times*, contributed to them. Other papers, Leigh Hunt's *Examiner* and Cobbett's various journalistic ventures, were inspired by a political creed and conducted primarily for the purpose of disseminating it. There was, too, a change of style; eighteenth-century newspapers were quite unreadable, and even the greatest writers must have seemed intimidating to the uneducated reader. Paine had initiated a plainer, easier way of writing and Cobbett wrote a prose which was vivid, simple and entertaining. In spite of taxation designed to raise the price of newspapers and make them too expensive for the working class, newspapers and pamphlets, especially Cobbett's, had an enormous circulation. Workmen formed clubs to buy them, newspapers were one of the attractions of a public house. The Press helped to canalize the general discontent into a demand for Parliamentary reform; the Tories had fewer newspapers and those they had, had a much smaller circulation than the Radical publications.

II

A great deal of the popularity of reform was based on false expectations, delusions and misrepresentations. But the popular agitation was reinforced by a formidable intellectual attack on the whole theory of English government launched by Bentham and his followers. It is never easy to assess the influence of ideas and probably the Utilitarians had little influence on the demand for reform, as they had none on the details of the Bill itself. But Utilitarianism captured nearly all those who thought about social problems and infiltrated the minds even of Tory Cabinet Ministers—and this before their triumphs after the Reform Bill when the Poor Law, local government and public health were remodelled by disciples of Bentham.

Bentham destroyed for several generations the intellectual foundation of the old Constitution. Attachment to it was based on sentiment and habit, on a reverence for the great traditions of the past and on an empirical approach to politics, ranging from the philosophic insight of Burke to the ordinary argument, 'after all, it works'. All this Bentham rejected with scorn, with no less scorn did he reject the whole theory of natural rights on which all political speculation had for so long been founded. His theory was rationalist and logical, based on an individual who is the best judge of his own interests.

He gave to the philosophic Radicals a philosophy which was 'scientific', even then a word of power, easy to understand and possessed of an answer to everything, apart from the advantage of containing a good deal of truth which had never been stated so plainly before. He did not deal in abstractions like rights, but went straight to the basis of any philosophy of society, to the psychology of man. Human nature is such that men always try to secure pleasure and avoid pain. The maximization of pleasure is happiness. Since society consists of individuals, the aim of government is the greatest happiness of the greatest number. This famous and familiar phrase contains the great discovery by which Bentham believed he had revolutionized political thought far more successfully than the Jacobins had revolutionized France. Bentham said he had found this idea in Priestley's *Essay on Government*. Priestley wrote: "The good and happiness of the members of any State is the great standard by which everything relating to that State must be finally determined." On reading this, Bentham tells us, he cried out "as if it were in an inward ecstasy"; it is not very easy to see why, as he could have found similar sentiments in many other writers, including Locke.

The principle of the greatest happiness does not necessarily lead to democracy, and Bentham himself had not originally been interested in political theories. He was first attracted to law reform and it was here that his most enduring work lay. But the hostility of lawyers, the indifference of politicians and the frivolity of such statesmen as he met at Lord Lansdowne's made him into a democrat. Although the principle of the greatest happiness does not involve democracy, the hedonistic psychology on which Bentham's theories were based makes it the only reasonable form of government. For as long as everyone must inevitably act so as to secure as much pleasure and as little pain as possible, each man must also be the best judge of his own happiness and therefore of his own interest. If any proposition is put to the vote, each man will vote according to his own interest and the decision of the majority must produce the greatest happiness of the greatest number. This is the only rational foundation for majority rule. If once it is allowed either that the Government or experts of any kind are better judges of what is good for him than the individual himself, or that men are not ruled by reason, there is no basis except convenience for accepting a majority decision.

Bentham threw himself into the campaign for Parliamentary reform and even condescended to popular propaganda in his *Dictionary of Parliamentary Reform*; but James Mill stated the utilitarian doctrine of government in its clearest form in a famous article in the supplement to the *Encyclopaedia Britannica*. He agrees with the Social Contract theorists that the object of government is the necessity of protecting men from one another, for otherwise the strong will tyrannize over the weak. But he does not place this contract at any particular date in the past. Indeed, he talked not of origins but of ends, and the end of government, of course, was the greatest happiness of the greatest number. How is government then to be organized? There is a difficulty here because, just as an individual will always subordinate the interests of others to his own, so will the men who compose the Government:

> If a Government is founded upon this, as a law of human nature, that a man, if able, will take from others anything which they have and he desires, it is sufficiently evident that when a man is called a king, he does not change his nature;

so that when he has got power to enable him to take from other men what he pleases, he will take whatever he pleases. To suppose that he will not is to affirm that government is unnecessary; and that human beings will abstain from injuring one another of their own accord.

It is very evident that this reasoning extends to every modification of the smaller number. Whenever the powers of government are placed in any hands, other than those of the community, whether those of one man, of a few or of several, those principles of human nature which imply that government is at all necessary, imply that those persons will make use of them to defeat the very end for which government exists.

This is very clear, very logical and very persuasive, particularly to anyone who has already decided that democracy is the best form of government, or the form of government which will suit him best. The argument implies, of course, universal, or at least manhood, suffrage; the Utilitarians were against giving the vote to women on the grounds that the interests of women and their husbands were the same, and therefore female suffrage was unnecessary.

Mill had equally logical arguments to meet any doubt which might be entertained about the ability of a democracy to conduct the affairs of the State successfully, or about the fate of such institutions as monarchy or the House of Lords if universal suffrage were adopted. To the objection that "the people are not capable of knowing what is agreeable to their interests", he gave the answer that he had irrefutably proved that if the power of electing the Government is placed in any portion of the community less than the whole, in other words, if the franchise is based on any qualification other than adult male citizenship, those who possess the franchise will pursue their own interests, and only their own interests, so that the interests of all other classes and of the whole community will be sacrificed to those of a particular section. This argument sounds like the modern argument that if any class is debarred from voting, its interests will be neglected. But Mill's argument goes much further. He says that the psychology of man is such that the individual must choose pleasure and avoid pain, and therefore that any collection of individuals which together compose a class must do the same. He interprets pleasure in the narrowest sense; it is probably from James Mill that people derived the impression that the Utilitarian philosophy was based on a crude selfishness. The belief that people pursue what is agreeable to them is perfectly compatible with the pursuit of various kinds of altruistic activities, because these may give as much or more 'pleasure' as purely selfish pursuits. The reformer can also be explained by the hedonistic calculation. Mill proved on his own assumptions quite clearly that it was impossible to stop short of universal franchise. He also proved that the whole people would be interested in good government, but even he failed to prove that they would be able to produce it; all he was able to say was that if the opponents of democracy were right, it was impossible to produce any good government at all. "If the powers of government must be entrusted to persons incapable of good conduct, they were better entrusted to incapables who have an interest in good government, than to incapables who have an interest in bad."

He still felt quite certain that good government was possible and would be furthered by universal suffrage, for the reason that "the wise and good in any class of men do, to all general purposes, govern the rest". This he interpreted to mean that working men would choose men from the middle class to represent them. ". . . There can be no doubt that the middle rank, which gives to science, to art, and to legislation itself, their most distinguished ornaments, and is the chief source that has exalted and refined human nature, is that portion of the community of which, if the basis of Representation were ever so far extended, the opinion would ultimately decide. Of the people beneath them, a vast majority would be sure to be guided by their advice and example."

We smile at the simplicity of Mill's reasoning, but this is the theory of democracy still held by many people. The *Daily Mirror* could rewrite James Mill in its own jargon without dissenting from any proposition except the one about the virtues and influence of the middle class.

III

⌈Most of the middle class and a large part of the working class were permanently dissatisfied with the political arrangements, a bad harvest and depressions in trade converted nearly everyone to reform. But it was by no means certain what exact character reform would take, or which party would introduce it, or even whether it might not be indefinitely postponed. There had been a violent agitation immediately after the war as a result of unemployment, depression and a bad harvest. The middle classes, however, had been frightened by the wild talk of Radical leaders like 'Orator' Hunt, Cobbett and Thistlewood. The Government repressed this agitation with the greatest firmness, not to say ruthlessness, and on the whole all the 'respectable classes' supported them. The French Revolution was too near for any sympathy to be felt for Thistlewood and his companions when they were hanged for plotting to murder the Cabinet, or even for rioters in Manchester or rick-burners in Sussex⌉The Tories had had to deal with 'disaffection' during the war too often not to be efficient, and Lord Sidmouth and his six Acts might be odious, but were certainly successful. When a reaction might have set in, the death of Castlereagh made Canning, who although adamant against Parliament reform, was a liberal and a reformer in all other directions, the dominant figure in the Government. From this period the Tory Governments pursued a social policy difficult to distinguish from that of Governments after 1832, except that it was less energetic and ruthless. There is little difference between the Government when Canning was Leader of the House and Liverpool Prime Minister, when Canning was Prime Minister with a mainly Whig Cabinet, and when Wellington was Prime Minister and Peel Leader of the House in a purely Tory administration.[6] This was one of the periods in the history of Parliament when the division between parties was neither distinct nor deep; although when Wellington quarrelled with Huskisson, and his friends, who had been like him followers of Canning, left the Government, it became more distinctly high Tory.

The slave trade was abolished in 1806, and the Metropolitan Police were established in 1829. In 1816 flogging was abolished as a punishment for women; in 1820 the first Act against cruelty to animals was passed; and in 1827 the habit of leaving spring guns in coverts to catch poachers was made illegal.

The Tories were much impressed by the arguments of the economists, and in 1825 there was a wholesale reduction of tariffs and the abolition of customs duties between England and Ireland. The first Ricardian Lecture was attended by Huskisson, Canning, Peel, and Lord Liverpool the Prime Minister. Under the influence of this liberal enlightenment the Combination Laws, which forbade combinations of working men and so made trade unions impossible, were repealed.

Some steps were even taken towards the reform of the law. This was a particularly thorny subject because lawyers naturally did not want a lot of ignorant laymen interfering. No doubt many of them thought that their interests would be affected, but they were also attached to the ancient traditions of English law, a sentiment which the Utilitarians could not believe to be either genuine or reasonable. The lawyers' position was strong because Lord Eldon was Lord Chancellor, and without the co-operation of the Lord Chancellor it is impossible to change English law. In Eldon the reverence for the whole corpus of English law felt by the average lawyer was intensified a thousand times and reinforced by a natural dislike to change of any kind and a conviction that any reform, however small, however limited, would mean in the end the downfall of the Constitution. Some breaches in the old system were, however, made; in 1823, for example, the death penalty was abolished for over a hundred offences; and in 1826 the Government adopted the proposals of the Parliamentary Committee on Law Reform. Not all these reforms were introduced by the Government. The private Members played a far greater part in legislation in those days, and the repeal of the Combination Acts, for instance, was moved by Joseph Hume; but the Government had to agree with the decision of the House of Commons, and had to allow the Bill to pass the House of Lords. Although some of the Reforms were not Government measures, they show how widespread the belief in reform had become. Nor was it all due to Bentham and his followers. The abolition of the slave trade was chiefly the work of Wilberforce and the religious humanitarians.

By these measures the Government had antagonized many of those to whom a Tory Government had to look for support. The police were particularly unpopular; the reaction was something like what it would be if a modern British Government attempted to introduce a secret police. Many country gentlemen had never forgiven Peel the return to cash payment, or in other words return to a gold standard, in 1820 with its deflationary consequences. More people were aware of the effect of changes in the value of money than might be supposed. In 1833 half the county Members voted for a motion for currency reform introduced into the House of Commons by Attwood. Sir James Graham demanded that the salaries of all officials should be reduced because the real value of money was rising. Lord Blandford, an ultra-Tory, was seduced by Attwood's currency theories and saw in them the salvation of agriculture.

But doubtful as the country gentlemen might be of Peel and even of Wellington, they were not prepared for the great betrayal of Catholic Emancipation. It is difficult now to understand the importance attached to this measure, but the supremacy of the national Church in religion was as much an article of the Tory creed as the supremacy of the land in politics. The Bill to relieve Catholics of their civil disabilities split the Tory party from end to end, particularly as Peel himself had always been an extreme Protestant and represented the University of Oxford, the core of opposition to the Catholic claims. Sir Charles Wetherall, the Attorney-General, refused to draw up the Bill and delivered a violent attack on the Government from its own front bench. The toast of 'Church and King' had to be abandoned at Tory gatherings, so violent were the reactions. The Duke of Cumberland, an ultra-Tory, said that Wellington's real object was to overthrow the monarchy. Peel lost his seat at Oxford. More important if less vivid than these demonstrations, many clergymen and many peers who had been the strongest supporters of the old Constitution, were convinced that if Catholic emancipation could be carried under the existing system there must be something wrong with it. Cobbett united with Lord Blandford in thinking that Catholics would buy up the rotten boroughs and this, together with the influence of great Catholic landowners, would make them dominant in the House of Commons. Catholic Emancipation and the difficulties of farmers so converted Lord Blandford that he became an honorary member of Attwood's Birmingham Political Union and introduced a motion into the House of Commons which combined Parliamentary with currency reform.

In spite, however, of the real desire of the country for reform and the doubtless transient enthusiasm of the extreme Tories, no one expected the fall of the Government in 1830. But for the obstinacy of the Duke of Wellington a less drastic reform might have been carried by agreement between all parties. Peel was not averse to moderate reform and in 1830 some of the Whigs offered their support to the Government if they would introduce some measure of Parliamentary reform. The Duke refused to consider any kind of reform. Even then there seemed no immediate prospect of any change of Government; indeed the Government seemed to be gaining support. But in 1830 George IV died. A change of sovereign in those days made a general election necessary.

The election coincided with the July Revolution in France which replaced Charles X with Louis-Philippe. It was widely believed at the time, although it is disputed by modern historians, that this revolution contributed to the victory of the reform candidates. Contemporary opinion regarded it as one of the main factors in the Government's defeat, for when the election results were known it was calculated that the Government had lost some fifty seats. Such calculation was then necessary as it was by no means plain which party any particular Member would support; they were still elected as individuals and hardly thought of at all, except for the leaders themselves, as members of a party.

Moreover, although the result was regarded as a victory for the reformers, neither party put any definite plan before the electorate. The opposition was divided into various groups of Whigs and Canningites. Lord Grey had introduced several proposals into the House of Commons in the early years of the war but had seemed indifferent about such ideas for some time. Lord John Russell had brought forward various Bills for minor electoral reform, but had never proposed any complete scheme. Even Brougham, whose election for the large and independent constituency of Yorkshire was regarded as the most startling and significant of the results, had not made any definite suggestions about the franchise although he stood as a reform candidate. It was not so obvious as it would be today that one party and one alone could form a Government. It was even thought possible that Wellington would exchange Peel or Goulbourn for some Whigs and introduce a limited measure of reform. The Duke himself made this impossible by a declaration that he would never lend himself to reform of any kind. After this it was only a matter of time before the Government fell. Although the actual occasion of Wellington's resignation was a minor defeat, which would not in ordinary circumstances have entailed a change of Government, it was by this time clear that the country would insist on some change in the franchise, which would go as far at least as representation for the new towns and the suppression of a number of rotten boroughs.

The King sent for Lord Grey, who made it a condition of accepting office that the King should support reform. His Cabinet was not merely composed of Whigs; Melbourne and Palmerston had been followers of Canning, the Duke of Richmond was an ultra-Tory, only Lord Durham, 'radical Jack', was a democrat. It was not surprising that this Cabinet should not have immediately agreed on a plan. Lord Grey then hit on an expedient, much used subsequently, of leaving it to a committee of four to draw up a Bill.

The Bill when finally introduced roused the utmost enthusiasm and the utmost horror.

Sixty-two boroughs with less than 2,000 inhabitants were to be disenfranchised altogether, and forty-seven of less than 4,000 inhabitants, were to return one Member instead of two. Most of the seats thus made available were to be transferred to the unrepresented towns, although additional Members were given to twenty-six counties and also to Scotland. Four new constituencies were to be created in London. These changes swept away most of the rotten boroughs, though not all of them. Calne, for example, in the possession of the whig Lord Lansdowne, was not in the schedule, as the Tories did not fail to point out.

The abolition of so many seats, however, and the halving of the representation of small boroughs greatly diminished the weight of landowners and of the southern counties in the House of Commons and transferred the influence they had exercised to manufacturing interests in the north. The Tories deplored the effects which these changes would have, and resented the abolition of rotten boroughs without compensation as an attack on property itself. But important as these changes were they could be reconciled with the old theory of representation. The most startling and far-reaching change in the Bill was the introduction of a uniform franchise in the boroughs, which had the effect of abolishing the existing working-class element in the franchise. The qualification was to be the payment of rates on a house of an annual rent of £10 or more. Those who had an existing right to vote were to retain it as long as they were residents, but when they disappeared, working men would be virtually excluded.

Angry and dismayed as the Tories were by the treatment of the rotten boroughs, much as they mourned the Members for the small boroughs, it was the uniform franchise and its implications which disturbed them most. For they saw, as did the Radicals, that such an arrangement must lead to complete democracy either by revolution or by another and wider extension of the franchise. They were, even the most 'aristocratic' of them, sincerely convinced of the danger of having no representation of working-class interests in the House of Commons. It was one of the main themes of Peel's speeches. "If you were establishing a perfectly new system of representation would it be wise to exclude altogether the sympathies of this class? How much more unwise, when you find it possessed from time immemorial of the privilege, to take the privilege away, and to subject a great, powerful, jealous and intelligent mass of your population to the injury, ay, and to the stigma, of entire uncompensated exclusion." He was not, as might be supposed, merely angling for popular support against the Bill. Lord Ellenborough, a man neither then nor now regarded as the possessor of much political wisdom, repeatedly made the same kind of remark in his diary, when there was no need for protestations. He said on one occasion that "in ten years the poorest class will be unrepresented and then we shall have a servile war or universal suffrage".[7] Nor was it only Tory politicians in the heat of the struggle who took this view. Walter Bagehot had come to think in 1877 that the fundamental mistake of the Bill had been "the vicious precedent of establishing uniformity", which had made universal suffrage inevitable. Even although the Bill of 1867 had only introduced household suffrage in the boroughs, he said "the middle classes have as little power as they had before 1832, and the only difference is that before 1832 they were ruled by those richer than themselves and now they are ruled by those that are poorer".[8]

If the object of the Government had been to prepare the way for democracy the limited but uniform franchise would have been a masterly stroke, but this was not the purpose of the Reform Bill; it was designed rather to prevent the development of democracy than to foster it. Or perhaps it would be truer to say that its fundamental purpose was to prevent a revolution on the French pattern. For even in 1831 the memories of 1789 exercised their influence. The Whigs had derived a moral from these memories different from that subsequently drawn; the lesson taught them was to attach the middle classes to the existing institutions so that any revolutionary movement would be as strenuously opposed by these classes as by the landowners themselves. Nor did they or their supporters make any attempt to conceal their motives as modern politicians might have done. Lord Althorp remarked during the debates that by 'the people' he meant the middle classes. The ideas which had inspired the Cabinet were stated by Macaulay with his accustomed clarity. He was not a member of the Government but he was particularly representative of the type of middle-class reformer who played so large a part in politics between 1832 and 1867. He said during the second reading debate: "We say, and we say justly, that it is not by mere numbers, but by property and intelligence that the nation ought to be governed. Yet, saying this, we exclude great masses of property and intelligence, great numbers of those who are most interested in preserving tranquillity and who know best how to preserve it. We do more. We drive over to the side of revolution those whom we shut out from power."⌐

IV

The Bill did just what it was designed to do; it included in the electorate all those who had sufficient intelligence and education to follow political questions with care and enough security to be most unwilling to embark on reckless policies. The success of the measure in attaching the mass of the new electorate to the Constitution was proved in the agricultural troubles which immediately followed the return of the first Reformed Parliament and in the Chartist movement of the 'forties. Any revolutionary movement was, as the Whigs expected, helpless without middle-class leadership.

In its immediate effect the Bill was an unparalleled success, but its ultimate results were exactly those predicted by the Tories. It did in the end lead to universal suffrage, to a decline in the power of the Crown, to the virtual extinction of the House of Lords, to an attack on property itself. They were only wrong in their timing of these developments; they expected the abolition of the monarchy and the House of Lords about 1840 and a socialist republic somewhere about 1845. Two of their prophecies indeed turned out to be incorrect, the disappearance of the Tory party and the weakness of the executive. Peel and Wellington thought that the party could hardly survive and even if a dispirited remnant managed to get elected they would never be able to form a Government. In fact Peel was Prime Minister with a Tory Cabinet in 1839, and it was not popular but royal dis-approval which prevented his being in office in 1837. The Tories, especially Wellington, also thought that the executive would be so weakened that it would hardly be possible to carry on the Government. Although there were symptoms of this between 1832 and 1867, democracy in England, in contrast to democracy on the Continent, has immensely strengthened the executive.

No doubt, if Wellington were alive today he would say that he had been right, for if the Cabinet is more powerful compared with the House of Commons, fear of public opinion has more than once prevented Governments taking action which they knew to be necessary.

The arguments of the opponents of reform made no impression whatever on the country. Let no one think that these arguments were all as strange as some of them now seem. The Tory defence of the small boroughs as representing something more valuable than could be calculated in mere numbers was repeated word for word by *The Observer* in opposition to the last redistribution.

A vast majority were enraptured with the boldness, the originality, the simplicity of the scheme. It still, however, had to get through the two Houses. Even in the House of Commons the second reading only passed by one vote and in committee the Government were defeated. The Tories still hoped that they might strangle the Bill, but the King instead granted a dissolution of Parliament. The election which followed was an overwhelming victory for the Government. Even before the results were known the country had clearly given its verdict. "The Bill, the whole Bill and nothing but the Bill" was heard on every side. Placards appeared in the most respectable windows with "No taxes paid until the Bill is passed". A great meeting at Birmingham stood with bared heads and pledged themselves to unending struggle and then sang a hymn composed for the occasion which ended with the words:

> God is our guide; from field, from wave,
>   The plough, the anvil and the loom,
> We come, our country's rights to save,
>   And speak a tyrant faction's doom.
>   And hark! We raise from sea to sea
>   Our sacred watchword liberty!

Armed insurrection was both threatened and feared. Francis Place devised a plan by which the ruling classes might be intimidated through a run on the banks; placards proclaiming "To stop the Duke go for gold" were actually distributed. None of this, however, turned out to be necessary, although the election results, by their overwhelming support for the Bill, showed half the arguments for reform to be unfounded. Over a hundred Members who had voted against the Bill lost their seats. Only fifteen of the eighty-two county Members had voted against, but of those, eight were defeated. Tory members lost seats they had represented for thirty years. The atmosphere must have been like that of the election of 1945, when all ordinary sentiments and interests were forgotten in the desire for change.

The verdict of the country was plain without mistake; but one of the Houses of Parliament is not bound to pay attention to any such verdict; indeed the Peers may well regard it as their duty to save the country from itself, and they did so in 1832. They were, however, far from being in a strong position. This was the first occasion on which the Lords had faced a House of Commons elected to carry out a policy of which they disapproved. Apart from the natural conservatism of men of mature years, as most peers naturally are, and of great possessions, which most peers then were, the House of Lords was predominantly Tory not only because of the long succession of Tory Governments but because the Younger Pitt had made peers with a hitherto unknown lavishness. He is reputed to have said that "any man with £10,000 a year has a right to a peerage". The dilemma of the House of Lords was not unlike it is today for one party was heavily over-represented compared to its representation in the country, though the lack of balance between the parties was not so great and the causes for it were quite different.

The Lords threw the Bill out. The country was enraged and the Government alarmed. Both the possibility of making sufficient peers to pass the Bill and the possibility of another Government were raised. But it was plainly impossible for an anti-reform ministry to rule the country and the crisis was finally resolved by the prayers of the King, who prevailed on the Duke of Wellington to persuade enough of the peers to stay away from the House to allow the Bill to pass.

The Bill had thus to be carried in both Houses by pressure from outside, than which nothing was more repugnant to the old theory of the Constitution. Such pressure went far to turn the members into delegates, not representatives. In this election candidates had been forced to give 'pledges' as to their future conduct, for the only issue was reform and electors even of that day would not elect a man without knowing his opinions on it.

The Tories had won some battles on the floor of the House. The number of boroughs to be abolished was reduced from sixty-two to fifty-six, the reduction of members for small boroughs from forty-seven to thirty-one. No alteration had originally been proposed in the qualification for the county vote except that lease-holders for more than twenty-one years with an annual rental of £50 were to vote, and 40s. copyholders were added to 40s. free-holders. By the famous Chandos Clause the Tories managed to give a vote to tenants at will with a rent of £50 a year. This enfranchised the bulk of tenant farmers and may seem a demo-cratic step. But it was generally believed that tenants were so much under the 'influence' of their landlords, however the word influence was interpreted, that this simply led to an increase in the weight of the landed interest.

Even when the 'ancient rights' voters had disappeared, the franchise would only be uniform in the boroughs. Without any growth of democratic feeling it might well be supposed that there was plenty of room for argument and comparison and that the settlement would in reality be far from that finality promised by the Government.

Two other steps were taken towards the modern system; voters were in future to be registered before they were allowed to vote. These registration lists were to be compiled by the overseers of the poor and in order to curtail the expense and disorder of elections, polling was limited to two days. Not of course the same two days in every constituency. One polling day for the whole country was not introduced until 1918.

CHAPTER IV

THE GOLDEN AGE OF THE PRIVATE MEMBER

I

IT has become the fashion to minimize the immediate effect of the Reform Act as much as nineteenth-century historians exaggerated it. The surface of politics, electioneering methods, the relation of a Member to his constituency, the influence of the local landowner were much as they had been before, not all even of the proprietary boroughs were abolished. But a shift in the relative position of the Monarchy, the House of Lords and the House of Commons took place and, more important, reform became respectable because it had been successful. To say that someone was proposing an 'innovation' was, in the eighteenth century, a reproach; after 1832 it became, if not the compliment it would be today, at least neutral. No longer was anything held to be outside the scope of improvement. The municipal Corporations, the Poor Law, the Irish Church and many other institutions were reformed in accordance with the new spirit.

Politics as experienced by the ordinary Member of Parliament were less altered than most people had expected. The £10 franchise meant that in the constituencies both the rich and the poor were swamped by the middle class, and this class, through its voting strength, became the predominant political class in the sense that it was the electorate. The new voters did not, however, use their new power to assert their class interests, but in purely political matters showed rather a tendency to follow the lead of the old political class. Radicals complained that there were still forty-two pocket boroughs returning sixty-nine members.[1] In most county constituencies and small boroughs the influence of the local landowner was still supreme; in some cases it had even been increased as in Malmesbury, where the 'influence' is said to have passed from the Corporation to Lord Suffolk. In the new towns and in large cities manufacturers occupied a position similar to landowners in the country. Advocates of a further extension of the franchise always said it was ridiculous to maintain that democracy meant socialism; on the contrary working men would vote for great employers of labour. Dod's *Electoral Facts* (1852) gives the prevailing 'influence' in each constituency after the results of the previous election. Of Tiverton it tells us that the influence was formerly divided between Sir John Muntze and the late Earl of Harrowby, "subsequently possessed by the Earl alone, but since the Reform Act is in possession of Mr. Heathcoat, proprietor of the great lace factory in the town". In the same way in Leicester, "formerly the families of Manvers and Frewen had strong interests here; but of late years the great dealers in hosiery and the heads of the stocking factories have possessed the predominant influence".

The electorate in most boroughs was still small, in some cases no more than 500 voters, so that either bribery or influence was easy to exercise. Bribery was just as common after 1832 as it was before and is quite plainly revealed in Dod, as where it is said of Totnes "as is the case in all small boroughs where parties happen to be almost equally divided, money has considerable weight in Totnes". The prices of votes varied in different constituences and were well known to election agents; £1 to £2 was sufficient at Leicester and York, while at Ipswich in 1841, £15 to £20 was given.[2] In addition to cash down, unlimited drink was provided during the election at the candidate's expense. The expense of elections was not much reduced from what it had been before reform, and this meant that parties still made arrangements to avoid a contest in some constituencies. Intimidation was also employed; gangs of men were hired by both sides to shout at their opponents, throw rotten eggs and indulge in all the traditional political activities as well as threats of more serious violence, which were quite important when voting was still open and not by ballot. 'Couping', i.e. making a man drunk and shutting him up until he had voted, had become, with the extension of the franchise, even more useful.

The Parliament elected by such methods carried through a vast series of reforms, many of them highly unpopular, especially with the class from which the new voters were mostly drawn' for although the repeal of the Corn Laws and the new Poor Law might be considered as framed to suit middle-class interests, other reforms, such as factory and sanitary legislation, were most repugnant to middle-class sentiment. The picture in broad outline looks curiously different from the picture in detail. *Hansard* is full of descriptions of bought votes and intimidated voters, and so are contemporary novels; but public opinion in the middle of the century probably agreed with Bagehot that the Reform Act had been eminently successful. "It is a commonplace to speak of the legislative improvement of the last twenty-five years. . . . Free trade, a new colonial policy, the improved poor-law, the encumbered estate acts in Ireland, the tithe commutation, municipal reform, the tentative but most judicious support of education, are some of the results of the reform of the House of Commons. Scarcely less important is the improvement which the Reform Bill has introduced into the general tone of our administration; our executive has become purer, more considerate, more humane."[3] In reality most of these things were due to the change in public opinion rather than the change in the qualifications for the franchise; the policy of reform had already begun before the Act. Peel, its determined opponent, was much more typical of the new age and the new attitude than Melbourne or Palmerston, its supporters.

The Reform Act is a landmark in English politics not because it introduced a change in policy, but because of the changes it made in the Constitution. In spite of bribery, influence and intimidation, its effects can be seen even before the next extension of the franchise. Before 1832 we are in an unfamiliar world which seems to us in some ways recklessly individualistic, in others intolerably authoritarian. After the Reform Act some of the familiar landmarks begin to appear. The changes may appear small if attention is concentrated only on the qualifications for the franchise and the conduct of elections. Although the franchise eventually determines all the other conditions of politics, it takes time to make itself fully effective; yet if we look at some of the other political factors, the revolutionary nature of the Reform Act is clear. The relations between different parts of the Constitution, between the King and the Ministers, between the Lords and the Commons, between central and local government, were altered. The series of economic and administrative reforms since 1782 had made it more difficult for the King to manage the House of Commons. The long supremacy of Pitt and the tie, which can only be called ideological, which bound his followers together, had also worked to undermine the power of the Crown. Whatever theoretical powers the King might have had in choosing Ministers, he could not have exercised them effectively if there had been strong party organization in the House of Commons. The Reform Act completed this development, although it did not at once become plain either to the King or to the party leaders. After 1832 the House of Commons chose the Government, and the Prime Minister had either to have a majority already in the House or to win an election. It was to the Prime Minister and not to the King that Members of Parliament would in future look for promotion. With the extinction of the King's power to bribe or coerce went a growing disinclination among Members to be bribed. A number of young Members shared the deep earnestness of Lord Ashley.

It has been pointed out by Mr. Enoch Powell[4] that the Reform Act emancipated the House of Lords from royal control as well as the House of Commons. Most of the Lords had thought that the Reform Bill would mean the end of their House; the Duke of Wellington's prophecies of doom are well known. It was true that the Lords had had to yield to popular clamour and allow the Bill to pass. They had sustained a public defeat and to this extent their prestige, if not their actual power, had been damaged. But the Bill made no inroads on their formal powers; it diminished although it did not altogether abolish the hold individual peers had on the House of Commons through their influence in the constituencies; it did nothing to lessen, it rather increased the influence they could exert by asking Members of Parliament to dinner. Bagehot said that one of the motives which led a man to the House of Commons was a wish to raise his social position and for this ambition invitations played a considerable part. No doubt if either of the two main parties had wanted to introduce democracy, or if a large section of the country had really believed in democratic ideas, a clash might have occurred between the two Houses in which the House of Lords would have been destroyed. As long, however, as large classes were excluded from the franchise, Radical agitation tended to be concentrated on electoral reform, both because it was more obvious and because it was more likely to be immediately rewarding. Even those who strongly objected to an hereditary second chamber thought that manhood suffrage would be a necessary preliminary to its abolition and on the whole there seems to have been little feeling against the Upper House. Its abolition did not figure even in the Chartists' demands.

The House of Lords seems an odd institution in a democracy, but it was not until the eighteen-seventies that even the Liberals admitted that they were democrats. Gladstone as well as Disraeli protested in the reform debates of 1866 and 1867 that he had no belief in democratic principles. The Whig Governments grumbled when the Lords refused to pass their Bills and a few Whigs, as well as Radicals, made suggestions for reforming the Lords, but the majority of Whigs were as loath as the Tories to have a full-scale clash. It was the constitutional right of the House of Lords to reject or amend Bills sent to them from the Commons, and although immediately after 1832 they acted with some caution, as soon as they realized the strength of their position, they made full use of their rights. They insisted on amending the Municipal Corporations Bill and the Reform Bill of 1867; they rejected Gladstone's proposal to repeal the duty on paper in 1860; they insisted on a redistribution Bill before they consented to the extension of the franchise in 1884. The management of the Lords was a preoccupation even with Conservative statesmen; in 1839 Sir James Graham asked despairingly how could they manage the Peers if the Duke of Wellington died?

The independence of the Lords contributed to the weakness of Governments between 1832 and 1867. The Tories had been right in thinking that the Reform Bill would weaken the executive, although this effect was only temporary. Governments no longer had the old means of securing a majority in the House of

Commons nor had they the new discipline of party. Members were still elected primarily as individuals and not as members of a party. The property qualifications and the lack of any salary meant that most Members would be men of substantial standing. No Government, no leader could depend on automatic obedience. Men on the Government side had to be persuaded to vote for Government measures, and men on the Opposition benches could be persuaded to vote for them. There was little means of either coercion or bribery and a substantial proportion wanted neither office nor titles. The local committees who chose Parliamentary candidates would have been astounded indeed if Sir Robert Peel or Lord Melbourne had attempted to censor their choice. The independence of the back-benchers was increased after 1846 because with the split in the Conservative party over the repeal of the Corn Laws, the Peelites formed a third party. Governments, whether Whig or Conservative, could only be kept in office by the benevolent tolerance of the Opposition. It has been said that Lord Stanley ruled England for twenty years from the Opposition benches. This period, which has been called the golden age of the private Member, was also the golden age of the House of Commons itself. It was the House, not the King as in the eighteenth century or the electorate as today, which chose Governments. Yet at the same time one of the influences which has encroached on the original powers of the House of Commons, public opinion outside the House, was beginning to appear in a more definite form.

To contemporaries the most startling thing about the Reform Bill was that the issue was decided outside Parliament. Public opinion had been important before; as we have seen, politicians were cautious about offending it, and Governments had withdrawn in the face of even ill-informed opposition as long as it was sufficiently widespread. But although they had bowed to organized opinion so far as to withdraw their own measures, the Reform Bill was different in that it was conceived in deference to popular agitation and forced on the Lords, and even on the King, by popular clamour. Nothing disturbed Conservative speakers more. Peel said in the House of Commons: "I see no prospect that the King will hereafter be able to exercise an unpopular prerogative however necessary that prerogative might be to the permanent interests of the country. . . . How can the King hereafter change a Ministry? How can he make a partial change in the administration in times of public excitement with any prospect that the Ministers of his choice, unpopular perhaps, from the strict performance of necessary duties, would be returned to Parliament?"

The reformed franchise gave the electorate a cohesion more like a modern electorate than anything which had existed before. Under the old franchise it would have been difficult to frame a party programme which would appeal to the whole electorate even if there had been any incentive to do so. Waves of feeling did sweep across the country, as the rise of Chatham showed; but they could express themselves only in a very limited way; the London mob, the county Members, independent alike of Court and Ministry, and the City of London were the three chief vehicles. But after the Reform Act the larger part of the electorate in the towns was composed of people with roughly the same interests and roughly the same scale of values. Even those without votes who agreed with the majority could ally themselves with the voters, and their support was valuable because the Government still paid attention to the views of the unrepresented. For example, Sir Robert Peel is said to have been influenced by popular feeling against the Corn Laws, although many of those who shared it did not have votes.

Peel was the first politician to recognize the new power of the electorate. No party leader had previously made a direct appeal through a public speech or a written manifesto and, not only because of the lack of facilities, it was held, indeed it was held even after 1867, that the proper way to address the country was through its representatives in the House of Commons. When Peel was asked to form a Government in 1835 he issued a statement on his policy; it respected the convention of the time to the extent that it was addressed to his own constituents, but it explained his attitude on the topics of the day, had been composed by the whole Cabinet and officially sent to *The Times*, the *Herald* and the *Morning Post*. The Tamworth Manifesto was the first sign of the tendency which has grown with democracy for party leaders to appeal directly to the whole electorate for general support, and thus to some extent to by-pass both the House of Commons and to distract attention from the speeches of Members even in their own constituencies. The implications of the manifesto were fully understood at the time, it was said in an article in the *Quarterly Review*: "In former times such a proceeding would have been thought derogatory, and impugned as unconstitutional, and would have been both; but the new circumstances in which the Reform Bill has placed the Crown, by making its choice of Ministers immediately and absolutely dependent on the choice of the several constituencies, and in the first instance, quite independent of the concurrence of the assembled Parliament, have rendered such a course not merely expedient but inevitable."[5]

In spite of this, however, there was no hint of the doctrine of a mandate from the electorate, nor was it even thought that a Government which wished to pursue a policy different to that on which they had been elected should go to the country first. The circumstances in which Peel was forced to repeal the Corn Laws were exceptional, but the reasons he gave for not having a general election show the gulf between representative government then and today. "I thought that such an appeal would ensure a bitter conflict between classes of society and would preclude the possibility of dispassionate consideration by a Parliament, the members of which would probably have committed themselves by explicit declarations and pledges."

Although some Radicals thought Members should be bound by the wishes of their constituents, it was still generally held that the electorate had no right to insist on pledges and this view was shared by the more thoughtful Radicals themselves. James Mill, for example, declared that "a man of conscience and known ability should insist on full freedom to act on what he, in his own judgment, deems best, and should not consent to act on any other terms".[6]

The extension of the franchise meant a shift in the sources from which politicians drew their support and power. Educated opinion, especially as expressed in newspapers and periodicals, became increasingly important, and popular opinion in the eighteenth-century sense less so. Nassau Senior said that the artisans and shopkeepers in London, the middle classes in the country and in the county towns were more influenced by the Press than other classes because they read little else, did not realize that newspapers were simply money-making enterprises and had few other sources of information. It was just these classes which formed the bulk of the new electorate. It was in the eighteen-fifties that Trollope, in *The Warden*, portrayed *The Times* as the 'all-powerful thunderer'. Riots, which in the eighteenth century had often caused Governments to retreat, had no such power in the nineteenth century. It seems unlikely that any eighteenth-century Government would have proceeded with the Poor Law Bill of 1834 in face of the intense opposition of the poorer classes. The new importance of the middle-class voter who had to pay the rates is, of course, only one reason, though it is an important reason. It was not only the memory of the French Revolution which caused people to look on mob violence with a different and a more serious eye. The religious revival made civil commotion not only a nuisance and a danger, but a sin. The economists were teaching all classes a respect for property quite different from the eighteenth-century attitude. By showing how dependent everyone was on industry, they induced an attitude of reverence towards it not unlike that which the balance of payments constrains us to adopt today. Governments were also far more capable of dealing with popular outbreaks. During the Napoleonic wars and the ensuing troubles they had to learn the technique of repression in order to survive. Of this technique the eighteenth century had been completely innocent. Even in the eighteen-thirties, Governments, while not sufficiently influenced by public clamour to repeal unpopular legislation, were unwilling to insist on its application to places where there was intense opposition; as there was, for instance, to the new Poor Law in Leeds and other industrial towns in the north.

The new importance of educated public opinion made it easier to organize movements to bring pressure to bear on Governments. The Anti-Corn Law League started the first campaign of this kind. The manufacturers wanted tariffs on imported corn abolished because they realized that if Great

Britain did not import from abroad they would be unable to sell to foreign countries (an example of economic intelligence which the manufacturers of other countries have since frequently failed to emulate), while to Cobden and Bright and, no doubt, to many of their followers, free trade meant far more than economic advantage; it meant freedom and a higher standard of living at home and peace amongst the nations of the world—peace, because free trade would teach the nations their dependence on each other. When Cobden said that it seemed to him that "a moral and even a religious spirit might be infused into that topic", he was speaking in all sincerity as a deeply religious man. But in spite, or perhaps because of, this idealistic basis, the League did not scorn to use all the methods of this world, including stirring up of class hatred and making lavish promises to every interest. Their speakers, for example, tried to persuade the farmers that it was only landlords who would be injured by the repeal of the Corn Laws. The League used public meetings as their chief method of propaganda, with both paid and unpaid speakers; they also issued vast numbers of what they called 'tracts', something between a pamphlet and the modern handbill.

The repeal of the Corn Laws was, of course, not solely, or even mainly due to this agitation. Peel and several other leading politicians had been half converted to free trade by Adam Smith, or at least by Adam Smith as interpreted by Pitt, Huskisson and Canning, and the failure of the Irish potato crop forced Peel to overrule his party.

The real importance of the Anti-Corn Law agitation in the history of democracy is that it showed the importance of the new method of communication—the speech delivered at a public meeting and fully reported in the newspapers. This method was first used in the agitation for Catholic Emancipation but the Anti-Corn Law Leaguers employed it much more effectively. It was not only the change in the electorate which made the public meeting possible and effective; many people who went to the meetings must have been without votes; it was the increase in newspapers and the habit of reading them which gave the platform its dominant position as a propaganda method; a position which it retained until the introduction of wireless and television.

The public meeting was a popular influence in every sense; it was an appeal direct to the people, whether electors or not; its entertainment value, which in the days before cinemas was very great, made it an extremely efficient agent for political education; moreover it allowed any Member of Parliament who differed from his leaders or wished to go farther or faster than they did to appeal directly to an audience outside the House of Commons. Joseph Chamberlain and Lloyd George both stampeded the more orthodox members of the Liberal party by their speeches in the country. The platform, unlike the wireless and television, was open to anyone known or unknown, Member of Parliament or not, who could hire a hall and make a speech. It meant that the leaders in any party could be challenged, and if the challenger succeeded in attracting support in the country, it was difficult for the official leaders to resent it openly or to counter it effectively.

The Anti-Corn Law agitation showed that political leaders could be made outside Parliament by purely popular agitation. Bright and Cobden were both elected to Parliament, as indeed other popular leaders had been. But unlike other popular leaders they were powerful figures there, and both became Cabinet Ministers in Liberal Governments, in spite of the dislike of the House of Commons, evident then as now, of men who come to it with a reputation made outside. The means through which ambitious young men can climb to power is an important influence on politics, partly because different means demand different qualities, and partly because the path of popular agitation produces special temptations.

The Chartist movement may seem to be another democratic agitation, but it was undemocratic in the sense that its appeal was made, and made deliberately, to those without votes and that its leaders threatened to use force if their demands were not granted. This put it outside the Constitution and made it like many other popular movements in undemocratic states, indeed like the movement for the Reform Bill itself. It could have happened at almost any time almost anywhere, and so did not show, as did the Anti-Corn Law campaign, how the new political conditions could be used.

Perhaps the most important of all the effects of the Reform Act was that, once the franchise had been extended, both political parties had an incentive to extend it again, especially as the new qualification, being based on a monetary standard, would fall with the growth in national income, and was bound to lead to complete democracy in the end. The next Reform Act, that of 1867, was passed not in response to any popular demand but as a result of the competition between the parties for popular support.

II

Long, however, before there was any question of a further extension of the franchise, reforms in local government had fore-shadowed modern developments in two directions. The Municipal Reform Act reorganized the government of boroughs on the basis of a uniform local government franchise. The Poor Law Amendment Act instituted a central Board with extensive powers over local authorities.

It was obvious that the new uniform Parliamentary franchise could not be reconciled with the haphazard methods by which Corporations came into being, ranging from a franchise with a qualification much lower than the £10 householder to Corporations which were self-perpetuating. Brougham, the Lord Chancellor in Grey's Ministry, was determined to reform local government. *The Times*, whether inspired by Brougham or not, took the same view, and it was naturally a cause that appealed to Radicals.

It was easy to find scandals, although it is now conceded that the Report on the Municipal Corporations gave a biased picture of the state of most towns. English urban life was not quite such a chaos of squalor, indifference and corruption as the Report suggested. A substantial proportion of the towns, whether incorporated or not, had tried to do something towards the sanitary reforms which were introduced in the eighteen-forties. Between 1785 and 1800 more than 200 private Bills had been passed to give commissioners or other authorities power to 'improve'. These powers were used for paving, for supplying water, for cleansing streets. But other Corporations made no attempt to do these things and used their funds for purposes which, though entirely legal, were no benefit to the town at all. Nor had there even been any symmetry between the electoral arrangements for choosing Members of Parliament and members of the Corporations. Towns with a wide Parliamentary franchise might be ruled by a close Corporation, as was, for example, Leicester, with a scot and lot franchise; it was one of the most Radical and Nonconformist towns in England, yet its local affairs were presided over by a close Corporation composed entirely of Tories and Anglicans.

In addition to these anomalies there was the problem of the new towns. Birmingham, Manchester and Leeds had Corporations but still lived under ancient manorial arrangements, with commissioners for special purposes. It was no easier to establish elected authorities in these towns in isolation than it was to give them Parliamentary representation without endangering the old system.

The Municipal Corporations Act was more democratic in intention than the Reform Bill itself, and more drastic. The right of trading in many towns was originally confined to freemen, although they were now chiefly important as possessors of Parliamentary votes. The Municipal Corporation Act took away any local government rights from the freemen and abolished all exclusive trading. It established elected councils and gave a local government vote to all male householders or occupiers of business property who had been in occupation for two and a half years and had paid rates on the property. Anyone who had received alms was disqualified. The most important form of alms was, of course, poor relief. The provision about the payment of rates apparently disqualified more persons than had been realized, partly because it was the custom in many places not to rate labourers' cottages, and partly because the overseers were in the habit of 'compounding' with landlords to collect the rates for them; if the landlord's name appeared in the rate-book, then he was legally the rate-payer. It was said at the time that about two million householders were disenfranchised under the rate-paying regulations.

These provisions only applied to 186 boroughs, did not include London, and of course made no difference at all in counties. The counties were, however, profoundly affected by the intrusion of the central government into local affairs involved in the reform of the Poor Law. It was this period, not the end of the century, in which the functions of the State were extended to the 'welfare' of people in the modern sense. The new Poor Law, factory legislation and sanitary legislation were all concerned with welfare, and the Poor Law and sanitary reform extended Government activity to spheres previously left to local authorities. Some degree of centralization was necessary; it was a condition for the success of such measures that they should be uniform over the country; this meant that the Government would have to coerce some local authorities and that they must set standards below which they would allow no local authority to fall. Some central control and central supervision, probably through paid inspectors, was essential although it was most repugnant to the spirit of the old Constitution. The centralization, however, was exaggerated because some of these measures were initiated and all were profoundly influenced by Edwin Chadwick. He was a disciple of Bentham, and Bentham had had no regard for local liberties, indeed he had little regard for liberty in the eighteenth-century sense at all. Chadwick was temperamentally a central planner who would have been more at home in 1946 than 1846. He pushed his plans with no regard for local susceptibilities. At the very moment when democracy secured a foothold in central and local government and seemed to have won a decisive victory over what then appeared the only alternative, aristocratic predominance, its other rival, the rule of the expert, first emerged.

Poor relief had become the main function of most local authorities, at least in the south of England. It was a function which they performed extremely badly. Expenditure on poor relief rose from £1½ million in 1775 to £8 million in 1833, with a national income estimated to have been between £200 and £300 million. This was somewhere between four and three per cent. of the total national income. Curiously enough the total insurance benefits paid in 1954 amounted to between three and four per cent. of the national income. The lavishness with which relief was distributed may be attributed partly to sympathy with the poor. Nassau Senior reported with scorn that "the answer given by the magistrates when a man's bad conduct is urged by the overseers against his relief is 'We cannot help that, his wife and family are not to suffer because the man has done wrong'."[7] Partly it was regarded as a form of insurance against discontent and revolution. The outbreak of rick-burning and machine-smashing all over the southern counties in 1833-4, however, showed the inability of the old system of poor relief either to make the agricultural labourer's life tolerable or to keep him contented. There was clearly no reason any longer to accept the waste, expense and inefficiency it involved. The Government appointed a Commission to examine the question and it produced a report, perhaps the most famous in the whole history of Royal Commissions. Nassau Senior and Chadwick, the most important members of the Commission, considered that the evil arose from the system of subsidizing wages and that the solution lay in making the situation of the pauper less 'eligible' than that of the wage-earner; the only way to do this in their view was to abolish all outdoor relief and force everyone who applied for help to go into the workhouse. The members of the Commission saw that the parish could not be expected to carry out this policy, first it was too small to be able to build and administer a work-house in which the able-bodied pauper should be adequately fed (but provided with neither tobacco, spirits nor tea) and in which children, the sick and the old should at the same time be properly cared for. This meant that parishes must be combined in unions. It was most unlikely that parishes would unite voluntarily; they already were permitted to combine to build workhouses, few had done so and those workhouses that had been built were far from being what the Poor Law Commission wanted. Parishes, whether combined or not, could not be expected to supervise them adequately nor could parish overseers be expected to carry out the principles of the new Poor Law, because the paupers were often their friends and always their neighbours.

Sometimes it was fear not kindliness that increased the amount of relief. In the southern counties farmers were afraid to refuse relief or to contradict their workers when they declared their wages to be lower than they were, in case their ricks or even their houses were burnt. It was said that insurance companies refused to reinsure farmers who had had their ricks burnt once, on the ground that they must have done something to make themselves unpopular. Under the 1834 Act the parish was replaced by Boards of Guardians elected by the rate-payers, and the old system of everyone or anyone acting in turn as an unpaid overseer was replaced by paid relieving officers. This is the first appearance of the local government official.

The Boards of Guardians were elected, even if they were elected by rate-payers, and it was by no means only the labourers who benefited from the system of outdoor relief. Farmers, shop-keepers, innkeepers either benefited or thought they benefited; farmers because they could pay low wages, shopkeepers and inn-keepers because it was there that the subsidized labourer spent the money the parish gave him. The magistrates, it is true, were exempt from these temptations and were responsible only to the Crown, but it was to their sentimentality and love of popularity that the Poor Law Commission attributed most of the trouble. The Act set up a Board with members appointed by the Govern-ment with extensive powers of supervision, entitled and able to see that the new Boards of Guardians carried out their duties in the proper way. The Board had power to compel unions to build workhouses, to regulate the time, place, quality and quantity of relief, and to frame and enforce general rules for workhouse management.

The Board was responsible to the Cabinet but was as independ-ent of the House of Commons as a nationalized industry, an institution which, in its relation to the Government and Parlia-ment, it somewhat resembled. There was, however, a drastic check on its powers, they were conferred for five years, after which they had again to be confirmed by Parliament.

The Poor Law Commissioners were successful in the southern counties but at the cost of rousing the utmost popular fury. In the northern industrial towns the new system could not be applied because here the rates had not been used to subsidize wages, except for the hand-loom weavers, a special case of a dying industry, but to help workers over periods of unemployment. Just when the Commissioners were ready to turn their attention to the north, the trade depression of 1841 began and there were large numbers of men who could not find work. In these circumstances it was impossible to refuse outdoor relief and attempts to do so caused widespread riots.

The Act antagonized many other people as well as paupers, it was the first attempt on the part of the central government to control local authorities since the similar efforts of the Star Chamber had been defeated. It was hotly attacked on the grounds of 'centralization', as was the Board of Health which had a similar organization, though its powers of coercion were less. In matters of health, too, local authorities and local interests of all kinds, from water companies to individual householders, had to be coerced. The arguments for central control of 'welfare' services are obvious and were the same then as they are today. The objections to it then, however, were not based on the evil of interference with local democracy but on the importance of maintaining local liberties in the eighteenth-century sense.

Administration by Boards of this nature was found to be impossible in the existing state of public opinion, and when the Boards' first five years came to an end the responsibilities of the Commissioners both for the Poor Law and for public health were transferred to a Minister who could be questioned in the House.

The most immediate effect of the Poor Law Act was to strengthen the Conservative party by breaking the alliance between the Whigs, the middle class and the working-class which had carried the Reform Bill. No doubt the working-class supporters of reform would have been bitterly disillusioned anyhow, but the new Poor Law made many of them take a new attitude to the Conservatives, which in its turn had a marked influence on the Conservative attitude to further extensions of the franchise and indeed to popular agitations in general. There was a section of the Tory party, of whom Disraeli was the most outstanding, who had almost flirted with the Chartists themselves. Two Chartist leaders originally called themselves Tories, though they were perhaps Tories of a peculiar kind. It was common for

Chartists, even those most opposed to Toryism in general, to work for Tories at elections, and where possible, to intimidate voters in their favour, in order to show their hatred of the Whigs who, they considered, had betrayed them.[8] Nor is this surprising. The old Poor Law subsidized wages out of the rates, and this meant, of course, that the rate-payer was subsidizing the farmer and the manufacturer. But this is not the kind of thing that is easily believed by those who are affected. The policy had been adopted by the magistrates with the best intentions, the Tory country gentlemen inclined to be more sympathetic to the pauper than the new Boards of Guardians elected by the rate-payers. Nassau Senior described the landowner as "the terror of the overseer", "the idol of the labourer for twenty miles", enjoying "power without appeal and benevolence without expense".[9]

It is not surprising that the paupers themselves took a different view, especially as their memories were constantly jogged by the Tories. The parish overseers were inclined to be lavish even without the intervention of the magistrates. In so small a community the most despised and helpless had some place, even if only that of having been known to the authorities all his life. The popular view of the Poor Law Amendment Act and particularly of the new workhouses is contained in *Oliver Twist*, which is not, as critics are so fond of asserting, a social document, but a folk-tale.

Although, as the Whigs pointed out, the landlords were the chief beneficiaries of the new Poor Law because it was on land that the main burden of the old system had fallen, and although Peel had not opposed the Bill and Wellington had supported it, Tory candidates used it against the Government in the election in 1837. Greville commented sourly that "it is this behaviour of the Tories which has shown me that there can be such a thing as a 'Tory-Radical'; for though I had heard the appellation I thought they were contradictory terms, which did not admit of a conjunction. A Tory-Radical is, however, a politician who for Tory party purposes endeavours to influence the mind of the people against the laws and their administration."

There had been more opposition in the Lords than in the Commons, and although most of it was based on a dislike of

'French centralizing measures', two ultra-Tory peers expressed sentiments which were then considered the height of reaction and now read as if they might have been said yesterday. Lord Wynford, for example, protesting against the abolition of out-relief, said the best principle on which the Poor Laws should be based is "that they should go to relieve the aged and infirm, and those who, having contributed by their labour to the wealth of the country, were no longer able to earn a support for themselves", and Lord Harewood pointed out the hardships which would be inflicted on the unemployed in industrial towns if they were denied out-relief.

Even apart from the question of Poor Law relief the Tories found, perhaps to their surprise, that there was much Conservative sentiment among working men. There was even in 1835 an association of Conservative Operatives in Leeds with a motto "The Throne, the Altar, the Cottage".[10] It is impossible to explain the actions of the Conservative party in 1865, when they produced a Reform Bill much more drastic than that on which their opponents had been defeated, unless this background is remembered. Most historians have accepted the Liberal argument in the 1868 election that the Liberal amendments made all the difference to the Bill, because they could not believe that the Tories were not frightened of a working-class electorate. Their real attitude can be more clearly seen in Lord Shaftesbury's speech opposing the Bill: "I have heard it said that the middle classes are not Conservative, but that if you go deep you get into a vein of gold, and encounter the presence of a highly Conservative feeling." To anyone who has ever listened to the private talk of politicians, these remarks have the authentic ring; we can almost hear the chatter of the Carlton Club.

III

The introduction of a uniform franchise made universal suffrage inevitable. While there were working-class constituencies, close boroughs and all the other variations, especially while the middle class were rather more likely to be excluded from the franchise than they were themselves, the working class might not have insisted on numerical equality. But to pronounce a whole class to be incompetent to exercise the right of voting is not so much an injury as an insult. In spite of the Whig talk of finality any practical politician must have realized it was impossible to stop at the £10 householder even without the Radicals constantly reminding everyone of the advantage of pure democracy. Between 1832 and 1867 the introduction of reform Bills was one of the constant occupations of both famous and unknown Members of Parliament.

Reform in 1832 was demanded by the whole country, in 1867 it was passed by the political parties. Disillusionment, revolutionary ideas inspired by France, unemployment and falling wages drove men into the Chartist movement, but after its collapse in 1848 there was little interest in politics. This was the period when it was impossible to run a class on politics at the London Working Men's College, though classes on geology, philosophy, history were eagerly attended.[11] There was in 1866 little popular excitement and no demand for an extension of the franchise except from Liberal Members of Parliament. Nor was household suffrage introduced in deference to any idea that every citizen had a right to take part in the government of the country. In the House of Commons most Liberals denied that they believed any such thing, even if some of them were near to proclaiming such a belief at public meetings.

In 1866 the Liberal Government introduced a Bill with more definite and far-reaching proposals than any suggested in previous Bills. It reduced the qualifications for the franchise in boroughs from a rental of £10 to a rental of £7; in the counties from £50 to £14. But, although the proposals in themselves were limited, those who hoped for or feared the advent of pure democracy realized that the process could only end in universal suffrage. Even the inclusion of women was prophesied by those who opposed the Bill. The debates were, therefore, not confined to the difference between £10 and £7 or to the kind of person who would be enfranchised, but ranged over the whole field of political theory and most of human history. Gladstone and

Disraeli, John Stuart Mill, Bulwer Lytton, Lord Shaftesbury and John Bright all contributed, together with a host of back-benchers whose names are now forgotten, but whose exact words on each clause can still be read.

Two main questions dominated these debates: the question of how far and in what proportions different classes should be represented in theory, and the question of the extent to which the working man there and then could be trusted with the responsibility of political power. No one, except a few left-wing Radicals like Bright and John Stuart Mill, and possibly Gladstone himself, believed in democracy. Indeed, if one may judge by the frequency with which it was used, the accusation that the reformers wished to introduce democracy or 'American' institutions was one of the most effective arguments against them. The second question, of how far the working man could be trusted, therefore became immensely important, and this was a question which was not at all easy to answer. There was no compulsory education, the Chartist movement not so long before had displayed both violence and foolishness, trade unions were still liable to fall into the hands of dishonest and incapable men, a campaign of murder had been waged in Sheffield during the eighteen-sixties by some unions against men who refused to join them. Against this formidable list, the chief examples quoted, even by the opponents of reform, were the Co-operative Society of Rochdale and the behaviour of the cotton operatives during the Lancashire cotton famine. Gladstone referred to Rochdale in his speech introducing the Bill:

> ... the town of Rochdale which has done more than any other town in making good to practical minds the case for some enfranchisement of the working classes; because it is the town where that remarkable system, and at first sight I do not hesitate to say, that most critical and even perilous system, obtained, under which the working class ousted the retail trader from his accustomed province; and where, through the extraordinary intelligence and self-governing power of these men, that system has been brought to a successful issue and has become a source of the utmost comfort and profit to themselves.

Bulwer Lytton, a Tory and an opponent of the Bill, spoke of the founders of the Co-operative Society in terms of even greater enthusiasm. "To artisans of that kind," he said, "whatever their political creed, I am willing to grant the franchise. Willing do I say? The word is too cold. I might almost wish that, like some old commonwealth of Greece, we could admit them to the franchise by acclamation, too proud of such fellow citizens to ask what rent they pay for their houses."

Liberal speakers frequently dilated on the behaviour of the Lancashire cotton operatives during the period of the cotton famine caused by the Northern States' blockade of the Southern ports. This had also made a great impression on Conservative speakers and on the opponents of the Bill. A back-bencher called Gregory, who was an opponent of the Bill, said: "Was not the great manufacturing heart of England paralysed a few years ago, and was not the conduct of the operatives in Lancashire characterized by a prudence, a moderation and an admirable bearing that must constitute with others, as it does with myself, the best argument that could possibly be employed for the enfranchisement of the working man?" Sir Michael Hicks-Beach, one of the leaders of the Conservative party, said: "I would without hesitation admit to the franchise the members of the Co-operative Societies of Rochdale and the elite of the Lancashire and Yorkshire operatives." Members of Parliament had not only been impressed by the restraint shown by the unemployed cotton workers, but also by their continued support of the Northern States who were causing their sufferings; because they believed that slavery was wrong they made no proposals, put no pressure on the Government to break the blockade.

The Bill was opposed by a section of the Liberals led by a man now forgotten, Robert Lowe. Long afterwards Gladstone said: "So effective were his speeches that during this, and during this year only, he had such a command of the House as has never in my recollection been surpassed." Owing to the desertion of this section of its supporters, the Liberal Government was defeated.

On the resignation of the Liberal Government, Lord Derby became Prime Minister with Disraeli as Leader of the House of Commons. To the astonishment of the political world they proceeded to introduce a Bill giving the franchise to all house-holders who paid rates. It puzzled his supporters at the time, and has still remained a puzzle, why Lord Derby agreed to put forward the Reform Bill of 1867 and accepted so easily the Liberal amendments which widened it still more. It is true that he had originally been a Whig and a member of the Government which introduced the Bill of 1832, and had left the Whig party on a disagreement about Church, not mundane, matters. But to be a supporter of the 1832 Bill did not make a man a believer either in democracy or in enfranchising the working classes. Disraeli's motives are clear. He had always believed in the appeal of the Conservative party to the working man, and Gladstone himself had pointed out during the 1866 debate that the larger the proportion of working-class voters the more likely was the seat to be represented by a Conservative. But Derby was not ambitious of office either for himself or for his party, and it is hard to believe that if he had really been con-vinced of the folly of giving a vote to the working man he would have consented. During the cotton famine Derby had been the leading spirit in the vast organization of help for the unemployed which was set on foot. He had given large sums of money him-self; he had secured large sums from others, and had worked, though he was ill at the time, amongst the Lancashire people. Saintsbury, who had himself been in Lancashire shortly after the cotton famine, suggested that it was this experience which made Derby ready to support the Bill which,[12] as its opponents reiterated, made universal suffrage in the end inevitable.

The 1867 Bill practically introduced household suffrage in the boroughs, with new qualifications for extra votes which the Government described as 'compensations'. These qualifications were £50 in the savings bank, a pension of £200 a year from the Army, the Navy or the Civil Service, or to be a schoolmaster; and anyone possessing these qualifications was to be allowed to add them together or to any other qualifications he might possess and to use as many votes as he had qualifications. The qualifi-cations were derided under the name of 'fancy franchises' and were struck out of the Bill by amendments in the House of Commons. The other compensation was the condition that in order to qualify, the rates must be paid in person, which meant not by the landlord; this condition, it was supposed, would disfranchise a very'large number of people who lived either in tenements or small houses. This was also struck out of the Bill, and household suffrage in the towns introduced.

The Act made far more difference to the electorate than the Act of 1832. It increased the electorate by 938,000, or 88 per cent. of the former voters, but the effect over the country was uneven. In some of the small boroughs the increase was very small, but in the new industrial towns the electorate was enormously increased. For example, the electorate in Bolton was five times larger in 1868 than in 1867; in South Shields and Oldfield six times; and in Merthyr Tydfil ten times. For the first time the working class was placed in a clear majority in the boroughs, and in order to have a majority in the country it was necessary to win at least some of the boroughs.

The eventual results of this Bill were clearly predicted by its chief opponent, Robert Lowe. He prophesied the inevitability of universal franchise and the consequent collapse of free trade, the institution of the closed shop and the introduction of an inconvertible currency. By inconvertible, of course, he meant inconvertible into gold, even the Cassandra of the Liberal party could not foresee a currency inconvertible into other currencies.

CHAPTER V

THE RULE OF MERE NUMBERS

I

AFTER the Reform Act of 1867 had given a vote to all male householders living in boroughs it could only be a matter of time before the franchise was extended to the counties, and then manhood suffrage could not be far off.

Between the second Reform Act and the next extension of the franchise in 1884 there was a gradual and almost imperceptible acceptance of democracy. It was no sudden or revolutionary movement; it is impossible to point to any particular date and to say that here democracy won its final victory. But the change, though slow, was complete. How complete is illustrated by the difference in the reception of the Bill of 1867 and the Bill of 1884. In 1867 politicians could still say that they were against the rule of 'mere numbers'; in 1884, although there were still men who were opposed to democracy, they were already considered as slightly eccentric. They were writers, professors or soldiers. No active politician could any longer be against democracy, although it was not yet necessary to be enthusiastic about it. The Representation of the People Act, 1884, was not opposed by the Conservative party either in the Commons or in the Lords.

The main factor in the acceptance of universal suffrage was that after 1867 Great Britain was a democracy, although a limited one. The majority of voters in the towns were working men and this electorate was naturally sympathetic to further extensions of the franchise and, although the Liberals had been in office for ten out of the sixteen years between 1868 and 1884, the new electorate had shown none of the tendencies prophesied by the opponents of reform. There was no visible growth of socialist ideas or of class antagonism. There had been attempts in some London boroughs to return working men to Parliament in the election of 1868. The Labour Representation League was formed to encourage working men to claim and exercise their votes, but although the Liberals seemed to have regarded the League as only interested in the return of working-class candidates, its declared object was the organization of the Labour vote "without reference to opinion or party bias". Working men showed no particular disposition to vote for working men. There was still a feeling that a Member of Parliament ought to be a gentleman and even in those advanced circles which had rejected this, it had been replaced by a rather pathetic reverence for 'education'. Not only were there no attacks on property, but the Conservative party had fared much better than anyone in 1832 would have believed possible. The Liberals might be in office more often, but they were never so predominant as to make Conservatism look hopeless and Conservatives always drew a large proportion of the urban vote.

Although democracy was not yet complete, the conduct of politics was already subjected to democratic pressures which perceptibly altered the shape of the political system. The new voters, partly through their numbers, made it necessary for parties to formulate much more distinctly the theories on which they based their policies. In the towns the electorate was so large that the previous method, which consisted in choosing some local worthy or some rich or distinguished stranger on his own character or his own wealth, had to be supplemented with some kind of programme and the appeal had to be simplified. It was not so much that the new voters were uneducated, which in most cases they were, but that they were unsophisticated. A simple moral appeal or a large expenditure of money was the way to their hearts, and rife as bribery in all its forms might be, the simple moral appeal gradually became the more powerful. There were men like Gladstone who had policies they passionately wanted to carry out, and there were the Tapers and Tadpoles who realized how essential a programme was to victory.

Under the 1832 Act voters had to claim to be put on the register. The register was published, and objections to claims could be made; the overseers of the poor were made the registration officers. They were probably incompetent and certainly corrupt.

A large field was thus open to election lawyers and party agents. When it was found that the people who had been prepared to use violence to obtain the vote were not prepared to bother to register, the field was further widened. The subject became so important that Peel once devoted a long passage in one of his speeches to the necessity of registering. Registration societies were formed in the constituencies, and by 1867 both parties had an organization of a kind. There was a mysterious figure called Bonham, variously described as a parasite, an agent and friend of Peel, who concerned himself with matters of organization in the Conservative party, and in fact acted as Chief Agent. He had suggested as early as 1835 the formation of "a very small but *active* Committee to obtain information and prepare for an election".[1] Parties at that time had almost no control over the selection of candidates, who were chosen by local committees and who paid their own election expenses, still there were candidates looking for seats and seats looking for candidates. Bonham appears to have brought the two together.

The Liberal party also had an organization, which by 1868 seems to have become more elaborate than that of the Conservatives. At least, when Gladstone answered the plaintive cries of his Whips for more money by asking how this "mysterious fund" was to be used, they replied that they kept an "office in London with a Secretary in communication with local agents giving them advice, supplying them with registration forms and looking up out-voters". They had also distributed pamphlets which they called "flying sheets".[2]

The political clubs, the Carlton and the Reform, were founded. In the eighteen-sixties, the age of the independent private Member, these clubs were useful in inducing a certain amount of cohesion in the Parliamentary party.

But this was merely the minimum organization necessary to any party. The essential power still lay in the local committees and in the Parliamentary party. It was the provisions for minority representation in the 1867 Bill which inspired the beginning of the Liberal 'caucus', the forerunner of modern party organization. There was at the time a general anxiety about the position of minorities under a democratic regime, an anxiety voiced by Mill in his *Representative Government*. Although the Liberal Opposition had refused to accept the provision for minorities contained in the 1867 Bill, a new device was introduced in the Lords. They carried an amendment providing that in those counties and boroughs where there were three Members, each elector should have only two votes, where there were four, only three votes. This was designed to ensure that in a three Member constituency, for example, Members of the majority party would give their two votes to the two popular candidates of the majority party, leaving the third to be defeated by the candidate who had received the largest number of minority votes, and thus allowing a minority candidate to slip into third place. This was the plan but the Liberals persisted in regarding these provisions as an attempt to minimize the influence of 'the people', and to obstruct social reform.

At Birmingham a movement was started to organize Liberal voters in such a way as to make the provisions ineffective. By careful calculations the Liberal committee decided how many votes each Liberal must receive to win, and instructed each Liberal elector which Liberal candidate to vote for in order that no Liberal votes should be wasted. If this arrangement was to be successful, it entailed the most careful organization, because large numbers of canvassers were necessary to track down the individual voter and persuade him to vote in the required direction. Harris, the Secretary of the Birmingham Liberal Association, transformed his Association into a party organization of the modern type based on ward committees. The slogan of the Birmingham elections was "Vote as you are told". The paradox of democratic party organization had appeared. Harris was completely successful; three Liberals were elected and the principle of minority representation successfully defied.

Harris had forged the instrument but Joseph Chamberlain was to use it, and he used it first for municipal, not Parliamentary purposes. The Association was made more democratic. The town was divided into wards. At the annual meeting of these wards representatives were elected to serve on the Central Committee. Any Liberal might take part in these meetings, and this is an important point because the officers of the Central Committee were accused in the great days of the Association of having a band of 'travelling' Liberals who went from ward to ward ensuring the election of those candidates acceptable to the executive. That's as may be, but the organization was certainly successful; it secured not only three Liberal Members of Parliament, but sixty-eight out of seventy seats on the Council. In local politics it was, of course, not only organization but Chamberlain's successful administration which procured this result, but the Birmingham organization might never have spread beyond Birmingham if it had not also represented the most radical wing of the Liberal party. In his early days Chamberlain was even Socialist in phrase, although not in intention, and the official leadership regarded this kind of Liberalism with deep suspicion. Gladstone himself was strongly against what he called 'constructivism', whether it appeared in the Liberal or in the Conservative party. The activities and the speeches of the 'man of Birmingham' had aroused much sympathy in other industrial towns, and the obvious course was to combine the other Associations in a great Liberal Federation. This Federation would represent the source from which Liberalism must now draw its power, the new voters in the towns, and the real control would be transferred from the Parliamentary leaders to the officers of the Federation. It would then no longer be possible for the 'Whigs' to obstruct the onrush of democratic reform. Chamberlain described the projected Federation in his speech at the Conference of Liberal Associations, called to consider the new plan, as "a real Liberal Parliament outside the imperial legislature and, unlike it, elected by universal suffrage".

The Liberal Federation was successfully formed and blessed by Gladstone himself. In its hey-day it claimed powers as extensive, if not more extensive, than those of the present Labour Party Conference and presented, at least in theory, a real challenge to the supremacy of Parliament. The Federation was to decide what policy the party should put forward and in what order it was to be introduced into the House of Commons. No candidate was to be approved who was not prepared to accept the authority of the Federation; this was no empty threat; a respected Liberal Member was driven out of politics because he refused to sign on the dotted line.

The political world was startled by these developments. The organization was attacked under the name of the 'caucus'; it was said to be copied from America, to be destructive of the dignity and power of Parliament and to be democracy in its worst form. Chamberlain defended the caucus as essentially democratic, being designed to make "more real, more direct and more constant the influence of the people in the management of their own affairs".[3] All political parties are now organized much on this model, and the effect has been neither to destroy Parliament nor to increase the influence of the people, but to augment the power of the official leaders and to add a new factor to political life, the party machine. The Liberal Federation itself, after its brief day of power, fell into the hands of the Parliamentary leadership. When Chamberlain left the Liberal party his own Birmingham Association followed him, but the Federation as a whole remained loyal to the party. This is one of the most dramatic instances of the hold which the Parliamentary leadership must always have over the party machine.

The Conservatives also started organization after 1865. Indeed, it was started earlier than the Birmingham movement, but the motive was different; it was to organize the support which Conservatives believed they had among the new voters in the towns. Without some organization these voters would have remained largely inarticulate, or even drifted over to the Liberals. The Conservative Working Men's Clubs, as they were called, were extremely successful. In Sunderland, for example, the membership is said to have been 25,000. After the rise of the Liberal Federation, Lord Randolph Churchill cast envious eyes on it, urged the necessity of organization, and had clearly cast himself for the part of a Conservative Chamberlain. For a moment the Union of Conservative Associations seemed prepared to play too, but when he resigned from the Cabinet the Union showed no desire to support him.

Organization in the country was reflected in the House of Commons in rather more distinct party divisions. After the death of Peel his followers gradually disintegrated and joined either the Conservatives or the Liberals. A man elected as a Conservative or a Liberal after 1867 was fully 'pledged', at least to his general conduct, and although the Whips had not a tithe of the power they possess today, even in the House itself the presence of party organization could already be felt.

The change in the political atmosphere led to some slight alterations in Parliamentary procedure. In the eighteenth century Government business had no priority, although 'public' Bills had some over private Bills. This procedure only worked because there was little in the way of legislation and Members themselves would not allow obstruction. In the great era of reform after 1832 the Government of the day found it necessary to reserve one day, and then, as legislation increased, three days for Government business. The real tightening up of Parliamentary procedure did not, however, occur until after the extension of the franchise in 1884 and was then due to persistent obstruction by the Irish Nationalists.

II

The average citizen took a more continuous and steady interest in politics than he had done before or has done since. Any leading political figure could expect an audience of two or three thousand when he spoke. The newspapers reported Parliamentary debates verbatim, not edited, as even *The Times* edits them today, according to what the editor may consider valuable or important. It is true that Parliament sat only for six months, but during the recess every newspaper filled columns with speeches of Members of Parliament, under the heading "Parliament Out of Session". And people did not keep a close watch on Parliament merely to safeguard their position or to snatch as much as they could for themselves. Nor did they believe in salvation through politics. Politics were simply the main intellectual interest of the majority of all classes. Nor is this so surprising as it may seem. It has often been pointed out that there was little entertainment open to the respectable either of the middle or working classes; no cinemas, no television, no Test matches, no football finals, the only national sporting event was the Derby. The religious teaching of the day regarded even those amusements which did exist as sinful. Serious persons of any denomination were unlikely to approve of racing, not in itself, but because it was an occasion of temptation to others. There were, indeed, theatres in London and other large towns and working men crowded to them, but they did not of course attract anything like the numbers which the cinemas drew between the wars. For anyone below the middle rank of life there were no respectable dances, and the Nonconformist conscience objected to dancing in itself. Really pious Nonconformists did not read novels; even Sir Walter Scott was regarded at worst as dangerous, at best as frivolous. Yet education was spreading, the chapels had aroused an appetite for discussion and debate. The early Methodists were extreme Tories, some of the more rigid sects forbade their members to take part in politics, but to the great majority it was a duty to do so. Gladstone mobilized the Nonconformist conscience for the Liberals and made an interest in politics almost a part of religion.

The enormous interest in politics made the speech outside Parliament the main means of party propaganda. It was becoming as important for success in politics to be a good platform speaker as to be a good House of Commons speaker. Cobden, Bright and Chamberlain made their reputations even before they became Members of Parliament; Cobden and Bright entirely by oratory, and although Chamberlain had also a reputation as a municipal reformer, it is doubtful how far this would have been heard of beyond the Midlands, but for his platform campaigns. The importance of the platform preserved the importance of the individual member; the man who could attract large audiences was important whether he was officially recognized as a leader or not. Lord Randolph Churchill, for example, enormously enhanced a reputation made in the House of Commons by his speeches in the country and thus gained an exceptional position in the Conservative party.

A passionate interest in politics encourages intimidation, and the growth of organization had done nothing to check bribery. The more democracy was accepted in theory, the more unseemly did the actual conduct of elections appear. No one could be satisfied with it, even if he were he could hardly say so in public; bribery and intimidation had indeed changed their forms, but they were as widespread as ever. The increase in the electorate certainly made bribery more difficult and less rewarding by making it ever more expensive and by making it difficult for the briber to make certain that the bribed fulfilled his part of the bargain. But indirect bribery such as 'treating', entertainment of all kinds, and lavish expenditure on conveying the voters to the polls, could still be employed.

Various attempts had already been made to discourage corruption, beginning with the Corrupt Practices Act of 1854; this Act is thought to have been effective to some limited extent, as from 1832 to 1852 there had been a continuous increase in the number of election petitions on the score of corruption, while from 1854 there was a decline. In 1852 twenty-three Members were unseated for bribery; in 1859 there was only one. The reform does not seem, however, to have been so complete as these figures would seem to indicate, at least if Trollope's experiences at Beverley in 1868 are any guide, although Beverley was famous for corruption and was disenfranchised as a result of this very election. One of the most obvious devices for checking bribery is the ballot, although it is not so completely effective as has been supposed either against bribery or against intimidation. The demand for the ballot had been a constant feature of Radical propaganda from its very early days in the eighteenth century, but many people were opposed to it in the first half of the nineteenth century, including John Stuart Mill and Gladstone. They both thought it would diminish the seriousness with which the good citizen ought to approach the solemn duty of casting a vote and that anything which tended to curtail the profound reflections which ought to precede such an act would be a mistake. The Duke of Argyll wrote to Gladstone that "the motives under which men act in secret are in general inferior to those under which they act in public", and this was a common view. Before 1867 the doctrine was still held that the elector was exercising his right, not only on his own behalf, but on that of the unrepresented also, who had a right therefore to know which way he voted. After 1867 both the objections tended to disappear. The high seriousness of Gladstone and Mill was not shared by the new generation; in the boroughs the majority of men were now voters, and the new Liberals were more impressed by the danger of losing elections through bribery and intimidation by their opponents than by the danger of tempting the elector to make a frivolous or selfish choice. Bright was in the Liberal Cabinet of 1868, and he had always believed in the full milk of the democratic word, of which the ballot was a part, and the radical wing of the Liberal party was growing at the expense of the 'Whigs'.

In 1870 the Government set up a committee of investigation which produced a somewhat tepid recommendation in favour of the ballot. They were not only concerned with bribery and intimidation, but they also thought that "the ballot would conduce to the tranquillity of elections". The Government accepted this recommendation, and it was finally passed "in spite of the utmost hostility of the House of Lords, the secret disapproval of the House of Commons and the indifference of the general community"; at least, that was the situation as described by the Annual Register. Intimidation is said to have been checked by the ballot, although it certainly did not stop it altogether; but it may have enabled some men to deceive their landlords or their customers. Intimidation by the mob still exists today; not that modern intimidation has any political importance, as it can only be practised in those constituencies in which there is a majority large enough to make the result of the election certain anyhow. Bribery was not eliminated either; indeed, it was suggested that the Act's chief result was to enable the voter to take bribes from both sides whereas previously he had necessarily been confined to one.

The Liberal Government made a more deliberate attack on corruption in 1883, in a Bill introduced this time before, not after, the extension of the franchise. This Bill laid down the main lines of modern election law. The penalties for offering bribes were made much more severe. The most important part of the Bill was, however, the provision that the candidate must appoint a single agent and conduct all financial matters through him. This meant that candidates could no longer employ a number of agents and profess to have no knowledge of what they did. The total amount which could be spent on an election was also limited, and certain practices, such as unlimited 'treating' in the public houses and certain forms of entertainment, were prohibited. From this date elections assumed their modern form, although they still remained much rowdier than they have been since the Second World War. But bribery and corruption in the eighteenth- and nineteenth-century sense had more or less completely died out by the end of the century.

III

Victorian reformers were as interested in efficiency as they were in democracy, and although the Civil Service reforms used to be presented in histories of England as part of the process of democratization, it was the demands for competent administration that they were designed to meet. The modern Civil Service is usually held to date either from the publication of the Trevelyan-Northcote Report in 1854 or from the institution of competitive examinations as the only method of recruitment in 1870. This tends to exaggerate the difference between the Service before and after these dates and to ignore previous reforms. The first inquiry into the workings of the Civil Service was held not in 1854 but in 1780. Perhaps the most important step was taken in 1816 when the miscellaneous methods by which Civil Servants had been paid—salary, commission, perquisites, fees for franking letters etc.—were unified into one method, payment of a salary by the Government.

In the eighteenth century each department was a self-contained unit which recruited its own staff. The usual method was nomination either by the political head of the department, by the permanent head, or by the commissioners who controlled some departments. This did not, as is generally supposed, lead to inefficiency, because heads of departments were vitally interested in a competent staff and although no doubt they had to carry some passengers inserted in the Government machine to 'oblige' someone, they would not deliberately appoint men incapable of carrying out their duties. In some branches there was a qualifying examination as early as the seventeen-forties.[4] The heads of departments controlled all promotion, so that although it was possible to enter the Service through the goodwill of some Minister, Member of Parliament or boroughmonger, success must have depended on the same qualities as it did in other walks of life. By the middle of the nineteenth century, however, there had grown up a system of promotion by seniority only.

The drive against corruption and nepotism had, by the beginning of the nineteenth century, resulted in most patronage being under the control of the Treasury. This had a worse effect than private patronage, which was exercised on personal grounds and therefore likely to involve some considerations as to fitness. Treasury patronage, on the other hand, was exercised for political reasons, into which no consideration of fitness entered. The extent and importance of patronage must not, however, be exaggerated. The agitation carried on since the seventeen-seventies against place-men, sinecures and Government patronage had already limited it. The constant complaint of Prime Ministers in the first half of the nineteenth century was that they did not possess the means, so widely attributed to them, of rewarding political services, or even merit in other forms, with agreeable and profitable situations. The positions still in their gift were either important, so that any Government was bound to choose not only an efficient adminstator, but one who was qualified for the particular situation, or ordinary clerkships. There were, however, enough places in some departments and enough political influence in appointments to give the Radicals material for accusations of jobbery. There was, indeed still is, a Minister at the Treasury known as the Patronage Secretary, but in those days he dealt with Civil Service appointments and tried to integrate them into the party organization. That austere character Sir James Graham, when he was First Lord of the Admiralty, carried on an almost constant war with the Patronage Secretary who tried to use the Admiralty patronage to reward supporters, and who complained: "I have undoubted authority that the Tories (then in opposition), are at a loss to divine any other motive in your recent dispensation of the patronage at the Admiralty than a desire to conciliate and cultivate the Conservative party. It is quite time that you should be made acquainted

with the rumours of your friends and the jeers of your enemies."[5]
Sir James replied that in future, appointments in the dockyards
would be made on the grounds of fitness alone, and this seems
to have become more and more the attitude of Governments.

There was, however, undoubtedly a good deal of anxiety
about the condition of the Civil Service both among the general
public and among politicians. There was even an association for
'administrative reform'. All through the 'forties there was a series
of select committees concerned chiefly with methods of cutting
expenditure but which gave Trevelyan, then one of the permanent secretaries to the Treasury, a chance to express his views on
general reorganization. It was not only that patronage was
becoming inconsistent with the general atmosphere and that the
conduct of the Crimean War by both the civil and the military
departments provoked public indignation, the Civil Service
was becoming more important. Contemporaries attributed this
to the frequent changes in government: "The inconveniences
which are inseparable from the frequent changes which take place
in the responsible administration are matters of sufficient notoriety.
It may safely be asserted that, as matters now stand, the government of this country could not be carried on without the aid of
an efficient body of permanent officers, occupying a position
duly subordinate to that of the Ministers who are directly
responsible to the Crown and to Parliament, yet possessing sufficient independence, character, ability and experience to be able
to advise, assist, and to some extent, influence, those who are
from time to time set over them."[6] The new responsibilities
assumed by the Government, under, for example, the Public
Health legislation, demanded more administration than the
traditional functions. Ministers and Members of Parliament
seemed to have felt that the powers of nomination still left to
them were an embarrassment rather than otherwise and exposed
them to the dilemma of offending friends or constituents or of
introducing unsuitable men into the public offices.

In 1853 Lord Aberdeen's Government asked Trevelyan and
Sir Stafford Northcote to undertake an inquiry into the Civil
Service and to make a report. Trevelyan was Assistant Under-
Secretary at the Treasury. Sir Stafford Northcote, though a

'stiff Conservative', had been at one time Gladstone's private secretary and Gladstone, still a Peelite, was Chancellor of the Exchequer and was deeply interested in the question of reform.

The faults of which Civil Servants were accused seem to have a not unfamiliar ring. "We often hear of official delays, official evasions of difficulty and official indisposition to improvement."[7] It was natural that many people should attribute all shortcomings to the system of recruitment.

The real trouble, however, lay elsewhere as anyone who reads the famous Report can see.[8] There was not sufficient inducement for really able men to enter the Service. The pay was low, there was no distinction of grade, everyone entered on the same basis and, as the typewriter had not yet been invented, everyone had to spend years copying documents. There was no general service; a man who entered one department, except in most exceptional circumstances, had to stay in that department. Civil Servants themselves clung to the system of promotion by seniority for the same reason as might some trade union. The heads of departments were usually brought in from outside, although there were some notable exceptions, because it was generally believed that the Service itself would not provide anyone of sufficient ability.

Mr. Trevelyan and Sir Stafford Northcote after some severe, indeed acrimonious, criticism of the average Civil Servant, recommended that the Service should be unified, that there should be two separate grades, that promotion should be on merit, and that entrance to both grades should be by competitive examination only. The lower grade should be subjected to a simple examination in handwriting, dictation and arithmetic, but the examination for the higher grade should be on the same level as that for a University Degree. The motives of those who advocated these reforms were not to open the Civil Service to men from all classes, but to make it efficient and incorruptible. There was in many minds another motive which had nothing to do with the Civil Service itself; this was to raise the prestige of education among all classes by showing that it paid. The Report itself had been published with a letter from Jowett welcoming it for its effect on the universities.

The Report, although received with enthusiasm by all

professors and headmasters, encountered much opposition. Nearly all the permanent heads of departments leapt to the defence of their clerks, and such a defence involved a certain scepticism about the advantages of examinations. Genuine doubts, particularly about examinations, were felt by many people. Apart from those who simply said "Let well alone", many people thought it was more important to get gentlemen with practical experience and all-round ability, than academic prodigies. It was asked what bearing had a knowledge of the classics on a man's character or on the duties he would have to undertake.

There was a sentimental as well as a practical objection to the abolition of nomination. Anthony Trollope began his article in the "Quarterly" attacking the Report thus: "Those who have read with pleasure the story . . . of Sir Walter Scott getting two cadetships for Allan Cunningham's gallant sons, or of Johnson exerting himself to obtain some little advantage at Oxford for the son of a worthy clergyman who had received him hospitably— of Sir Robert Peel giving a place in the Treasury to poor Haydon's son in the dark hour of calamity and distress . . . may naturally have supposed that such transactions reflect credit upon all concerned and are honourable and useful to society."[9]

Attention was mainly concentrated on examinations; equally if not more important, however, was the suggestion, which at the time no doubt seemed to most people merely a matter of internal reorganization, that there should be two separate grades recruited from two quite different social and intellectual levels. It was this which made it possible to recruit some of the best brains from Oxford and Cambridge and so to justify examinations.

All the proposals were accepted in the end, although it took nearly twenty years before they were completed in 1870 by the abolition of all nomination and the introduction of competitive examination as the only means of recruitment.

The general tendency to look more and more askance at patronage of any kind would probably have ensured that the system of examination was adopted in the end, but the distinction and prestige of the Indian Civil Service certainly helped the advocates of this reform. The open competitive system had been adopted as soon as the Crown took over the administration of

India from the East India Company, and the Service succeeded in attracting men of great intellect and personality.

The reformed Civil Service not only became the instrument through which the people could implement the wishes they expressed at elections, but also had influence in moulding the wishes themselves. The success of centralized bureaucracy in administering Government services greatly affected the direction of Socialist thought; it was, for example, largely the foundation of the Webbs' philosophy. The bias towards administration and the idea that all problems can find administrative solutions spread far beyond declared Socialists. It can be seen in Lord Beveridge's study of unemployment,[10] with its suggestion that the establishment of Labour Exchanges would make a serious contribution to lessening unemployment, and in the new school of economic historians who did so much to popularize Government intervention in industry. They do not discuss at all the incentives offered to innovators, an aspect of the Industrial Revolution so prominent in modern studies.

The Civil Servant, especially the Colonial Civil Servant, became for the middle class the type of achievement which largely replaced both the saintly clergyman and the successful manufacturer or merchant. Never has any country, except perhaps China, consecrated so much ability to the task of pure administration; of merely administering policies which were at any rate supposed to be conceived and decided elsewhere.

IV

These various developments prepared the way for the modern State even before the next extension of the franchise. By 1884 the anomalies of the electoral system had become more and more glaring. Men in the same occupations, earning the same wages, in some cases living on opposite sides of the same street, could or could not vote according to whether they were technically in a borough or in a county. For example, a miner who happened to live within the borough of Merthyr Tydfil could vote, whereas a miner who lived outside could not.

The Reform Act of 1885 did not involve any departure in principle. The permanent exclusion of the agricultural labourer could not be defended; it was not a question of whether, but when. In 1867 no one had proposed that the county and borough franchise should be the same, except the academic believers in universal suffrage; it was then agreed by all practical men that the agricultural labourer's view of life was too limited and his opportunity for acquiring political information too small to make him a desirable elector. The Liberals, too, felt that, while the working man in the towns was largely emancipated from the control of the upper class, the squire and the parson were still supreme in the village. But by 1885 changes had occurred even in the countryside. There was political agitation in parts of the country in the 'seventies as there had not been since the rick-burning of the 'forties. Joseph Arch started an Agricultural Workers' Union in Norfolk in 1871. Land had ceased to be the main source of wealth, but politics are nearly always concerned with past not with existing conditions, and agitation against property before 1914 was almost entirely directed against large landowners.

This curious time-lag was helped by the disciples of Henry George who were, in the closing years of the century, numerous and influential. Henry George is now so completely forgotten that it may be necessary to say that his idea was that the landlord, both agricultural and urban, received an income from the value of his land which had been entirely created by the activities of others. He also thought that the whole revenue needed by the modern State could be raised by taxing these values. The excitement which the idea aroused is now hard to understand and, as Clapham said, the view on taxation could have been refuted by five minutes with the income-tax returns.[11] It is, however, an historical fact that no one spent those five minutes, and Henry George was far better known than Karl Marx. His ideas not only spread in an almost miraculous way among working men, but both Morley and Chamberlain were interested in them.

It was probably the doctrine of the taxation of land values which turned Chamberlain's mind to the nationalization of land or compulsory acquisition and the establishment of peasant holdings. With these proposals he not unnaturally thought the

Liberals could win the agricultural labourer's vote, and the Radicals thought they saw a great opportunity to strengthen the position of the Liberal party in the country and their own position in the Liberal party through the extension of the franchise. As the 'Radical Programme' put it: "The leverage which the Reform Acts will place in the hands of the Democratic Leaders will be immense, and will make them the controlling power in the State."[12]

It had become impossible for any party to set itself against electoral reform for fear the new voters should remember and resent it. The Conservative party had by now adjusted itself to democracy, or at least to democracy as it appeared in the eighteen-eighties, and even apart from the hopelessness of struggling against the inevitable, probably realized that if they had managed to retain so large a share of the working-class vote in the towns, they had little to fear from the agricultural labourer. Although Conservative speakers in the debate pleaded for some form of proportional representation, both as a safeguard for minorities and as a bulwark against the rule of mere numbers, the real struggle was not over the franchise but over the question of redistribution. Conservatives contended that, unless there were a redistribution Bill, the voters who were really urban working men but who happened to live in an area where the local authority was a county not a borough, would swamp the true agricultural voter; and thus agriculture would be put at an unfair disadvantage as compared with industry and the towns.

Liberals refused to introduce redistribution before the Bill was passed, and the Lords refused to pass the Bill until redistribution was introduced. The conflict between the two Houses was only solved by the personal intervention of the Queen. A compromise was reached by which the franchise was extended, as the Liberals wished, and redistribution took place at the same date and not after the new franchise had come into force.

Local government in the counties was now completely out of harmony with the other institutions of the country. The magistrates had, after the Poor Law Amendment Act, suffered no further diminution of their powers but still presided over the police, granted licences to public houses, supervised the roads and levied the county rate. This was clearly not in accordance with democratic theory, especially as the different Boards—School Boards, Health Boards and Boards of Guardians—which then did much of the work now done by local authorities, were all elected. The Radicals had from 1832 onwards made continuous efforts to introduce democratic local authorities. They had not succeeded because although there was from time to time agitation against the magistrates, they were, as they had been in 1832, on the whole popular. Agricultural labourers seemed to have little desire for representative institutions until the 'seventies, and then only in some counties. The Radicals thought that the rate-payers should have some control of the level of the rates and of how they were spent. This propaganda appears, however, not to have got much response from the countryside, probably because the magistrates were among the largest rate-payers and were most unlikely to be extravagant in expenditure or excessive in assessment.

Democratic local government was, however, made into a real political issue by Joseph Chamberlain, and appeared in the 'Radical Programme' inspired by him in 1885. A passionate belief in democracy was the most genuine part of his political creed and he took it with him to the Conservative party in 1888. It was the Conservative party which introduced representative institutions in the counties and, although Chamberlain was the main architect of the reform, no more eloquent testimony could be given to the universal acceptance of democracy. The Act of 1888 created County Councils elected by rate-payers; this meant, of course, household not manhood suffrage.

After 1885 substantial democracy existed in England, and this is true however democracy is defined, although both Lord Coleraine[14] and Mr. Aneurin Bevan[15] deny this and say that democracy was not introduced into England until 1918 because the electorate did not include the whole adult population. The vote was, however, possessed by the majority of adult males and the franchise was withheld from no one on the grounds of his station in life, unless the provision that those in receipt of Poor Law relief could not vote, is considered such. The working class were in the majority in nearly every constituency, except the residential areas of large towns, seaside towns like Brighton in which they are in a minority today and the centres of cities which were dominated by the business vote until 1948.

The franchise could be regarded as undemocratic because it excluded women or because it allowed some men more than one vote, or because the numbers of voters in each constituency were not equal so that the value of a vote was different according to the constituency. It is not possible to say that a political system is undemocratic because women do not vote, unless the word democratic is used as a synonym for 'admirable' or 'ideal'. It seems difficult to maintain that Switzerland is not a democracy today or that France was not a democracy before the war. Opposition to women's suffrage was not based on any political theory, but either on mere unreasoning prejudice or, in the minds of Liberals, on a shrewd suspicion that women were more likely to vote Conservative than Liberal.

The extension of the franchise added a number of other voters to the register but did not abolish the rights of the 40s. freeholders in the counties, so that it was still possible for a man to vote in any constituency where he had property and to vote as a university graduate as well. Now when all polling is on the same day the impossibility of being in two places at once would place a drastic limitation on this right, but then polling days might still spread over some three weeks. Liberals complained bitterly about this franchise and maintained that it consistently favoured the Conservatives.

'One man one vote" was the Liberal slogan. "One vote one value" retorted the Conservatives, for it was the Conservative party who now upheld the 'equal electoral districts' part of the democratic creed. The existing system favoured the Liberals because the Irish constituencies had many fewer voters than suburbs of large towns and other constituencies in England where the Conservatives had at least an equal chance with the Liberals.

Equal electoral districts has always been part of the democratic programme, but in a country like Great Britain with vast towns and a much more sparsely populated countryside, they are not a practical proposition, especially when the most lonely country-sides are in Scotland and Wales—the numbers of whose representatives in relation to those of England have to be fixed by agreement with Scotland.

The Crown and the Lords were indeed inconsistent with this system; but most advanced democrats thought that the monarchy would disappear by a natural process, and anyhow to most people it appeared a mere ornament. Such influence as Queen Victoria possessed was not wielded in public.

The House of Lords was clearly the next target for the Radicals; even so 'conservative' a Liberal as Gladstone had more than once threatened to reduce its powers or alter its composition, and the Radical Programme of 1885 plainly said that if the House of Lords attempted to block the measures of a Liberal Government it would be abolished. But even the most advanced felt that there was no hurry, power at last lay in the hands of the people.

England was a political democracy, a democracy as the early Radicals had imagined it, a country in which there were no longer legal privileges except in vestigial and trivial forms, and in which differences in rank and wealth were softened because ultimate political power lay with the majority. Of course the legitimate and, critics said, the illegitimate influence of rank and wealth still existed. Men still voted Conservative because their wives wanted to be asked to the Duchess's Ball, and some working men even in the towns were still prepared to vote as their employers did. There was still a tendency, more powerful in Scotland and the remoter counties, but perceptible everywhere, for farmers and farm labourers to follow the lead of their landlords. Liberals said that Conservative landlords, with the usual Tory disregard of human rights, brought pressure to bear by threats of eviction from cottages and farms. Conservatives said that Liberal landlords, notoriously harder on their tenants than Conservatives, refused to renew the leases of those sturdy farmers who had refused to vote Liberal at their behest. This influence, however, could in reality only be exercised with the consent of the electorate. After the introduction of the ballot it was a weak-kneed farmer indeed who could not vote as his convictions dictated, a worker singularly devoid of guile who could not vote against his employer's party if he wanted to.

Democracy was not confined to the central government, local

authorities were elected by household suffrage and so were the Education Boards and Poor Law Boards. In one aspect local authorities of all kinds were even more democratic than they are today, for they were far more independent of the central government. Centralization appeared to have been finally defeated. Sir John Simon said in his book *English Sanitary Institutions*, published in 1890:

"At the present time there prevails a pretty general consensus of opinion, that matters of individual interest are in general better cared for by individuals (separate or in combinations or through elected representatives) than they can be by the officers of the central government—that the essential condition for effective local self-government is the form of local intelligence and will—and that to despair of local energy for local purposes would be to despair of the purposes themselves. . . . If at the present time proposals were put forth, such as the Board of Health made in its reports of 1850 . . . that the duty of providing drainage, the duty of burying the dead of the metropolis and of supplying water should, in all their respective details, be done or directed by officers of Her Majesty's Civil Service, the proposals would seem to have come from the moon."

The Liberals were naturally anxious to remove any undemocratic elements which still existed in the electoral system and the Government introduced a Bill in 1906 which abolished plural voting. This Bill was thrown out by the House of Lords. Other Bills in the same sense were introduced by private Members but none succeeded in reaching the statute book. The interference of the House of Lords roused no indignation except among Liberal M.P.s because those who had previously been most interested were now beginning to be interested in quite another kind of equality. Indeed some, under the influence of Marx and the French syndicalists, were turning from the Parliamentary method and reverting to revolutionary ideas not heard in England since the days of the Chartists. These were a minority but everywhere there was a new attitude which could almost be regarded as a counter-revolution against Liberalism.

From 1846 onwards both political parties had been liberal in the widest sense, believers in free trade, competition and the liberty of the individual. Their disagreements were rather as to how these concepts were to be interpreted. From 1918 all parties became collectivist, but the change was already beginning in the eighteen-eighties. This is often attributed to manhood suffrage; it is not, however, necessary to be quite so cynical. Power, it is true, lay with the majority and the majority were the working class or the poor, as they were then usually called. This meant that party programmes had to be drawn up with an eye to their approval and that the championship of the poor, instead of being, as it had in Shaftesbury's day, the end of ordinary political amibitions, was one road to power. But the forces at work were more complex and far-reaching than can be explained merely by the weight of the working-class vote.

v

The altered view of the nature and functions of the State ran right through the political and intellectual spectrum; it appeared not in one but in two new theories, Socialism and Imperialism. The trade difficulties which lasted from 1873 to about 1896, and which included the great depression, went far to disillusion not only working men but their employers with the system of free enterprise. Although falling prices meant that real wages actually increased, unemployment also rose. Profit margins fell sharply and did not recover. British industry found itself faced for the first time with foreign competition. especially from Germany. There was a general loss of confidence apparent among business men both in the system of free competition and in themselves. When business recovered there was still unemployment; rising prices reduced real wages although money wages rose.[15]

There were many people inclined to look to the State for help, whether the help took the form of tariffs, of minimum wages or of old age pensions, and there was a variety of theories which helped them to formulate their demands and to provide a theoretical basis for them.

In the eighteen-eighties the public conscience became pre-
occupied with the problem of poverty. Poverty had of course
been a constant worry during the whole of the eighteenth
century, particularly during the last twenty-five years, and so it
was during the early nineteen-hundreds. But it had been only
one form, and not the most serious form of suffering. We, who
take drugs when we have a headache, have our teeth taken out
under an anaesthetic and treat even our dogs with penicillin,
can hardly imagine the suffering everyone encountered in one
day, suffering which it was impossible to relieve. Nor did wealth
make much difference. The rich man could provide himself
with enough to eat, but if he got appendicitis or even toothache
there was little he could do.

Even a happy and healthy life was full of pain unknown to us.
The pain of animals also was ever present and impossible to
relieve. When misery, intolerable and hopeless, was ubiquitous,
not safely confined to concentration camps in Russia or villages
in China, those who wished to retain their sanity had to acquire a
certain callousness. In the eighteen-eighties all this was changed.
Whereas in 1780 the child of the richest man in England had a
better, but not much better chance of survival than the child
of poor but careful parents, in 1880 the nursery was nearly as
safe as it is today. Disease and pain had been forced to relinquish
their universal grip, and poverty had become the chief and
obvious cause of suffering. It was brought home to the whole
reading public by the publication of Charles Booth's *London Life
and Labour* in 1892. This book describes the life of the working
class with actual figures of income and expenditure. The
interest in the problem was not confined to politicians, social
workers or philanthropists. Popular novels, for instance those of
Mrs. Humphrey Ward, were full of it; so were plays.

This preoccupation appears in the most unexpected places.
The 'temptation' of the heroine in a novel by Charlotte Yonge is
no longer as it was in 1860 to learn more Latin and Greek than
was becoming for a woman, but to do social work outside the
direction of the Church. "And this is all I am doing for my
fellow creatures," she muttered half-aloud. ". . . not a paper do I
take up but I see something about wretchedness and crime, and

here I sit with health, strength and knowledge, and able to do nothing, *nothing* at the risk of breaking my mother's heart! . . . when I see children cramped in soul, destroyed in body, that fine ladies may wear useless lace trimmings! . . . when I know that every alley and lane of town or country reeks with corruption."[16]

And few now believed, as had the Liberals in the first half of the nineteenth century, that the problem would automatically be solved by the growth of national wealth. The process had indeed been slower than had been expected, but the pessimism about economic advance seems to have been accentuated by ignorance about what had actually happened.

Chamberlain could say, even when he was President of the Board of Trade, that the poor were getting poorer and the rich richer, a statement now known to be quite false. Sidney Webb in 1910 asserted "that we have had to admit that all the discoveries of physical science and all the mechanical inventions in the world, have not lightened or by themselves never will lighten, the toil of the working classes. A scientific discovery or a mechanical invention, though it may revolutionize the processes of industry and vastly augment our productive power, does not in itself affect the terms of the bargain which the employer of labour is able to make with the wage-earner; does not make the profitableness of 'the marginal man' to the employer any greater than before; and accordingly, does not by itself make the working day shorter or the wages greater."[17]

To people as well-meaning and as blind to plain facts as these the only hope lay in intervention by the Government; they had therefore every motive for wishing the state to be strong. As for liberty, it had ceased to be important because it seemed to be safe. Even the autocratic States were civilized. Germany, though in some ways verging on an absolute monarchy, was as much subject to the rule of law as Great Britain. So was Japan, according to its own conception of law. Apart from decayed Asiatic countries like Persia and Turkey, the only police State was Russia and everyone believed the Czarist regime to be in its last days.

The element of social reform was moreover only one in the complex of ideas working against liberalism in the old sense. The theory of majority rule has in itself an authoritarian element, as it has in Rousseau, and this element was much stressed by some Liberals. Joseph Chamberlain went far in denying the rights of minorities. He was, in the eighteen-seventies, the most powerful figure in the Radical wing of the Liberal party in this period. He said in 1883: "I have observed that some of my political friends have been much exercised of late with regard to what they call majority representation. I really feel this anxiety is altogether premature. What we have to deal with, the evil against which we are protesting, is the inordinate influence and power which minorities have obtained in our system. Majorities must not be thwarted by minorities. They (minorities) are trying to devise some ingenious machinery by which minorities may be saved from the natural consequences of being outnumbered."

There is, of course, something undeniable in all this, especially when he goes on to say that someone must decide, and it must be either the majority or the minority, but his exaltation of the state went deeper than this and must have played a considerable part in his breach with the Liberal party over Home Rule for Ireland and his rejection of Free Trade in favour of Imperial Preference. He once expressed it in a talk with Balfour: "I think a democratic government should be the strongest government from a military and imperial point of view in the world, for it has the people behind it. Our misfortune is that we live under a system of government originally contrived to check the action of Kings and Ministers, and which meddles far too much with the Executive of the country."[18]

Chamberlain was a politician anxious for power, but there were intellectual influences also working in the same direction. The dominance of German philosophy is enshrined in the epigram: "Bad German philosophers when they die go to Oxford." The characteristic of German philosophy, which still meant Hegelianism, was the extraordinary position it gave to the state. The state in this view did not exist primarily for the benefit of its citizens, as had before been stressed in all political theory even the most authoritarian. On the contrary the citizens existed only to serve the purposes of the state because the state had an identity quite separate from that of the total identities of all its citizens. They bore the same relation to it as the cells in the body of a plant or animal bear to the whole organism, and its life was more valuable than theirs in the same way as the life of the organism is more valuable than the life of one of its cells. How all-pervasive German philosophy was can be seen in, of all places, the *Cambridge Modern History*, dedicated to the most austere impartiality. It is clear that in 1910 Hegelianism was so dominant that its intrusion was not considered to be an infringement of this impartiality. The chapter on eighteenth-century political philosophy almost sneers at Locke. Its author, Arthur Lionel Smith, perhaps more representative of the period because his name is not now widely known, said:

> However Hobbes may have over emphasized a true theory, it was a different matter when Locke's influence set a false theory in its place. Very convenient it was, certainly. Sovereignty limited, could square with the Bill of Rights; revocable that the nation might hold over William and the Georges the threat of a notice to quit; partible, the very thing to suit the great Whig houses. But like some other convenient fallacies, it led to more than inconvenience in the end, and had to be corrected by more and more stress on the omnipotence of Parliaments. . . . We are coming to see that what we want is not less but more central power, now that it is in the hands of the community. . . . The more united and the more developed a people, the more active is its sovereign power, and the modern sovereign power comes more and more to add the work of legislation to its older executive and judicial work. The political development of a people may be measured by the urgency of its legislation.

The admiration of all things German went far beyond those who were directly influenced by Hegel. Liberals were influenced by the State system of education; the advocates of compulsory elementary education in the 'seventies relied heavily on the example both of Saxony and Prussia. Matthew Arnold published in 1871 *Friendship's Garland*, in which he held up Prussian land legislation and Prussian education as a model. In his essay on democracy written in 1861 he pleaded for more state intervention especially in education. This was probably, at the time, needed, but he goes on to maintain there could never be any danger of too much State interference in England, a Victorian variant of 'it can't happen here'. "It would really be wasting time to contend at length, that to give more prominence to the idea of the State is now possible in this country, without endangering liberty. . . . Here the people will always sufficiently keep in mind that any public authority is a trust delegated by themselves, for certain purposes and within certain limits." This would certainly meet with the agreement of modern advocates of state intervention and in some ways Matthew Arnold resembled them although his main purpose was different. He was a Civil Servant, an inspector of schools, and in him can already be seen the outlines of a certain type of Fabian Socialist. Fastidious, reserved, cultivated, he shrank from the philistine vigour of the commercial classes; he had the contempt for trade of some continental aristocrat and he did not suspect that the philistines might solve the social problem merely in pursuit of their own selfish ends.

The worship of the state had its effect in producing the two characteristic political ideas of the period—Imperialism and Socialism. Imperialism was transient and always slightly unreal, Socialism we are now living with.

Nationalism in its modern form has grown out of democracy which, by making the government and the people one, at least in theory, has immensely strengthened the emotion of unity within the State. Imperialism was in one sense the English version of this new patriotism, in another it might have been an alternative to it, but as a creed it was killed by the 1914 war. It was never really strong in England, partly because it was not new, a feeling of being English and by nature superior to the rest of the world was more widespread in the eighteenth century. It also offended the sentiments of just those classes which in other countries have been most influenced by nationalism. A Conservative could be an Imperialist, because his belief in democracy was, at its most ardent, limited and was sometimes merely the acceptance of the inevitable. Liberals, however, could not resist demands for self-government. In those days they came from Ireland, but from wherever they came they could not be refused by those who really believed in democracy, not as a convenient method of getting on with the rather tiresome business of government but as a way of life, almost as a means of salvation.

The legacy left by Imperialism to modern politics is Imperial Preference and other forms of tariff legislation. The conversion of Chamberlain and of a section of the Conservative party to protection showed how widespread the desire for State intervention had become and how variegated the forms in which it might show itself. After the immediate agitation over the repeal of the Corn Laws had died down free trade was as much a part of the Conservative creed as of the Liberal; it was a subject on which both parties agreed as firmly as they now agree on the system of national insurance against old age and unemployment.

The turning from economic liberalism to State intervention was so far a change in sentiment rather than in policy. The *Economist*, it is true, said in 1894: "Little by little and year by year the fabric of State expenditure and State responsibility is built up like a coral island, cell on cell." But Governments even in the age of triumphant liberalism had not hesitated to introduce legislation which drastically interfered with industry, with the lives of the people and with property rights. Sanitary legislation, however much its results were welcomed, made inroads on private life and even as in the Burials Bill, on religious sentiment. The Encumbered Estates Act had interfered with the existing rights of landowners in Ireland. This kind of legislation was, however, regarded as an exception to the general trend of policy and if there was a choice, public opinion was in favour of leaving action to individuals. Now a philosophy of the state was growing up which preferred it to intervene even where the same end might be produced by other agencies.

VI

In a society which combined complete acceptance of democracy in theory, a widespread philosophy which idealized if it did not deify the state, and great economic inequality, the emergence of

Socialism was probably inevitable. Both political parties, however unwittingly, contributed to the creation of the Labour party. They both exaggerated their appeal to working men. The Conservatives seem to have been dazzled by their unexpected survival in a democratic state; having retained so large a share of the working-class vote, they assumed that they would retain it indefinitely, which in a sense, of course, they have. But they failed to see that while a paternalistic Conservatism might well win votes against the austere Liberalism of the early part of the century, it would have to struggle much harder against a Liberalism which was rapidly becoming socialist; that it was socialist in phrase not in intention only made it certain that a real socialist party would appear. Besides the Irish question split the Liberals and obscured the social and economic issues for many people.

It now seems incredible that Liberals could have so misjudged the temper of the working class, and it was not the 'Whigs' but the Radicals who showed themselves singularly ignorant of 'the people's' real aspirations.

The Radicals used language which would have been suitable as a preparation for Communism rather than for giving County Councils powers for the compulsory acquisition of land. It is true that it was owners of land alone against whom they were fulminating, but it is inexplicable how they can have failed to see that the same phrases would very shortly be used against themselves, or, indeed, were being used at that very date. As Mallock said: "Birmingham capitalists denounce landlords as robbers, and far more logical Socialists denounce Birmingham capitalists." It seems hard to see what one of Chamberlain's own employees was expected to make of the following statement: "If you go back to the early days of our social system, you will find that . . . every man was born into the world with natural rights, with a right to a share in the great inheritance of the community, with a right to a part of the land of his birth. Private ownership has taken the place of those communal rights, and this system has become so interwoven with our habits and usages . . . that it might be very difficult if not impossible to reverse it. But then I ask what ransom will property pay for the security which it enjoys?"[19] In a subsequent speech he suggested the ransom, which was the somewhat moderate one of free education, democratic local government in the counties, compulsory powers of the local authorities to acquire land, and state supervision of housing for the working class. It was hardly likely that an unemployed man, familiar with Socialist theories, would be content with this sort of thing.

Lord Hartington, though a 'Whig', had a juster appreciation than Chamberlain. He said "the worst of Chamberlain's speeches seems to me the enormous difference between the general declaration of what has to be done and the measures which he proposes. If they are carried how far should we have got towards reducing the difference between the condition of the rich and the poor which shocks him so much, and what will the poor say when they find out how far short of the end promised the remedies fall?"[20] What they thought was shown in 1894 when the Independent Labour Party declared "plutocratic Liberalism, which takes £250 million per annum in the form of interest, is in every way as bad, as wicked and as harmful, as aristocratic Toryism, which takes a similar sum in the form of rent".

Lloyd George, in 1907, was still harping on the perfectly irrelevant topic of land tenure; he called "drink and this vicious land system" the main cause of "slums and widespread destitution", and the same diagnosis was the basis of his famous budget in 1909.

Men who worked in factories and lived in big towns were unlikely to find their lives any pleasanter because large county estates had been broken up, and even the taxation of site values in towns would have made little difference. It is true that the Liberal Governments after 1906 made some steps towards the Welfare State by introducing old age pensions and unemployment insurance; but even these hardly seemed an adequate fulfilment of the promise held out in the Liberal song:

> The Land! The Land! 'Twas God that made the Land;
> The Land! The Land! The ground on which we stand.
> Why should we be beggars with the ballot in our hand?
> God gave the Land for the people.

"Why should we be beggars with the ballot in our hands?"
Why indeed? There were already signs that many of the men to
whom the Liberal party looked for support were turning elsewhere.

Real Socialism was reaching them from two different sources,
from the disciples of Marx and from the Fabians. Marx had only
died in 1883 and besides founding a school he had influenced many
people outside it. In discussing working-class unrest contemporary
opinion concentrated perhaps excessively on poverty. If there was
poverty there was also the chance of a decent if narrow life and
even of a modest prosperity. Charles Booth in his *London Life and
Labour* defined the poor as consisting of two classes, the first ill-
nourished and ill-clad, the second neither "ill-nourished nor ill-
clad" according to any standard that can reasonably be used, and
not in "want although its members would be much better off
with more of everything". He calculated that 37.3 per cent. of the
working-class population of London consisted of either one or the
other. These are frightful figures but it is not always noticed that
they also mean that 62.7 per cent. were living above this standard.
The democracy in which these men lived, while it gave them
political power, did not offer many opportunities for the
exceptionally gifted, nor did it provide an accepted picture of
society which would make the average workman, even if he was
successful in keeping a decent job and bringing up his family,
contented with his life compared with that of other classes.

Men from working-class families did make large fortunes, but
although it is not possible to support the impression with figures,
it seems as if in other walks of life there were more barriers than
there had been. There were eleven working men in the House of
Commons in 1890 who all accepted the Liberal Whip, but they
had little influence. It is suggested that the growth of party
organization worked against the choice of working-class candidates because it meant that candidates were chosen by the
Central Committee and not, as they were before the development
of the 'caucus', by local committees. Conservative working men
still held as part of their political creed the necessity of aristocratic leadership and Conservative working-men candidates
would not have been popular in many places, although the

Secretary of the Cotton Operatives once sat as a Conservative Member.

The years of reform shut more doors than they opened. Two distinct grades in the Civil Service, with a competitive examination as the only means of reaching the higher, had closed the Civil Service to anyone whose parents could not afford to send him to a university—in England to Oxford or Cambridge. The Civil Service examinations had been devised to attract men from these universities and therefore they still favoured them. Universities had become much more expensive and the reform of university education had, by raising the standards of scholarship, practically limited them to boys from public schools and a few of the larger grammar schools. Neither Samuel Johnson nor William Collins would have got there in these years. Only in Scotland did the son of working-class parents still find his way to a university. The growth and increasing organization of science made it impossible for working men to contribute to it, as they had previously. No hand-loom weaver became a distinguished chemist nor son of a parish clerk a Professor of Greek. In the eighteenth century patronage coupled with the flexible not to say haphazard administration must have disseminated hope. When a Prime Minister could be congratulated on giving a living to the Professor of Arabic at Cambridge who had originally been a carpenter, on the grounds that such 'creditable exertions' should be rewarded, and although "his knowledge of Arabic was not profound but it was hardly to be expected in the circumstances"* nothing could have appeared out of reach. The knowledge of the marvellous luck with which some men had met must have had something of the same effect as the possibility of winning a football pool. While making no actual difference to 99.9 per cent. of the population, it yet adds something to life that such a chance exists.

From the eighteen-sixties to 1914 there were neither football pools nor patrons. Nor was there much in the way of secondary education. Even if a boy from a poor home could win a scholarship to a local grammar school it meant a real sacrifice to most

---

* It is fair to Professor Lee to say that the *Dictionary of National Biography* does not agree with this judgment.

homes to relinquish his earnings, a sacrifice often too heavy to be borne.

The mere growth of population must have tended to submerge individual ambition among working men. Anyone who has lived in Scotland knows that a small country makes individual effort seem much more possible than a large one. Everyone at least knows of everyone else. Scottish ploughmen take a vivid interest in the careers of Scottish Members of Parliament. University professors are quite likely to have cousins and even brothers-in-law who are shepherds. In these conditions to carve out a career for oneself seems both more possible and more worth while. The population of Great Britain had grown from an estimated six million in the middle of the eighteenth century, to thirty-three million in 1891 and forty-one million in 1901 and had tended more and more to live in towns which accentuated the effect of the growth in population itself—large anonymous masses, who, if not miserable themselves, lived side by side with misery and separated from other classes.

The one advantage which authoritarian or hierarchical societies have over modern democracy is that they provide a social map or picture in which the average, as apart from the exceptional, person can find a satisfying image of himself. The eighteenth century had been well furnished with these ideal stereotypes, as had the first half of the nineteenth. The faithful servant, the honest workman, the independent farmer, the liberal* and enlightened landlord existed in everyone's imagination if not in everyone's experience. Now they had vanished. No longer did "God make high and lowly and order their estate". Anyone could try and be a success, and a success in any field commanded the respect which it always has, but there was no longer an ideal picture on which the average person could model himself. To the rich, who could do as they liked, this did not matter, nor to those in interesting professions, but it mattered enormously to working men and to many intellectuals. The honest worker, the faithful servant had disappeared, killed by fierce Socialist ridicule and replaced by a collective not an individual ideal.

* Liberal in a financial not a political sense, of course.

The bright colours and clear outline of the social picture had become smudged, and this mattered to the intellectual classes as much if not more than to the working classes, for they are more dependent on it. Bertrand de Jouvenal says that the alliance between the worker and the intellectual dates from the French Revolution of 1830 but in England the conversion of writers, lawyers, teachers in large numbers only began in the eighteen-eighties and did not become overwhelming until the nineteen-thirties.

Writers have, of course, always criticized the social system in which they happened to live and there were from the eighteen-forties onwards men who, like Carlyle and Matthew Arnold, attacked not only specific evils but the whole basis of the existing system. Most of those engaged in what may be described as intellectual work, writers, ministers of religion, lawyers, journalists had, however, accepted more or less wholeheartedly the existing social structure. There was now a change. The kind of persons described as 'intellectual middlemen',* that is, those who do not themselves produce ideas but who explain, amplify and pass them on, had greatly increased. The growth of the Press was one element in this, and the spread of State education another. These men tended to be attracted by ideas of a complete social transformation; the teachers because some of them at least knew the misery in which a section of the poor lived; others because they felt, as the same kind of person so frequently does today, that the rewards of a successful business man were out of proportion to the social value of his activities, which compared poorly with their own.

From the electoral point of view the conversion of ministers of religion, who still had considerable influence, was probably more important. The new religious schools, Methodist and Tractarians, of the eighteenth and early nineteenth centuries, were profoundly Conservative. From the eighteen-sixties, however, although many Church of England clergymen remained high Tory, or at least as high Tory as it was still possible to be, others, even of the High Church party, were attracted to various forms of Christian Socialism. The chapels had become pre-dominantly Liberal and from a certain sort of Liberalism it was only a step to Socialism.

* By Professor Hayek.

The change in atmosphere was undoubtedly to some extent connected with the decline of religion itself. Philanthropy, which in the days of Shaftesbury had been nearly always inspired by religion, had by the eighteen-nineties become a substitute for it. Thoughtful and serious people who would in other periods have been prominent in church or chapel were now nearly always 'free-thinkers'. Even those whose faith remained unimpaired by conscious doubts were affected. The message of Christianity, as that of Stoicism, is to the individual soul. The Stoic said, as the Christian must say, "the good man is happy even on the rack". Such lesser suffering as poverty, ill-health or political oppression is a matter of indifference for it cannot hurt the soul. Once admit it can and Christianity as well as Stoicism is undermined. The Evangelical movement had recognized this; it was essentially a reassertion of 'primitive' Christianity against the social religion of the eighteenth century and this is why its leaders revived the controversy, so barren to us, of the relative importance of faith and works. It is alleged that there used to be a hymn containing the words

> Doing is a deadly thing
> Doing ends in death

in which doing means doing good. None of this had any bearing on actual conduct, the Evangelicals were as famous for 'doing' as the Tractarians; but it had an influence on political attitudes. A Wilberforce or a Shaftesbury might agitate against slavery or conduct a campaign for shorter working hours but they would certainly neither formulate Socialist doctrines themselves nor encourage them in others.

Christian Socialism was to some extent an attempt to attract working men to Christianity by agreeing with their politics or their supposed politics. The 'intelligent artisan' was as much if not more affected by the spread of the new scientific ideas, such as the new theories of geology and Darwinism, as the intelligent middle class. Geology and natural history had been their favourite sciences, as archaeology is now, and for the same reason, it opened to them wholly new worlds. It was only the minority even of artisans who had been attracted to such reading, but they were likely to be the leaders of opinion. It was the chapels who had clung most closely to the literal inspiration of the Bible as the centre of their creed, and the destruction of Biblical chron- ology by geologists struck hardest at the faith of those who knew the Bible by heart and got their science from popular handbooks. The exhilaration of throwing over the authority of parson and minister must have attracted many who were really quite indifferent to religion or science. Two possible solutions were open to those who worked among such people, to try and establish a Church which retained the ethical values of Christianity without its supernatural elements, or to try and show that belief was not incompatible with the most advanced political views.

Apart from the spread of new ideas, industrialism had so changed the conditions of life as to make the collective aspect more important for everyone. It was not only that the municipal council swept the streets: the State since 1870 educated your children, and the trade unions already negotiated your wages. Individual effort had ceased to be the only way of organizing the framework of life. No longer was it necessary for you to have your own horses or to walk if you wanted to go anywhere, other people organized and ran a system of railways, all you had to do was to take a ticket. The police were as effective as they are today. There was a whole range of commodities, from bread to ready-made clothes, to replace those produced by the household. A change of policy in Germany, or the United States, could result in unemployment, lower wages, lower profits or even bankruptcy. And everyone was made aware of the international origins of various troubles by the newspapers. In difficulties produced by events abroad it was natural to turn to the Government and this again emphasized the collective aspect of life and made everyone more conscious of their common interest. It is true that this awareness often showed itself in the acceptance of doctrines of class antagonism, but this is not as paradoxical as it may seem for they appeared to explain both the divisions of society and the strong feeling of mutual dependence. These doctrines were the more easily accepted because the old theory of representation, itself based on classes, must still have been familiar to everyone; they must have heard their fathers and mothers and the older Members of Parliament talk in its terms. This theory looks superficially not unlike the Marxist doctrine, and for practical purposes the substitution of inevitable conflict for mutual co-operation was all that was necessary. A theory which not only was but which sounded completely novel, would have taken much longer, as for example did the new psychology, which it is true affronted deeply-rooted sentiments, but also called for a strenuous mental effort to understand at all.

All the new factors which had emerged during the nineteenth century seemed to make for some form of collectivism or at least an extension of Government activity into fields which it had never yet invaded. There still existed, however, a strong traditional conservatism; the Liberal party only got an effective majority in the election of 1911, which was fought on the position of the House of Lords, because the Irish Nationalists, who numbered eighty-two, supported them; without them their majority would have been reduced to two. There also persisted the Radical attitude which was opposed both to legal privilege and to Government interference and wanted equality of opportunity not equality of income or condition. If England had followed this path she would have become a country more like the United States or Canada. Which way England would have developed if there had been no war it is hard to say. Everything always seems inevitable once it has happened. Although the pre-war Liberal Government introduced some measures which now seem to be the first step towards the Welfare State, the political situation was complicated by questions which have vanished. Ireland and proposals for the disestablishment of the Church of England, following its disestablishment in Wales, roused passions as fierce, or indeed fiercer, than economic questions.

The politics of the early years of this century were marked by more deliberate violence than they had been at any time since the seventeenth century; strikers, Ulster Unionists, suffragettes, even the Conservative leaders were all prepared to threaten to use force to resist the Government or to obtain their ends. This violence is often explained in terms of the fashionable psychology, as a desire to escape from the boredom of a too long peace, of an unconscious desire for war. It is, however, not necessary to appeal to these obscure and invisible motives, the strains and stresses were due to the sudden advent of complete democracy. Practical men in all parties had persuaded themselves not only that there was no danger in universal suffrage and one-chamber government but also that it would involve no essential changes. Liberal Cabinet Ministers saw a vision of a country in which the professional middle classes elected by the votes of the people would gradually ameliorate the hardships of poverty out of funds chiefly provided by the taxation of land. This was not an ignoble dream but one which unfortunately bore no relation to any reality. The House of Lords and the Conservative party did everything they could to exasperate the Liberal Government and its supporters, but the Government failed to see that in depriving the House of Lords of most of their powers they were changing the Constitution from one in which there was a balance of different powers to one in which a small and temporary majority could make vast changes which, among other things, might inflict serious injustice on individuals. There is no other democratic Constitution in which the power of the majority is so untrammelled. The United States retains the old theory of the Constitution in a different form. European democracies have fundamental rights written into the Constitution.

The Parliament Act had another and more practical consequence. To no one had the Lords' veto been more useful, although they failed to realize it, than to the leaders of progressive parties when they were in office. Any pledge which in the heat of an election had become too far-reaching, or which roused too much opposition in the country, could be dropped because of the implacable opposition of their Lordships and no blame could attach to the party leaders. No longer was this possible, and Asquith's Government nearly brought the country to civil war because they had to implement their promises to the Irish Nationalists on whose votes they depended. The disregard of constitutional propriety by Bonar Law and the other Conservative leaders has often been commented on; when it is realized that they felt that the Liberals had by the Parliament Act undermined the Constitution and drastically interfered with the rights of minorities, it is easier to understand their attitude. It was always one of the main themes of Bonar Law's speeches, as for instance when he said in Ulster: "The Government by the Parliament Act have erected a boom against you: a boom to cut you off from the help of the British people". However unlimited in theory the power of Parliament may be, there are strict limits in practice to what any Government in a civilized State can do, however great its majority. The Government of the day seems to have failed to realize these obvious facts. Complete democracy brought with it as serious a crisis in this country as elsewhere, a crisis which was solved only because it was submerged by the 1914 war.

The Home Rule controversy left a legacy to modern politics in the form of the doctrine of the mandate, which was evolved by the Conservative party as part of their campaign against the Government. They maintained that the Government had no right to introduce a Home Rule Bill because the last election had been fought on the House of Lords and the electorate had not been plainly told that a Liberal victory meant Irish Home Rule. This doctrine is a departure from the older ideas and, in theory at any rate, entails a considerable limitation on the powers of any Government. Usually employed by an Opposition against the Government, it is widely accepted, although many constitutional theorists consider that there is no basis for it. It would on the whole be considered improper if a Labour Government nationalized the banking system, for example, if they had not included such a proposal in their manifesto, or if a Conservative Government similarly abolished family allowances. The doctrine can only be applied to domestic affairs for foreign policy must be decided in the light of actual events.

The war broke down any lingering feeling against complete democracy. It was felt in all parties absurd that men who had risked their lives for their country should not have a voice in deciding its policy and that women too, who had done so much work of which they had previously been considered incapable, should continue to be shut out from political life.

The Representation of the People Act of 1918 was based on the recommendations of an all-party committee. It swept away all previous electoral qualifications and introduced universal suffrage with the exception that women could not vote until they were thirty. Even now, however, there were, apart from the continued existence of the House of Lords, some small exceptions to the universal rule of democracy. People could still have three votes and could still use two, although not in one constituency. The occupation of business premises carried a vote with it both for Parliamentary and local government elections. The University constituencies were not abolished. Indeed the Act created four university seats, the English Universities, the Welsh Universities, Queen's University in Belfast, and the National University of Ireland. The constituencies remained, moreover, far from equal in numbers, although the normal unit was supposed to be 70,000.

The present system of registration, by which the list of voters is compiled by an official, although it still remains the responsibility of the electors to make certain that they are on it, was also introduced. Polling in future was to be on the same day in all constituencies. Those who are not familiar with politics may suppose this provision made no difference, but it is a fact that polling spread over several weeks gave a considerable advantage to the party which took an early lead.

The last barriers against pure democracy, except for the brief delay which the House of Lords could still command, were removed in the Representation of the People Act, 1948, when the University constituencies and the business vote were abolished. We have now arrived at "One man one vote" and the Government of the day made an effort to produce also "One vote one value". Electoral reform was combined with redistribution and constituencies were made as far as practicable, equal. A commission was set up with instructions to redistribute the constituencies every five years.

The Local Government Act of 1945 made a drastic breach with all previous ideas of local government representation, by giving everyone on the Parliamentary register a local government vote. Occupiers of business premises are still allowed to vote in local elections as long as they do not use their residential vote as well, even if it is in another constituency.

CHAPTER VI

TRADE UNIONISTS, BUREAUCRATS AND BOSSES

I

THE foregoing account of the inception and development of democracy is based neither on the 'Whig' historians' vision of ever-widening freedom, nor on the Marxist picture of classes struggling to preserve or to gain economic advantages. Different as they are in their approach, they both share the assumption that history is a steady progress from worse to better and that a total victory is possible. This is not a useful background for the consideration of modern problems; it does not so much exaggerate the virtues as conceal the problems of democracy. It makes it fatally easy to confuse the idea of liberty with the idea of equality and thus Socialism appears inevitable because it seems to be only another extension of freedom. Having attained political equality the working class naturally go on to demand economic equality. If we confine our attention to Europe this indeed is the way the story seems to run. But if the horizon is widened a different picture emerges. There is no serious Socialist movement in the United States or Canada.

Nor do these theories make any allowance for chance or for the guises in which chance may appear, ambitions, enmities, loyalties, and perhaps most important of all, misconceptions. Groups and individuals, when they demand any change, do not always understand what they are really asking for, and still less do they see its more distant consequences. No nineteenth-century democrat saw a state like modern England as the culmination of his efforts; if they had, some of them would have revised their views. Even the early Fabians might have been slightly startled by the results of Socialism in practice.

Socialism itself is not a spontaneous creation of the working-class mind, still less the kind of Socialism which is the basis of the Labour party's creed. Some of the Chartists were Socialists but there were not many convinced Socialists among working men from the eighteen-fifties until after the 1914 war, and those that were believed in syndicalism rather than in state-organized or state-supervised industries. Socialism in the eighteen-nineties was a theory developed by middle-class intellectuals, who found it by no means easy to persuade working men to accept it. Even the formation of a separate working-class party does not seem to have been inevitable. The most important step towards the establishment of the Labour party was undoubtedly the conversion of the trade unions. Most of them had no desire whatever for Socialism and the Labour party did not officially become a Socialist party until 1918. On the whole the trade union leaders before 1914 supported the policies of the Liberal party, but they thought it did not provide for a sufficient number of working men to become Liberal candidates. For this they blamed the Liberal party organization, then known as the caucus; even Threlfell, the trade union leader who was Chairman of the Labour Electoral Committee, affiliated to the Liberal party, attacked it. "It is a curious commentary on this ideal system," he said, "that of the thirteen Labour Members representing England and Wales in the present House, four ran in opposition to the caucus, five represent constituencies where the miners absolutely dominate the position . . . and only four either captured the caucus or out-generalled it."[1] This desire for working-class representation was not primarily concerned with differences in policy, the Liberal party was prepared to accept the advice of trade union leaders on trade union legislation, and the trade union leaders on the whole supported the Liberal programme.

It is said that the other motive which led the trade unions to consent to the attempt to create a separate working-class party was their fear that the contemporary American attacks on trade unions might be copied in England, and that a 'Labour' party would be a better defence than universal suffrage without separate working-class representation. Although the party was not Socialist in origin, it offered a great opportunity to the theoretical Socialist. From the first there existed inside the party a dedicated group filled with proselytizing zeal and ready to take advantage of any industrial trouble, of any worsening of the wage-earners' position to propagate their faith. And trouble far worse than anything even the Socialists expected followed soon after the inauguration of the Independent Labour Party. A reluctance to change, a clinging to established institutions and habitual methods is a characteristic of either supremely successful, or of decadent societies. Great Britain between the two wars was neither. Her people still had sufficient energy to try and find other institutions when the traditional ones seemed inadequate; and they seemed more and more inadequate from 1914 onwards. The war itself, once the first enthusiasm was spent, appeared to be a betrayal of civilization. Even to those who remained certain that the Allies were engaged on a crusade, the mere fact of war meant that the social order had failed. More disillusion followed the peace. British industry never fully recovered. Even before the great depression the staple industries, coal, cotton and steel, were depressed and the figures for unemployment never fell below a million. When the depression engulfed even the United States the whole economic system seemed to have collapsed and there was now, as there had been in the days of the French Revolution, an alternative way of life. There was a general loss of confidence, which made working men vote Conservative, and writers, journalists and scientists become Socialists, Communists, or fellow travellers of varying degrees of sincerity.

Before 1914 collectivist ideas sprang from a wish to use the power of the State to mitigate or abolish suffering of all kinds, but especially suffering caused by poverty. Between the wars, although this motive still existed, there was a tendency to look to the state to solve problems which seemed to have become too big for individuals; it was not only social reformers who now demanded state intervention but business leaders, writers and farmers. Stronger on the Continent, this tendency also affected Great Britain and its influence can be seen in legislation. For Englishmen, however, the experiences of the twentieth century were not so devastating as they were for Russians and Germans, so that the element of hysteria was absent. Here people were not seeking a new religion but measures to protect or help particular interests, or at most a planned and directed economy. Even in this limited form it was a change from the traditional attitude and worked to strengthen the power as well as to increase the functions of Government.

II

If the machinery of Government allows it, democracy itself tends to increase the power of the State over the individual; since the Government is chosen by the people, the old safeguards no longer seem necessary. There are authoritarian elements in democratic theory; the concept of majority rule means that the majority has a right to disregard the wishes of any minority, whether it is large or small and whether its views are well or ill founded. Expedience is of course another matter, and in a civilized country no Government can act to the full extent allowed in theory.

The whole tendency of modern life, however, is to strengthen the collectivist aspect of society. We have been taught the value of discipline and co-operation in two wars, and this experience is confirmed by the extreme specialization of labour; a railway or a 'bus strike soon reminds the most arrogant or the most individualistic of their dependence on others. If there is a deficit on the balance of payments everyone is inconvenienced, from the housewife, who has to pay more for a saucepan, to the chairman of an industrial company, who cannot get credit from his bank.

The century of the common man is distinguished by the most aristocratic culture that has ever existed, aristocratic in the sense that it has no popular roots and that the average person can neither understand nor enjoy it. In nearly every other period in English history, pre-eminently in the eighteenth and nineteenth centuries, anyone of intelligence who could read found no difficulty in contemporary novels and poetry and could even follow scientific developments. Not only were Sir Walter Scott and

Wordsworth, Dickens and Tennyson perfectly comprehensible, they would have been ashamed to think that anyone, whatever his 'station', could not enjoy their writings. Today, most serious writers would feel uneasy if they were popular with either stockbrokers or coal-miners. Until a short time ago new painting was even more beyond the sympathy of the average person.

Perhaps literature and art have always been, save for exceptional artists and at exceptional periods, for a minority. The basis and mainspring of modern civilization, science, is however even more remote from ordinary understanding. Everyone can see the transformation which science has produced and some of its application can even be understood, but the theories on which it is based are beyond the comprehension even of those with a good general education. The discoveries of Newton diffused a sense that everyone was sharing the new understanding of God's universe, because they explained the movements of the planets by the same laws as the fall of an apple.[2] Relativity and quantum mechanics have no such homely illustrations. To most people they cannot be explained at all and, even more disconcerting, what glimmer of meaning does emerge seems to show them as repugnant to ordinary experience and to common sense. "A modern theory—whether it be psychoanalysis or relativity or quantum mechanics—is very abstract, not only its basic concepts but also the hypothesis it allows us to frame, and consequently the data for them are removed from familiar experience."[3] The impossibility of judging or testing for ourselves the theories which are the basis of material and intellectual advance produces a curious authoritarianism in the fabric of modern society, an authoritarianism quite different from the hierarchy of knowledge in the Middle Ages but which has something of the same psychological influence. It undermines that crude self-confidence which was the mark of the Englishman in the eighteenth and first half of the nineteenth centuries, and which formed the soil out of which democracy grew. Theories which stress the importance of the community and the dependence of individual achievement on the social setting suit better the modern situation, the situation in which no one feels himself to be of much individual importance. They are suited to the needs of a mass society in which people believe that everyone is equal and yet can find nothing for themselves in the predominant branches of science or in the literature and painting which experts admire.

All this may seem remote from politics, but submission to the demands of experts for only half-comprehended reasons makes people willing to accept the orders, legislation or policy of any properly elected Government. The modern habit of doing without much fuss what the Government commands is not a revulsion from the idea of democracy. The whole democratic process of elections is still highly valued; but after the election, although the average citizen may still try to assert his rights, he will not usually find much sympathy. He may even be dissuaded from opposing measures which he knows will injure him. It appears that in the agitation against the plans to make an airport at Gatwick a number of residents refused to take part on the grounds that air transport was a technical subject about which they knew nothing, while the Government must have had the best advice before taking their decision.

III

The administrative necessities of a Welfare State demand that the Government should be more powerful than the Governments of the Liberal era. Measures which are purely political such as Catholic Emancipation or the extension of the franchise are, once passed, self-regulating; nothing more needs to be done by the Government. Even social reforms like the abolition of the slave trade or the repeal of the Combination Laws, as long as they only abolish privileges or repeal prohibitions, require the minimum of administration. Welfare legislation, however, must also be administered. The simplest Factory Act involves inspectors to see that the law is carried out; so does even the most obvious kind of sanitary legislation or the smallest provision for elementary education. The further the Government goes towards the Welfare State the heavier becomes the burden of administration. The more elaborate the framework of social services the more varied and complicated are the circumstances in which they have to function, and the more powerful the apparatus of government.

The Government now does a great deal that used to be done by individuals or private organizations. It also does a great deal that previously was not done by anyone. A considerable proportion of industry is organized into public corporations for which Ministers are responsible to the House of Commons. The Government has accepted, has indeed snatched the responsibility for the overall direction of the economy. The Chancellor of the Exchequer, not the governor of the Bank of England, fixes the bank rate and supervises the other activities of a central bank. The central government has absorbed many of the functions of the local authorities; the extension of social insurance has transferred the provision for old age, unemployment and sickness, except in special circumstances, from local councils to departments of the central government.

These new functions in themselves involve a substantial degree of interference with individual choice. Choice is at this stage a better word than liberty because it is frequently argued that such institutions as compulsory social insurance, the closed shop in industry, or the present level of taxation increase the sum of 'real' liberty. No one, however, can maintain that they do not cut down the number of choices open to the average citizen. They place the State in a paternal relation to him and thus sanction prohibitions and orders on a wide and increasing range of subjects. That the Government is filled with the best intentions means that the citizen is disposed to obey and that the administrator is convinced that recalcitrance is either silly or wicked.

Some local authorities carry this interference into the most intimate and the most trivial details of everyday life. They regulate the affairs of those who live in their houses in a way which no eighteenth-century landlord would have contemplated for a moment. They refuse to allow the tenants to keep dogs or cats, to plant flowers in their front gardens, or they dictate what flowers are to be planted, and in a famous case evicted a man because he kept beetles in glass cases. Some of these restrictions have been made on private houses, but to be valid these must have been enumerated in the lease, while local authorities can change the conditions for the occupation of their property at any time.

The modern state is also forced to disregard property rights. Authorities, both central departments and local councils, must have powers for the compulsory acquisition of sites for hospitals, offices, municipal housing schemes, testing new weapons or building atomic energy stations. This list shows that it is not only the welfare aspects of the state that entail such interference with private property, but also the needs of defence. Contrary to what most people believe, however, these powers are not completely new.

Even Blackstone, after declaring the rights of property to be inviolable, said "if a new road for instance, were to be made through the grounds of a private person, it might perhaps be extensively beneficial; but the law permits no man, or set of men, to do this without the consent of the owner of the land. . . . In this and similar cases the legislature alone can, and indeed frequently does, interpose and compel, but how does it do this? Not by absolutely stripping the subject of his property in an arbitrary manner; but by giving him a full indemnification and equivalent for the injury thereby sustained . . . all that the legislature does is to oblige him, the owner, to alienate his possessions for a reasonable price." This is all, in theory at least, the legislature obliges the owner to do today. The difference is that when Blackstone wrote each case required a special Act of Parliament, so that the aggrieved owner was certain at any rate of prolonged discussion; today the legislature has conferred wide powers on Government departments and local authorities, and in the last resort it is the Minister and not the House of Commons who decides.

The most striking illustration of the changed attitude to property is, however, not compulsory acquisition, for after all this has always existed in emergencies, but the use of taxation not to ameliorate hardship or allay suffering but with the deliberate purpose of lessening inequality. Liberals had already started in this direction even before the 1914 war, and today the majority of Conservatives would probably accept it and would certainly see nothing strange in the idea. Yet even up to the end of the nineteenth century the majority, even of the serious and high-minded, thought that taxation should not be progressive but proportionate. A proportionate tax is a tax under which all incomes are taxed at the same rate, a progressive tax one in which the rate as well as the absolute amount of tax increases with the income. Under the proportionate system the high incomes will still pay the highest amount of any direct taxation, but unless the bulk of the population pay no tax at all, it will not alter the previous distribution of wealth. John Stuart Mill thought that progressive taxation was definitely wrong. He said: "To tax the larger incomes at a higher percentage than the smaller, is to lay a tax on industry and economy, to impose a penalty on people for having worked harder or saved more than their neighbours. It is partial taxation which is a mild form of robbery."[4] The opponents of progressive taxation were partly inspired by the fear that it would have an unfavourable effect on the willingness to work and save; but their fundamental objection was that it was not the function of taxation to alter the relative position of different tax-payers. The accepted maxim was that taxation should be for revenue purposes only, because it was no part of the function of the state to safeguard particular industries or to redistribute property.

The idea that taxation should be used to promote economic equality gives the state unlimited powers, for it could be pushed to the point where individuals are ruined, where there are no property rights left at all.

The change in both the nature and scale of Government activities has made a breach in the traditional relation between Parliament and the executive. It was for long a constitutional maxim that Parliament alone should make laws and that they should be so drafted that no discretion should be allowed to the executive in their interpretation or application. If any doubt arose about the exact meaning of a clause it must be decided by the Courts of Justice. This meant that there could be no delegation of power from Parliament to any Minister, Civil Servant or authority of any kind. When these ideas were most strongly held Parliament was not much given to legislation and when it did pass any Act it attempted to provide for all possible contingencies and to lay down exactly what should be done in each case. This is an ideal which is in practice unattainable and it would make the administration of any social service extremely difficult. Eloquent statements about this difficulty have been made by all those concerned with administration, for example by Sir William Graham-Harrison, then First Parliamentary Counsel, who, giving evidence before the Committee on Ministers' Powers in 1932, said: "Speaking from practical experience, which now extends to a period of twenty-seven years, of the work of getting legislation through Parliament I have no hesitation in saying that it would be impossible to produce the amount and the kind of legislation which Parliament desires to pass, and which the people of this country are supposed to want, if it became necessary to insert in the Acts of Parliament themselves any considerable proportion of what is now left to delegated legislation. As classical examples I would refer to the vast bulk of the National Health Insurance Regulations and special orders, which run to more than 1,000 pages, and to the 800 pages of the Orders setting up trade boards."[5]

Accordingly, in nearly every Act concerned with the social services and in some concerned with other subjects, for example the Transport Act of 1929, the Minister is given power to make rules, regulations and orders. Perhaps the real importance of this procedure is its effect on the rule of law, this will be discussed later but it has also the effect of removing in practice a considerable part of the activities of the executive from the control of Parliament. As the Treasury Solicitor said before the same committee: "The greater the complexity of our civilization and the wider the range of our legislation, the more difficult it is for a popularly elected legislature to exercise complete control over administrative policy."[6]

When it is said that the 'Government' has become more powerful than it was, it is the executive which is meant, for legislature cannot administer; they can only legislate.

The House of Commons as the body from which all the more important Members of the Government must come, has retained, has even increased its standing, but both the House as distinct from the Government, and the individual Member are less important than they have been at any time since 1688. For this there are many reasons. Delegated legislation means not only that Ministers have powers which were previously reserved to Parliament, but also that it is with the Minister or his officials and not with Parliament, that anyone affected by departmental rules and orders will negotiate. This is something which has grown out of the social policy of every modern Government but, policy apart, conditions today make the function of representation less necessary.

A representative house originally grew up because it was so difficult for the executive to communicate with any part of the country except the town in which the King happened to be at the moment; he had no means of knowing the opinions of anyone except the great barons who habitually attended the Court. It was therefore convenient to have someone from each town or county to state his neighbours' views to the Government and to carry the Government's views back to them. The representative continued to be the Government's chief means of contact with local views and opinions even when power passed from the King to the House of Commons. The growth of the Press during the nineteenth century gave public opinion another means of expression and it also allowed Ministers to speak directly to the whole country, over the heads of Members of Parliament.

Modern means of communication allow the party leaders to appeal even more directly to the individual voter. Wireless and television have the advantage of letting the ordinary citizen hear and see the man himself. Admittedly both have their limitations; neither is kind to oratory of the traditional sort and both enforce brevity. Gladstone's public speeches lasted two or three hours; a television appearance lasts fifteen minutes and demands the equipment of an actor rather than an orator. They are not, however, edited by the Press; the public hears what the leader himself wants to get over, not what some editor considers 'news'. Nor are policy or ideas filtered through Members and candidates, for who is going to listen to Mr. Smith when he can hear the Prime Minister himself? The back-bencher remains a back-bencher even in his own constituency.

Until the end of the nineteenth century geography remained the most important factor in most people's lives; they belonged to their town or to their county rather than to their class or profession; 'foreigners', in many parts of England, did not mean people of an alien nationality but people from another county or another town. Today, however, many people feel themselves to be more truly represented by their trade or professional organization than by their Member of Parliament. Collectivism, unless it is combined with political tyranny, is inclined to accentuate as much the importance of the group as the importance of the state, and this accords well with the prevailing English atmosphere. The ideal is no longer the independent individual, responsible to his own conscience alone, but the team and the team spirit. We may owe this originally to the public schools but football and cricket have spread it to everyone, at least to every man. It is strongest among working men for it coalesces admirably with trade union ethics. The ultimate appeal to the trade unionist in industry or politics is "you must stick by your mates". Personal success may be regarded with doubt or even suspicion, but even in the most Socialist of working-class circles no one is blamed for sticking up for his side. Or if he is, it is merely a conventional political gesture; the real resentment is caused by those who ought to be members of the workers' team and yet let down the side by refusing to join a union or by working when their mates are on strike. This sentiment is equally the basis of the criticism which used to be heard before the war of those officers who went to the staff college, that they put personal ambition before the 'regiment', and of the extreme umpopularity which pursues any politician who changes his party.

A strong, planning, interventionist Government makes it advantageous, even necessary that everyone who can should join a group which will protect his interests. Every step which the Government takes to modify the workings of the economic process, whether by tariffs, subsidy or regulation, benefits or injures someone, and these effects spread far beyond the primary intentions of the particular Bill. It is natural that people with the same interests should form associations and that these should add negotiation and argument with the Government and Government departments to their other activities. Labour Governments are predisposed in favour of associations by their affiliation with the trade unions but all Governments find it useful to deal with organized bodies. No Government wants to irritate any section, at least without some strong necessity; prior consultation with a trade union or a trade association, with the Farmers' Union or the British Medical Association, can keep such disturbance to a minimum. These bodies also perform the function, necessary with any Government, of preventing it making a fool of itself.

Such associations have always existed but in some periods public opinion was less sympathetic and sometimes it was definitely hostile. The general approval they evoke today gives them respectability and allows them to work in the open. Members of Parliament make no bones about speaking for particular industries if they are important to their constituents, particular classes if they were returned to represent them, or any section or group with whom they have links. Trade unions have their own representatives in the House of Commons and refer to them on occasions as 'our M.P.' or even as 'one of our M.P.s'. Trade associations cannot do exactly this because their members are never numerous enough to dominate any constituency, as members of one trade union sometimes do, but secretaries of trade associations sit in the House and put, with complete frankness and sincerity, their association's point of view. The Farmers' Union similarly tries to safeguard the interests of its members, and M.P.s for agricultural seats regard it as their duty to speak for agriculture in the House. We are largely returning to the eighteenth-century idea that interests should be represented rather than individuals. The interests are, of course, different and there is no class which corresponds to the old landed interest; but the atmosphere is more akin to eighteenth- than to nineteenth-century ideas. Few would now agree with Dicey that "citizens should be looked upon primarily as persons, secondly only as members of classes".

All this of course must be seen in the context of universal suffrage. Universal suffrage means the rule of the majority in the sense that all Governments and all parties have to adjust their policies to the wishes and even to the prejudices* of the majority of the people; and this majority is composed of weekly wage-earners. Anyone can see the effect which this has on all parties; an effect which can only be partially offset by the influence of those organizations which represent other interests.

Organized groups are powerful even at elections, but it is not here that most of them deploy their real influence, for great waves of popular feeling can overwhelm the anxious considerations of special interests, as they did in 1931 and in 1945. During an election any politician has the chance of appealing straight to the voter over the head of his trade union, his trade association or whatever organization usually moulds his ideas. But even when some tidal wave has submerged the familiar landmarks, after it has passed they tend to reappear. A Conservative Government must not offend the trade unions; a Labour Government cannot completely ignore the views of industry and finance; and neither can forget the National Farmers' Union.

If these groups represent those who would tend to be submerged by mere numbers they are a safeguard against the tyranny of the majority. It would perhaps give a better balance if the most powerful of organized groups were not composed of weekly wage-earners who are also the most numerous element in the electorate. Trade unions are powerful not only because of the key position of workers in an industrial state but because public opinion regards them more favourably on the whole than it does other associations, although this benevolence is being changed by the exasperation felt by the professional middle class with strikes and wage claims.

Proposals for legislation are always submitted to those whom it will affect before they are sent to the House; in some cases the Minister is obliged by law to consult certain bodies. If the trade union or the professional organization is able to convince the department that their suggestions ought to be incorporated in the Bill there is some implied obligation on the Government to see that they get through the House. The practice is sensible, indeed in present conditions it is essential, but it is direct contact between

* Conforming to prejudice is known as taking psychological factors into account.

the Government and the citizen, cutting out the citizen's representative. Group organization tends to reduce the power of the Government. The most striking difference between government in the eighteenth and nineteenth centuries and government today is the increase in the Government's power over individuals and local authorities and the decline in its power over organized groups. These organizations lessen the Government's power to do what it likes, but they strengthen the Cabinet as against the House of Commons. The mere multiplicity of activities expected of a modern state have anyhow raised the prestige of the 'Government' as compared with that of Parliament in the eyes of the electorate. It is after all the Civil Servant, who is the agent of the executive, with whom the average citizen comes most in contact rather than the Member of Parliament, and the Civil Servant is one who has authority over him, while the Member is dependent on his vote and is normally met with in the position of a candidate seeking support.

IV

The power of the Cabinet is enhanced and the importance of the private Member diminished by purely political developments, by the growth of party organization and party discipline. Members are not chosen in order to exercise their own judgment on events but to support their party and to follow the decisions of the party leaders. This does not mean that the back-benchers are merely voting machines, nor that the exceptional Member may not establish a position of influence; but Members are now elected as Conservatives or Socialists. This is not a perversion of democracy but the inevitable result of the whole idea of a programme on which the electorate is invited to pass judgment; it is pointless to complain about party discipline unless you are prepared also to abandon the party programme. If a party puts a definite list of measures before the country and is elected on it, then it must get the measures through the House of Commons.

Modern politics affect everyone's life and interests. Electors must in these circumstances be more interested in measures than in men. How could the Liberal Government of 1905 or the Labour Government of 1945 have got their proposals made law without the discipline of the Whips? As every member is already pledged to support or oppose the Government on every major issue the power of the Cabinet is obviously very great, much greater than it was before the rise of the modern party when it frequently had difficulty in persuading even its own supporters to vote for any particular Bill and when the electors often voted for individuals rather than for parties. Universal suffrage with its demands for policies of social amelioration makes a party programme inevitable, and all parties must put before the electorate a programme which will contain some proposals which require legislation. This forces a Government not only to see that all the members of its party vote for that legislation, but also to absorb nearly all the time of the House. Modern Governments are always short of time, for their innumerable activities have to be debated as well as carried out. A Minister could say even in 1930: "Every government wishes to pass more legislation than there is time for, and if a department has one big measure allotted to it in the course of a Parliament, it is considered to be lucky. We in the Ministry of Transport had the Electricity Act. Naturally, all the other Ministers make it their business to see that one department does not get more than one Bill of that importance in order that their own departments may have opportunities. That is the real explanation of why the Transport Bill was left over for two or three years."[7]

The pressure has become worse since 1930. The sheer amount of business which has to be got through has made it progressively more difficult for private Members to introduce important legislation, as Plimsoll did on the overloading of ships and Sir Alan Herbert on divorce. Public opinion acquiesced in this Government monopoly to the extent that even those who complained most bitterly about the strictness of party discipline were shocked when the Eden Government, after a motion for the abolition of capital punishment had been carried on a free vote, allowed Mr. Silverman, the proposer of the motion, to introduce a Bill himself. Many people seemed to think that there was something derogatory in permitting a mere private Member to pilot such an important Bill through the House.

Before 1880 a man was chosen as a Parliamentary candidate largely because he already had a position, independent of his membership of the House of Commons. In those days a large proportion of the House had no wish for office and no desire to speak; they regarded themselves neither as prosecuting nor defending counsel but rather as a jury. Even between the wars some of the country constituencies still returned this type of member. Today constituencies do not want them and they themselves could probably not afford to be M.P.s. The increased intensity of political life, the sessions which take up most of the year, the Government business which absorbs all Parliamentary time, mean that the Members must always be at the House ready to vote and make it increasingly difficult for anyone to combine membership of the House with earning a living outside.

The difference between then and now should not be exaggerated. Even in the nineteenth century Members valued their seats and there was always a certain mortification at being rejected by the electorate. It was, however, comparatively easy for the average Member to be independent, not only because he had less to gain from the favour of the Prime Minister and Cabinet, but also because he had less to lose by the last threat open to the Whips—a general election. It is no slur on the integrity of a Member of Parliament to say that a professional politician of today is less willing than a Victorian squire or large employer of labour to risk the displeasure of his party leaders, especially when these leaders form the Government of the country. Even if he is quixotic enough to disobey or annoy the Whips, it is by no means certain that he will do any good to the cause for which he is willing to sacrifice his career. For example the attempt of a number of Conservative back-benchers to persuade Sir Winston Churchill's Cabinet to change their decision to evacuate the Suez Canal Zone evoked no response and hardly any attention in the country. This would have been inconceivable in the nineteenth century and unlikely even between the wars.

But even when Governments are pledged to support a particular policy they usually have a measure of choice as to time and means; it is there that back-benchers will be able to influence decisions. Members quite frequently threaten to abstain from voting, and even if this does not mean a defeat no Government likes a majority much below what it could be. Ministers will listen both to party meetings and to individual Members. There are few Ministers and few Governments who will force a decision which is really unpopular with their party. In some cases, particularly in foreign affairs, a Government may be forced by sheer pressure of circumstances to disregard those protests. The Labour Government's attitude on German rearmament, the Conservative Government's persistence on the evacuation of the Suez Canal are examples; but no Government will do this sort of thing unless it has to. Conservative back-benchers induced the Churchill Government, for example, to abandon more than one minor Bill and to re-establish the Liverpool Cotton Exchange, and the Eden Government of 1955 to modify their proposals on the borrowing powers of the National Coal Board. If a certain course of action is unpopular with the party in the House, it will almost certainly be so with the party in the country. Mr. Morrison has said: "A Cabinet that proceeded to ride rough-shod over the feelings and wishes of its supporters, relying on the Whips to enforce its will, would be asking for trouble; and it would not be long before it got it."[8] A Minister is not anxious to be unpopular with his own party in the House and he knows that his colleagues, including the Prime Minister, are likely to feel that he could have handled the back-benchers more tactfully. Unpopularity also lessens his weight in the councils of the party; evey consideration, personal and political, dictates conciliation rather than intransigence.

In details, and details are often very important, the private Member can move amendments which may be accepted by the Government and incorporated in the Bill. Anyone who doubts that the ordinary Member has any scope should read the debates on the committee stage of any Bill. The Member will fight for the special interests of industries situated in his constituency or for individual constituents, with all the means in his power—questions to Ministers, letters, speeches in back-bench committees and on the floor of the House. The hold he has on his Member of Parliament is one of the few means by which the individual, as apart from the group or association, can protect himself against the state or even bring his own grievances to the attention of the Government. The man who writes to the Minister for Cultural Recreation and gets a printed reply to the effect that his communication has been received and will have his attention, will find that his Member of Parliament gets a different reception.

The general public are largely unaware of the give and take between the Government and its supporters. Some of the more simple-minded democrats may think that all this should take place in public; but open disagreement with the party on the floor of the House has much the same effect as actual abstention from voting, and on serious issues affects both the Member himself and the Government disagreeably. Any Member who constantly voices his disagreement is liable to lose his influence both with his leaders and with other members of his party.

The real limit to the power both of the ordinary back-bencher and of the House as a whole is the Member's own loyalty to his party. The Cabinet is in the end dependent on the House and at first sight it might seem as if this would be sufficient to make the legislature always the more powerful, as it is in France. It is, however, only in the most exceptional circumstances that the Government's own supporters will turn on it, because in England the defeat of the Government would mean an election, and an election in such circumstances as would almost certainly end in defeat. If the situation is sufficiently serious and the Government's policy evidently disastrous, even the strongest loyalty will snap; the replacement of Chamberlain by Churchill is a recent example and the same kind of thing might happen even in peace. It is possible to imagine circumstances in which a large number of Members might consider the fall of the Government and the loss of their own seats less disastrous than a complete repudiation of the party principles.

Nerves may also give way if public opinion seems hostile. The position of a private Member, when his party is in office, is to-day one of great difficulty. Political issues are terribly grave, taking the word 'terribly' in its most literal sense, and on some questions at least the ordinary Member may be no better informed than anyone else. The tightness of party organization and the publicity always given to any hint of disagreement make speakers or voters against the Government far more important than they used to be when Members voted first with one party and then with another. A Member's conviction that the Government is wrong may be strong, and yet it may be based on insufficient evidence. No theory or convention lays down what rules he must follow, but on the whole the danger at present seems to be that Governments should be rendered too averse from taking action for fear of revolts or splits rather than that Members should be too subservient to the Whip. Failure to do anything at all in a crisis is much less likely to cause trouble than taking any step in any direction; if only because it is difficult to protest effectively against a passive waiting on events.

v

The power of the central government over the local authorities has increased even more than the powers of government in general.

Exactly the same influences which have destroyed the self-sufficiency of nations have worked, and of course more powerfully, on the county and borough. Modern communications have done much to diminish the importance of locality itself. In the Middle Ages towns and villages were self-sufficient in a way they have long ceased to be, and much of this self-sufficiency remained until the railways were built. Roads, for example, when all transport was horse-drawn were mainly the concern of the immediate neighbourhood, though even in the late eighteenth century fast coaches had already made towns on the main roads closer to each other. As transport developed, so the financial burden on the local authorities increased, and might have become intolerable if the trunk roads had remained in the hands of the local authorities. In 1936 the Minister of Transport took over the maintenance of certain trunk roads, and by the Trunk Roads Act of 1946 the Minister became responsible for all those roads, although he still employs the counties and county boroughs as his agents for maintenance and repair.

Further inroads were made on the functions of local authorities as a result of nationalizing the gas and electricity industries. One of the main arguments for nationalization was the superior efficiency of a National Board, which could survey the whole field and plan development in the public interest, uninfluenced by private gain or local prejudice. This demanded that gas and electricity undertakings operated by local authorities should be nationalized as well as those operated by private companies.

The other great influence curtailing local independence has been the Government's responsibility for the welfare of citizens. Even in 1834 the Government felt they could not allow the parishes to continue to administer poor relief, or in the eighteen-forties to take on the new responsibilities for sanitation. In the latter part of the century, it is true, local authorities were considered more capable, but once politics themselves became concerned with the social services, the Government had to see that their intentions were adequately carried out. And they had to supplement local funds, which were never, even before 1914, large enough to finance the new schemes.

Today all responsible people have a passion for uniformity; nothing disturbs them more than an anomaly, but even to those who do not share this passion, it is plain that if the services provided by local authorities are likely to make a real difference, so that the chance of being born in Northumberland rather than in Kent might decide a boy's whole career or whether a woman lived or died, some attempt must be made to keep the standards of all local authorities not too far out of line. This has been mainly achieved through the grant in aid, the grant which the Treasury gives to local authorities to perform certain functions. It would be possible for the Treasury to give such grants without attaching any conditions to them, but the Treasury must remember that the Government and the local authority are spending the taxpayers' money. Even the most pedestrian, the least authoritarian of Governments will make some effort to see that the grant is not wasted. Modern Governments, however, are inspired with ideas, sometimes to the extent of fanaticism, and a grant from the

Exchequer is a method of encouraging certain kinds of expenditure and discouraging others.

A Government which plans or guides the national economy must keep a close supervision over the expenditure of the local authorities. In 1954 local authorities spent £844 million on goods and services in their ordinary day-to-day activities, or roughly one-fifth of the annual budget of the central government. In the same year they spent £497 million on capital investment, about one-fifth of the total expenditure of Government, nationalized industries, private industry and local authorities together. It is clear from these figures that the local authorities could frustrate the efforts of any Chancellor to control either inflation or deflation. The difficulty is most likely to arise in inflationary conditions—it would probably be easy enough to persuade them to spend more; but their spokesmen have shown little understanding of the part they should play in reducing their capital expenditure in an inflationary boom.

The post-war attempt to give all comparable authorities much the same income also increased central government control by abolishing the oldest of all the local authorities' powers, that of assessment for rates. One of the main difficulties of local government has always been the difference in the wealth of different areas. The less the rateable value the greater was the need to provide for poverty; the greater the rateable value the less need had the rate-payers for any of the social services. The difficulty was met partly by grants from the Treasury and partly by a scheme by which the richer local authorities transferred some of their rates to the poorer. Under this scheme it is obvious that the system by which local authorities undertook the assessment of property values in their area might give rise to complications, so by the Local Government Act of 1948 those functions were transferred to the Inland Revenue. This step had the further advantage of ensuring that standards of valuation are uniform.

When all this is said, and when all due weight has been given to the Government's reasons for a close supervision of local government, it does seem to have been carried to somewhat excessive lengths. Even when modern developments have shorn the county or the borough of its past self-sufficiency, local government is, after all, one of the best ways of associating the ordinary citizen with the work of government, and this is particularly important now when people are only too apt to feel that events and institutions are too complicated for them to understand, much less to influence. Democracy without local government loses many of its virtues without acquiring those of any other form of government. Local authorities still carry out functions of importance, and though it may be necessary to make certain that they do not fall below a certain standard, some post-war legislation seems to give the Minister or the department a power of interference even in details which must do a good deal to undermine the responsibility of local councillors, without making any substantial contribution to efficiency or anything else. For example, the Education Act, 1944, gives the Minister of Education powers to direct a local education authority to provide transport to enable children to go to school. One would have thought that this was a question eminently suitable for local decision. The Local Government Act of 1929 laid down that the County Councils and the County Borough Councils were to draw up schemes showing how they were going to carry out the functions transferred to them under the Act and gave detailed instructions as to the way in which they were to do this.

The National Health Service went even further. The Act which established it transferred the hospitals under the control of the local authorities to Hospital Boards and Hospital Management Committees whose members are all appointed by the Minister of Health. If the Minister ". . . is of opinion . . ." that these have failed to carry out the duties imposed on them, or have in carrying them out "failed to comply with any regulations or directions", he may not only "after such inquiry as he sees fit" declare them to be in default, a power Ministers have previously had in respect of certain services, but he may "in lieu of enforcing the order by mandamus or otherwise, make an order transferring to himself such of the functions of the authority as he sees fit". In previous legislation of this kind the Minister had the power to appoint new members to the Board; but this did not mean the complete supersession of local influence by central control. These powers were actually inserted in the Acts, local authorities can also be compelled to do things, or refrain from doing them, by departmental decisions. The habit of delegating to the Minister power to make rules and regulations as "he see fit" or as "they may be necessary" affects local councils in much the same way as it affects individual citizens. These regulations have the force of law and may, as Mr. D. N. Chester has said, introduce "an element of arbitrariness in central-local relations".[9]

VI

Just as the old Constitution had its own political theory, a new theory seems to be growing up to explain and defend the new organization of English politics. This, whether it is expounded by Conservatives or Socialists, stresses the importance of "the community as a whole", that favourite though otiose phrase, against the rights of the individual. In this system of ideas the word 'liberty' has changed its meaning; the most important kind of liberty is no longer the liberty to choose for oneself but the liberty to combine with others or to join an association. Thus Mr. Kenneth Younger, replying to Professor Lionel Robbins, said: "Mr. Robbins also insists that unless there are great private fortunes there can be no centres of power capable of standing up to the Government. . . . The independent political influence of, say, the cotton industry or the farmers or the Press, is in no way dependent on the leaders of these pressure groups being personally millionaires".[10] As the despotism of the Tsars was said to be tempered by assassination, so is the tyranny of the majority by the organization of special interests.

Mr. Younger is a Socialist, but it is by no means necessary to believe in economic equality to agree with him. Government departments have argued that delegated legislation was no menace to the rights of the citizen because all relevant organizations are always consulted before the rules, orders or regulations are drafted. For example, the Ministry of Health furnished the Committee on Ministers' Powers, 1932, with a memorandum which said: "Emphasis should at the outset be laid on the point . . .

that the matters with which regulations made by the Ministry deal (and the same is no doubt true of other Departments) are almost without exception under the continuous scrutiny of powerful associations and bodies representing Local Authorities, manufacturing and trading interests, officers of Local Authorities, and members of the public, whether as owners of property, rate-payers, professional men, insured persons and the like." This view was also adopted by Professor Wade in his introduction to Dicey's *Law of the Constitution*. "The exercise of the law-making power by Parliament is controlled almost exclusively by the government of the day, placed in power by the possession of a majority in the House of Commons. But it is only used to coerce the subject after the subjects—through Chambers of Commerce, Federations of Industry, Trade Unions . . . professional, technical and manual—have been consulted."

With this new conception of liberty it is not surprising that the old idea of the rule of law has been neglected, if not deliberately dropped, because the rule of law is essentially concerned with individual rights. Blackstone derived the Constitution itself from these rights, and he was followed in this instance by Dicey. As Professor Wade pointed out, no one could suppose this to be true of the modern Constitution and even in 1938 he referred to "the difficulty which any literal acceptance of the rule of law causes today" because "a system of law, which like the common law is based on the protection of individual rights, is not readily compatible with legislation which has for its object the welfare of the country, or a large section of it, as a whole." Since 1939 this difficulty has increased.

The revolt against the idea in theory has gone even further than its abandonment in practice, to the extent that some writers seem to have forgotten the meaning of the term. It does not mean that the Acts of the Government conform with the rule of law if only the proper legal forms have been observed. If, for example, Parliament passes an Act making it illegal for any red-haired person* to stand for Parliament under penalty of incurring a heavy fine and at the same time making the Act retrospective.

---

* Substitute Jew for red-haired person and the example does not seem quite so fantastic.

This would violate every canon of the rule of law but it would not be illegal in the sense that any Act would be illegal if the House of Commons chose to disregard the necessary formalities of allowing the House of Lords to consider it and the Sovereign to give her consent.

Since the Crichel Down case there has been considerable discussion about the rule of law, concerned chiefly with delegated legislation and Administrative Tribunals. These may or may not conflict with the rule of law but the rule itself is not concerned with particular cases; it is a criterion by which particular laws can be judged. "The whole idea of the rule of law or of the Rechtstaat implied an ideal standard by which the actual legal position was judged."[11] To conform to this standard laws must be general, that is, framed so that they apply to all citizens. They must be equal and they must be certain. At first sight 'equal' looks as if it was the same as 'general' but it is slightly different—'general' means that laws must be framed in universal terms, 'equal' means that there must be no exceptions, that, for example, Government officials must not be put in a special category as they are in some continental States. The term 'certain' speaks for itself; the negation of certainty is the unlimited power of the Government in a totalitarian state to do what it pleases, regardless of whether, for example, the action it wishes to punish was previously illegal and known to the public to be so. These three principles are in reality three aspects of one central idea, the idea expressed by Locke when he said: "Freedom of men under government is to have a standing rule to live by, common to everyone of that society, and made by the legislative power erected in it: and not to be subject to the inconstant, unknown, arbitrary will of man."

The doctrine of the separation of power follows from these principles. "The first maxim of a free State is that the laws be made by one set of men, and administered by another; in other words that the legislative and the judicial character be kept separate. When these offices are united in the same person or assembly, particular laws are made for particular cases, springing often from partial motives and directed to private ends. Whilst they are kept separate, general laws are made by one body of men, without foreseeing whom they will affect, and when made

must be applied by the other, let them affect whom they will."[12]
Laws ought to be enacted by the legislature not only because it is
here that the people can make their wishes known but also
because the decisions are arrived at in public, the law is known
and therefore certain. If a dispute arises between the Government
and any citizen which involves a doubt as to what the law really
says, it must be decided by a Court of Justice because if the
Government is left to decide, then it is judge in its own case, and
even in a democracy much injustice might be done.

Stated in this general way most people would probably think
that the law of England complied with all these requirements and
find it hard to understand the present agitation. This is because
the breaches which modern legislation have made in the rule of
law have not been concerned with fundamental rights such as
freedom of speech and freedom from arbitrary arrest; and though
numerous, have never been made with evil intent and often with
the cordial approval of a large section of public opinion. But
particular laws have been made for particular cases. In 1949
certain industrial companies proposed to make large payments
to their Chairmen in return for assurances as to their conduct in
hypothetical circumstances in the future. These payments under
the existing law would have been tax free. It was clear that the
intention was to evade the heavy taxes levied on high incomes.
The Government of the day brought in a Bill to make the
payments subject to income tax and made this Bill retrospective.
This was clearly in direct conflict with the rule of law, the preser-
vation of which is much more important than whether or not a
few men manage to secure more money than other people. Even
more dangerous were the provisions of the Parliament Act,
passed in 1949, limiting the power of the House of Lords to delay
legislation to one year, which were made to apply retrospectively.
This was a most drastic breach with the rule of law.

Many of our accepted institutions seem to be in conflict with
the rule, for example, the power of the Chancellor of the
Exchequer to prevent companies going to the market to raise new
capital. This power clearly allows discrimination between persons;
the reasons for the Chancellor's decisions are not known and
there is no appeal against them. This procedure may be necessary

and no one would maintain that circumstances might not arise in which even the rule of law must be abrogated. Such abrogations, however, are not usually defended on such grounds, but either on that of some higher equity or because it is necessary for the full implementation of the Government's policy. The Capital Issues Committee and other institutions of the same kind are in theory at any rate devised to deal with abnormal circumstances and are usually concerned with great affairs. In another category are the powers of Administrative Tribunals and some of the powers given to Ministers by delegated legislation; they are commonplace, inconspicuous and in thousands of instances do not result in injustice to anyone. They do, however, put unprecedented power in the hands not only of the Government, but also of innumerable Civil Servants.

When these tribunals were introduced, there was never any intention either to undermine the liberty of the subject or to increase the power of the executive. They were established simply as a matter of convenience. Social service legislation has been described as designed to produce "by detailed regulations certain intricate patterns of social conduct", but it is certain to produce also disputes and disagreements, especially when the Government possesses wide powers over all kinds of property. The form in which legislation is often drafted, giving the Minister power to make rules, or to do what he thinks fit, or to do anything which is necessary, often makes it doubtful what is or is not included under the Act. Decisions on these points must be taken by someone, and it is true that in many instances they are not particularly suitable for the Courts if only because of the time and expense involved; cases under the old Unemployment Insurance Act, the present National Insurance Act and other social service legislation, are examples.

Those who are familiar with the work of these tribunals stress the informality and the way in which those who appear before them are helped to state their case by the Chairman, in a way which the rigid forms of a court of law forbid. The difference between a tribunal and a court of law are indeed illustrations of the different social philosophies which underlie them.

The English common law was largely developed in the struggles with the Crown; legal procedure and legal philosophy assume a dispute between citizen and citizen or between citizen and the Crown. This dispute is decided by purely formal rules; the Judge must not look beyond the evidence presented and must not take into consideration any effect his judgment may have on the success or failure of the Government's policy. The citizen is regarded as a responsible, intelligent being, capable of conducting his own affairs, the Judge is not supposed to think about his 'real' welfare. It is under this procedure that a criminal may escape punishment by what to the man in the street seems to be a mere quibble, or that a case may be decided in a way which may inconvenience the Government of the day. The rules under which the court works are, however, known to everyone interested, the hearing is public and the reasons for the decision are always given. Each side has also had his case presented as well as can be done by a professional advocate to an arbitrator who has no interest of any kind, personal or political, in the outcome. The law is certain in the sense that while no one knows what will be the result of any particular case, the law which governs it and the rules by which it is decided are known in advance.

An Administrative Tribunal, on the other hand, is not bound by any formal rules of procedure, for it is not merely interpreting a code of laws; it can, indeed it must, take the effects of its decisions on Government policy into account. Often the proceedings are in private and reasons for its decisions are not always given. Nor are tribunals necessarily bound by their own past decisions. If a court of law gives a judgment which inconveniences the Government or conflicts with its policy, the law itself must be changed if the Government wants to continue with the policy. The Minister can presumably give to Administrative Tribunals instructions which might change with changes in Government. There is, therefore, an element of uncertainty about the decisions given which may, in the eyes of the citizen, even wear the aspect of caprice.

It is now often contended that the merits of judicial procedure have been exaggerated, that it is too formal and that the attitude of judges is pedantic, even when they are not prompted by sinister motives, as the Association of Labour Lawyers apparently believe them to be. In the evidence they gave before the Franks Committee on Administrative Tribunals, their spokesman said: "I am quite certain that some of the Judges in the Divisional Court consciously or unconsciously—I think Judges are often operated on by unconscious motives which they don't understand—dislike all these new Tribunals. . . . The Court of Appeal's decisions are tending at the present time to be fairly liberal. Nearly all the decisions of the House of Lords I would describe as thoroughly reactionary, and to expose these new statutes of social reform to the hazards of the courts, with lawyers' approaches as we know them, I think is appalling."[13]

This seems somewhat exaggerated, but serious arguments have been put forward, by more authoritative opinion, that considerations of policy should enter into judicial decisions or into decisions which, while not technically judicial, are of the same essential nature. Professor Robson, for example, although he believes that certain safeguards should be introduced into the system of administrative law, thinks that one of the main advantages of tribunals is that a tribunal "can enforce a policy unhampered by the rules of law and judicial precedent . . . of all the characteristics of administrative law, none is more advantageous, when rightly used for the public good, than the power of the tribunal to decide the cases coming before it with the avowed object of furthering a policy of social improvement in some particular field, or of adapting their attitude towards the controversy so as to fit the needs of that policy."[14] Professor Robson also argues that even the most austere Judge is influenced by considerations of policy, if policy is interpreted in the widest sense, and that it would make no essential difference if this influence were conscious and avowed. Even in the most moderate statement of this position, however, it is assumed that there is a policy of such overwhelming value and importance that nothing, even the liberty of the individual, can be allowed to hamper or to postpone its application.

This again is based on another assumption, that the Government knows best, knows what 'the public good' is, and 'will rightly use' the powers given to it. This really means that citizens have no rights at all; at the moment this chiefly applies to property rights but there seems to be nothing in principle which would prevent it also applying to freedom of speech. It is doubtful how these ideas can be reconciled with democracy. It is true that Governments depend on the electorate, but a great deal of 'policy' in the sense used by Professor Robson is carried on from Government to Government; and the whole apparatus of administration throws an immense amount of power into the hands of each succeeding Minister, for which he is responsible to no one, neither to the House of Commons for they have delegated their powers to him, nor to the electorate, unless the particular issue has been raised at the election. However justifiable or necessary this may be, it is at least a modification of democracy.

VII

Democracy in England has not produced the kind of State which its friends hoped or its opponents feared, and it does not conform to any standard or ideal, although it is too often discussed as if it was built to the original specifications. Democratic theory was originally based on the individual, who was held to be the best judge of his own interests; but it was not realized that he would feel his interests to be best served by forming associations to protect them. This blindness was, of course, partly because it was the democrats who denied that democracy would inevitably produce Socialism. In the system imagined by Bentham, Cobden and the Gladstonian Liberals there would have been little benefit from forming a pressure group because the Government had so little to give away; without protection, tariffs, subsidies, progressive taxation, what would there have been to press for? Liberals thought that universal suffrage would dissolve pressure groups, not create them. Although from an electoral point of view 'mere numbers' are sovereign, from another aspect we have retreated from the idea of the sovereignty of the majority to that of a balance of powers and interests. It is true that the balance is achieved outside, not inside the Constitution; but whatever the theory, a majority in the House of Commons cannot ride rough-shod over the trade unions nor, although private industry itself is threatened with extinction by a majority vote, could any Government ignore in practice the views of such industry as remains unnationalized. The Labour Government of 1945 largely relied on industry itself to administer various forms of rationing and control, and the employers' organizations were given as many representatives as the trade unions on every consultative body set up. Any future Labour Government, however far to the left it might be, would probably find it even more necessary to listen to the Federation of British Industries and kindred bodies, because although they might find that their policy was modified by listening, refusal to listen might lead to such economic confusion as would force a change of Government.

The nineteenth-century democrats thought that universal suffrage would ensure that Governments did less not more, and they never considered Socialism as a serious possibility. Nor, although some of them were prepared to push landowners outside "the pale of the Constitution", did they think a political creed would cause such deep divisions as Socialism must.

Even those politicians who want to do what the people want, rather than to persuade them to do what the politicians want, often do not know what it is. One of the disadvantages of group organization is that the officials may quite unconsciously misrepresent their members. The leaders of trade unions are more definitely Socialist than the average member. The average member may want higher wages, more social benefits, even more economic equality, without being at all prepared to sacrifice anything else for them, while some of their leaders would probably be prepared to give up a substantial amount to attain a Socialist state. The bigger the organization the more likely is there to be this division between leaders and led, and the whole electorate is very big indeed. This situation gives an unprecedented scope to interpreters of public opinion, journalists, psychologists, editors. The propaganda of political parties is largely controlled by this kind of interpreted opinion, for what else is there? It is expressed on the wireless, in newspapers, from the pulpit but never by 'the people', if by the people is meant the mass of the electorate.

To a great extent this must be so; ideas must be formulated and shaped so that they do not conflict with each other, an operation which has to be undertaken by some kind of intellectual middlemen. The growth of Socialism is an illustration. Economic equality seems such an obvious idea to us that we find it hard to realize that for many centuries no one, not even those to whom it might seem it must occur, the poor and oppressed, had any conception of it. It had to wait for middle-class intellectuals to organize the aspirations of the poor for a better life into this particular form.

The trouble, however, is that those who live by formulating and expressing opinion, not only on occasions, particularly important occasions, misrepresent the mass of the people, but they become an interest similar to other interests. Like the others, the Press, regarded as an 'interest', has its purely practical and its idealistic aspect, but unfortunately unlike the trade unions, the House of Commons, big business and every other British institution, the Press is never subjected to criticism. "Dog does not eat dog" is the sacred formula of Fleet Street. This is relaxed, it is true, to allow comment on the 'capitalist' Press in some left-wing journals and sneers at the cheap dailies can be encountered in some periodicals, but serious criticism of the respectable newspapers is never printed. This immunity, of which journalists are only half-conscious, leads to a remarkable lack of self-criticism and to an enormous mass of comment with no basis of real knowledge.

The failure of many newspapers to take sufficient care before they make pronouncements must have a perceptible effect in diminishing the power of the ordinary citizen to make sensible judgments on political events. This only applies to foreign and colonial affairs, in home affairs people are able to judge from their own experience, but in these other matters most of them must depend on information supplied by others. This would not matter if everyone could read and digest several periodicals, and could listen to more than one talk on the wireless, but most people are too occupied to be able to do more than read one morning and one evening paper, even if they can do that.

No newspaper ever allows that it has been wrong. Everyone must now agree that the decision to leave the Suez Canal base was a mistaken one. As every party, every 'practical' man, and practically every organ of opinion were equally wrong, as only the eccentric and reactionary turned out to be right, one would, have thought *The Observer* for example, would have pointed out, however much its leader writers may have disagreed with the Government's subsequent actions, that the policy they themselves had advocated was also bankrupt. The failure of any newspaper to do anything of the kind, which amounts to claiming an infallibility possessed by no human being, does a real disservice to democracy because it discourages serious consideration of the issues involved. The shock of reading in a leading article a "we were mistaken on this point, partly because our information was inadequate and partly because we misjudged the President's character", would stimulate the reader into making some mental effort himself. It would also give the man in the street some awareness of the insecure foundations on which political judgments have to be made.

It has turned out to be more difficult to organize democracy than anyone anticipated. It is, for instance, often pointed out that although there is universal suffrage, the voter can only vote for a candidate from one of two parties, neither of whom he may like; but this is only one aspect of the problem of public opinion. However democratic the Constitution, the initiative does not lie with the people but with governments, officials, leaders, active members of parties. The representative, especially in this country where there is a tradition that he is not a delegate bound by instructions, may have a different outlook and different values even from his most enthusiastic supporters. Active, energetic men and women who fill the local parties may be as completely unrepresentative of the average voter as the Member of a pocket borough. It is an assumption always made but never examined that those who are interested in politics have the right to cajole, bully and argue their fellow citizens into voting and supporting one party or the other. It is not easy, on any democratic theory, to see why, still less why they consider themselves superior to those who prefer football.

None of those who founded democracy ever thought that politics would become a profession. They retained the old idea that the House of Commons would consist of ordinary men and women who happened to be chosen to represent their fellow citizens, and it was usually assumed though not always stated that it was the fellow citizens who would do the choosing. On the whole it was thought that politics would become less professional rather than more, in the sense that the Member of Parliament would no more belong to a special political class, although he would be more professional in the sense that he would be more public-spirited and diligent. Professional politicians are less like the people they represent than the old county Member, and the more the pressure of political business prevents them having the ordinary contacts which come from earning a living outside politics, the more unrepresentative they become. Any group of this kind tends to develop interests and preoccupations of its own which may conflict with those of 'the people' at large. The idea of a political career as an end in itself, as a kind of game, which is very common among politicians, further separates the representative from those he is supposed to represent. We are always reading in Memoirs of retired politicians about "the great game of politics" and complacently they look back at their part over the last fifty years. This may be natural but democratic government is not supposed to be a game.

These developments are not undemocratic in the sense that they were constructed to impede popular government; they are developments of democracy itself; but they have modified previous ideas about how democratic government should work. Although they have not yet done anything to damage seriously the democratic framework, it is quite easy to see how they might do so in the future.

CHAPTER VII

THE FUTURE

I

DEMOCRACY may seem to be so deeply rooted that there can be no doubt about the future. It is now firmly established both in practice and in public opinion. There is no anti-democratic sentiment even to the extent that there was between the wars. The last few years have seen a revival in the traditional concern for liberty. Belief in equality is likely to deepen and to spread. Habits of compromise and tolerance are ingrained. The basis for all successful politics, great and increasing wealth, is there.

If Great Britain were an isolated community, or if the world were composed of Great Britain, the United States, Canada and Australia, we might hope that the Constitution would remain indefinitely in much the same state that it is today. The world, however, is nothing like this. Representative government everywhere is menaced by Communism and Russia herself is a threat to the continued existence of independent European States. The threat may be contained but catastrophe remains a possibility. Even without total disaster the conditions of the world may cause a reaction against democracy which, if previous experience is any guide, would affect opinion here also.

It is hard to see how democracy, at least in any form we should recognize, could survive complete Socialism because it would put such immense power into the hands of the State. It would even destroy most of the organizations which now serve to modify the omnipotence of the Government: read the list of organizations which are consulted according to the Departments themselves and cross out all that would cease to exist with a completely nationalized industry, education, medicine. Only the trade unions are left, and although the whole population might then be organized in them, they are not meant to be, indeed cannot be guardians of individual liberty. Such a system might call itself a democracy, indeed it would certainly do so; but it is difficult to see how it could retain the values as distinct from the organization of democracy. It is doubtful how far democracy can exist without substantial economic inequality; prosperity seems to be bound up with inequality of income, liberty with inequality of property. The economic case for paying more for the exercise of talent and responsibility than for routine work is now conceded even by convinced Socialists. The present attack is concentrated on accumulated and inherited wealth, but a system in which no one had any resources to fall back on, in which everyone was dependent on salary or wages, would make independence of mind or character difficult if not impossible. It ha been demonstrated again in the past few years that large aggregations of property, so far from being a threat to those with little or none, are their only defence against the injustice of the State. Because Commander Marten, the owner of Crichel Down, possessed of some influence and some spare cash, was able to present his case to the House of Commons and public opinion, Mrs. Woollett, a smallholder who had neither, also got her land back. Property may equally be the main defence of freedom of thought. Any State system of education involves grave dangers, as John Stuart Mill pointed out. The only safeguards against them in the modern world are independent schools, which are able to exist because some parents can afford to pay for them.

It may be, however, that the whole idea of liberty, at least in the older sense, is an illusion, or that it was never really an essential element in any form of democracy. It is undeniable that all the conditions of modern life work against it and seem to make it an anachronism. For many people this is sufficient. If there are strong tendencies in any direction it is considered to be the duty of any Government to strengthen them further; anything else is called putting the clock back, trying to sweep away the Atlantic with a broom, or going against the tide. It seems more reasonable to argue that the purpose of government, once it extends beyond defence and the criminal law, is to offer some counterweight to the prevailing forces; otherwise events would be much the same

if it did not exist. It is still important, therefore, to decide whether
there remains any value in the older ideas or whether we should
adjust our conception of democracy to make its foundation
equality rather than liberty. The clash between the two, although
it may be obscured by passing events and deliberately evaded by
politicians, is the main theme of modern politics. One way of
resolving it is to deny its existence by extending the meaning of
the word liberty to cover things previously designated by other
terms. This method is widely used in left-wing propaganda, as for
example in the Labour party publication on personal freedom,
where it is said: "The Welfare State and Full Employment
have undoubtedly widened personal freedom." It is, however,
by no means confined to the literature of persuasion; some professional philosophers strongly support this form of argument.
In their view the expression liberty or freedom is incomplete
unless it is also explained freedom from what. The old use of the
word merely meant freedom from the interference of the
Government. "But as well as freedom from . . . there is also
freedom to. . . . Freedom to . . . ought to mean, as it does in
ordinary life, that you are able to do anything, not merely that the
police will not stop you. To put it shortly, the Capitalist idea was
that freedom from . . . was very important and freedom to . . .
rather a luxury, except in so far as it was a kind of freedom
from. . . . The Communist view now reverses this valuation, and
Capitalism, in so far as it has come to accept New Deals and
Welfare States, has considerably changed its position."[1]

This is extremely persuasive: at first sight something new seems
to have been said about liberty. On further reflection, however,
these remarks do not seem to be so illuminating. They contain a
comparison between freedom to do something, which means
that there are no prohibitions against it, that no authority stops
you, and ability to do something, which means not only that
no one stops you but you have the means to do it. Between
ability to . . . and liberty to . . . there is surely a wide difference.
I am perfectly free to make a contribution to mathematical
theory; there is no law against my doing so, nor is anyone
interested in stopping me; there exist, however, insuperable
barriers. There was surely a difference between the situation of a

woman or a Roman Catholic who wanted to go to a university in the eighteenth century and a male member of the Church of England who could not afford to do so, and that difference is connected with personal liberty; all that the most extensive political liberty can do is to remove legal barriers and prohibitions from as many activities as possible. It is essentially concerned with seeing that policemen stop you from doing as few things as is consistent with the liberty of others. A policy which aims at giving everyone who can benefit by education a chance to go to a university is based on another and different idea, that of equality of opportunity. Nor does there appear to be any advantage in reducing our political vocabulary by calling it liberty; at worst it is a kind of double-think, at best merely a metaphor. The argument is no way advanced by saying that a man's freedom is increased by making him pay a proportion of his wages in compulsory State insurance. A more sensible way of defending the system is surely to say that though his freedom is curtailed to a slight but definite extent, the advantage to him of a certain income in old age, sickness and unemployment more than outweighs the disadvantage. He and everyone else can then argue whether this is so or not.

To call everything desirable 'liberty', obscures the very important fact that some of these other values can be had without liberty. There is a real sense in which a man in Russia, even if his standard of living were as high as the American, would be less free than a man in America. A patient in a lunatic asylum has all the material security, if not all the material luxury, he may desire, but no one would say that he was free, they would not even say that he was free if the material luxuries were added. A doctor may tell a man with heart disease that he ought to give up his work or be careful never to feel any strong emotion. The man may refuse to obey; if he were compelled, he would certainly be more secure, but he would not be freer.

There are, of course, more fundamental arguments against the whole idea of liberty than this juggling with words. The political philosophy derived from Hegel, whether it retained its original conservative hue or acquired a scarlet tinge, denied that the individual had any rights or indeed any real existence. The state, society or community was supposed to be a higher form of life than the individual, in the same sense in which a human being is a higher form of life than one of the cells of his body. This philosophy is widely discredited, but many writers on sociology and psychology have reached conclusions about the relations of the individual to society which are not very different; although for Hegel's state they would substitute the culture pattern or the social group. The part played by society in moulding the individual personality is so great that if all the elements that are merely reflections of social forces were removed, there would be nothing that we should recognize as a personality left. These forces comprise both the culture pattern and the position occupied by anyone in relation to other social groups. The greatest poet would be dumb without the language in which he writes, and language is essentially a social product. The successful business man could not operate without the particular framework which society provides. Character and temperament, even in matters seemingly so fundamental as sex, may be quite different according to where one happens to be born.

Whatever validity these arguments have in their own field, they have little bearing on political liberty in the twentieth century. The individual must exist in a physical sense before he has a personality to mould, and difficult as it may be to distinguish between the social and the individual elements in any personality, that personality exists or ceases to exist in a perfectly definite sense. It is as a safeguard of physical existence that the main value of the traditional liberties lies today. It is not surprising that many people should have looked with complacency on the expansion of the power and activities of the State before 1914, when even authoritarian Governments were civilized and when everyone thought, as they had thought in the eighteenth century, that never again would men and women be killed and tortured because they disagreed with the Government. But remembering what has happened, what is still happening, it seems a curious occupation to argue away the principles which stand between humanity and the horrors of modern tyranny.

Of course this is the point where the reader says "it couldn't happen here". And it is true that it is unlikely to happen here in its full dimensions or in a few years. But the reason it would not, is the wide diffusion of the respect for personality which was inculcated by the individualism of the eighteenth and nineteenth centuries. Tolerance, however, is not natural; men and women, particularly men, have to be continually reminded of other people's right to disagree with them. No one who has talked to some of the more unsophisticated and enthusiastic members of the Labour party, in some ways the most high-minded and idealistic of us all, will think that a constant and unremitting preaching of the value of liberty is unnecessary. Even Sir Stafford Cripps and Lord Attlee were once led by their acceptance of the overwhelming importance of equality into proposals for curtailing traditional liberties, which must surprise Lord Attlee when he remembers them.

But even granted that no Government, however powerful, would in this country infringe the basic civil rights, would never, for instance, interfere with Habeas Corpus, or freedom of speech, there still remains a large area in which the traditional view considers that government should be limited. Is there still any validity in this view?

Today in England people still seem to resent the interference of the state with what they regard as their own rights, even if they are cheerfully indifferent to interference with the rights of other people. It is clear that for some time to come Cabinets will have to remember that the English citizen still believes himself to have rights. But this does not dispose of the theoretical argument; the citizen may be wrong to feel as he does, there may have been no injustice in any of the cases with which we are familiar—or even if injustice existed in some superficial or temporary sense, it may disappear on a clearer and more dispassionate view. Commander Marten's real will may have been in full agreement with that of the Commissioner of Crown Lands. The liberty of the individual may be an abstraction without value or reality. Experience has proved that Governments can allay discontent not by altering their policy in accordance with the wishes of their subjects, but by altering the wishes. It might well be possible in about twenty-five years to destroy, or at any rate to attenuate, the sentiment for individual liberties, while retaining a democratic form of government. It has been repeatedly pointed out that had Commander Marten not been in possession of sufficient funds and numerous important friends, neither he nor Mrs. Woollett, who had neither, would have had their land returned to them. Every instance of this kind encourages intransigence, while every failure discourages it. Greater economic equality, or even a persistent refusal by the Government to yield, would probably create greater acquiescence, and propaganda would do the rest.

Is this the road we ought to follow? Is there any value in liberty when people can apparently be made quite happy without it?

One of the difficulties of discussing political theory is that there is today no agreement about ethics, and judgment on the purpose of the state ultimately depends on moral judgments. But any form of ethical theory, whether it is based on the Will of God or the pursuit of happiness, requires freedom of choice. If happiness is the end of life and the purpose of the state is to secure the greatest happiness of the greatest number, free choice in the things which matter to the particular individual is clearly an ingredient, and an important ingredient. Any democratic government must have some regard to individual happiness, even if only because it is something in which the electorate is interested. To say that people prefer to do as they like may seem a crude and unsophisticated observation, but introspection and experience seem to confirm its truth. There are exceptions. We all know people who cling to someone who can tell them what to do; but even they seem to prefer to choose the someone. The wish to decide for oneself is strongest for the things in which one's interest is most intense, and tends to fade away where things to which one is indifferent are concerned. Fortunately, everyone's interests are not the same; most people are, for instance, not interested in the problem of sanitation as long as the drains are in order, but to the expert it is a matter of passionate concern. It is the complaint at the moment that the majority of people are too passive, too acquiescent, but this is a complaint that their interests are too narrow, not that they do not wish to exercise a free choice about the things they feel really matter to them.

The sensation of free choice may be an illusion; the culture pattern may in reality dictate the determination of the English housewife that she will feed her family on butcher's meat as rigidly as the Government dictated that she should not. But as on this theory the culture pattern equally dictates the views of those who compose Governments, it offers no presumption that they will make a better choice, and therefore provides no argument for allowing the Government, in normal circumstances, to prescribe the country's diet, whereas we do know that the people dislike their doing so.

Democracy itself grew out of a regard for individual happiness but even democrats have chosen other aims. Many political philosophers have thought the fullest development of individual personality to be the purpose of social life. This demands government of some kind to provide a background of law and order, but it also requires that the ambit of the government should be strictly limited and that a wide area of free choice should be left to the individual. Some writers have rejected the whole idea of individual happiness or development; others have, without formulating their reasons, chosen other goals, such as the greatness of the nation, or the creation of a particular kind of civilization, or an idea seldom expressed but widely held, the production of great art. Contrary to the views of nearly all who have held this kind of theory, there is good reason to believe that even these austere and remote goals require individual liberty if they are to be successful.

It has always been a puzzle why long-continued and well-organized authoritarian systems have so often been accompanied by a cultural and economic decline; why the most anarchical feudalism has been more prolific of discoveries and inventions in government, in economics, in literature and art than the Roman Empire after the Antonines, or than the Ottoman Empire, originally so highly efficient, or even than China.

The answer may be that Governments or other authorities cannot solve all the problems of any society—not only because no man and no body of men are infallible, but because there is a limit to the number of tasks which can be performed by any hierarchical organization from the centre, and any attempt to supervise and control the whole economy leads not only to positive mistakes but to a slowing down of the whole machinery of life. We have had some experience of this since 1945, but Professor

Polanyi had already provided the theoretical explanation. He illustrated it by examples taken from engineering and mathematics, but the simplest example, that of the problem of piecing together a jig-saw puzzle when for some reason its completion is urgently required, shows clearly the limits of successful centralization.

We would no doubt engage a team of helpers; but how would we organize them? There would be no purpose in farming out a number of sets of the puzzle (which could be duplicated photographically) to several isolated collaborators and then adding up their results after a specified period. Though this method would allow the enlistment of an indefinite number of helpers, it would bear no appreciable results. The only way to get the job finished quickly would be to get as many helpers as could conveniently work at one and the same set and let them loose on it, each to follow his own initiative. Each helper would then watch the situation as it was affected by the progress made by all the others and would set himself new problems in accordance with the latest outline of the completed part of the puzzle. The tasks undertaken by each would closely dovetail into those performed by the others. And consequently the joint efforts of all would form a closely organized whole, even though each helper would follow entirely his own independent judgment.

Moreover, it is obvious what would happen if someone believing in the paramount effectiveness of central direction, were to intervene and try to improve matters by applying the methods of central administration. It is impossible to plan in advance the steps by which a jig-saw puzzle is to be put together. All that a centralized administration could achieve, therefore, would be to form all helpers into a hierarchical body and direct their activities henceforth from one centre. Each would then have to wait for directions from his superior and all would have to wait until a decision is taken at the supreme level. In effect, all participants except the one acting as the head of the organization would cease to make any appreciable contribution to the piecing together of the puzzle. The effect of co-operation would fall to zero.[2]

This argument is the essential basis not only of the justification of a free economic system but of democracy itself. It was the contention of the Utilitarians that by allowing each citizen to make a separate contribution to the total through his vote, a better Government would be attained than by authoritarian direction either by one individual or by a particular class; although a higher degree of 'co-ordination' would result from the authoritarian method.

The stultifying effect of despotic government is partly explained by Polanyi's illustration, and the effects increased by the influence which the slowing down of the whole apparatus of life has on individuals. If individual decisions are superseded by Government decisions and the results are bad the individuals will either feel acute frustration or will cease to take any interest in the particular field which the Government is 'co-ordinating'. If the reaction is frustration the society will be unstable; if it is apathy there will be a progressive deterioration. In addition to its inability to solve problems, a centralized system thus tends to depress and emasculate all the other sources of energy in the country. The deadening influence of centralization is made worse because as long as people resent the barriers to action the Government is unsafe and modern Governments have the means of converting the majority of their citizens by a mixture of propaganda and coercion.

It is true that in the decline of Rome, new forms of art and religion were created; but they did not attain their full scope until the collapse of the central government had produced anarchy rather than despotism. These movements grew, moreover, because people had, in despair of the state, turned away from politics to philosophy and religion. Modern despotisms do not allow their subjects thus to escape them.

England in the eighteenth century was far from being an ideal state, but Englishmen created the new industry which was to transform the world. The Industrial Revolution did not only consist in the inventions which everyone knows about, for example the spinning jenny and the steam engine, but in a constant solution of problems of technique and organization all over the country. The economic historians and economists who have studied the period, especially those who have discussed it in connection with the industrialization of backward countries, are agreed that the social atmosphere was one of the most important factors in stimulating it or allowing it to develop. Of course freedom was not the only ingredient in this atmosphere; Professor Ashton has stressed the high value assigned to wealth; but it was the absence of legal impediments to anyone getting wealth, if he could, that made this preoccupation stimulating. The importance of liberty, in the sense of absence of regulation, can be seen even in detail. The new industry tended to go to unincorporated towns because trade in the boroughs was still controlled by statutes passed under the Stuarts.

Liberty looked at in this way is not identical with political liberty in the ordinary sense, still less with democracy. If the sphere of Government could be confined to making regulations about things to which everyone is indifferent, except their agreement that regulations are necessary, as for example the decision as to whether one should drive on the right hand or the left, it would not much matter if the Government was authoritarian. Equally democracy is no guarantee that the sphere in which people are free to act as they like is large enough. An autocratic Government, which strictly confined itself to defence and administration of the criminal law, would be less destructive of the values of civilization than a Socialist democracy which combined a passion for equality with the religious and moral outlook of the Puritan settlers in New England. Some periods of autocratic government have also been periods of great intellectual achievements because Governments confined themselves to strictly political questions and did not attempt to control every form of human activity or if they did try, did not possess the resources to be successful. Humanity owes much to the inefficiency of government.

There are, of course, activities which can only be undertaken under some kind of central direction; war is the obvious example, but the one most common in ordinary life is sanitation. If each town is regarded as a unit, the cleaning of streets, the disposal of refuse, the provision of drainage require some form of central direction. The success of municipal councils in this activity led some early Socialists, like the Webbs, to think that municipal councils were suitable bodies to supersede the private production of consumer goods also. Both war and sanitation, however dissimilar they may appear, have this in common: that they have a simple and universally shared objective, victory in the one and a clean and wholesome town in the other. Compare this to the situation in either economics or sciences, where no agreement can be reached as to the ends to be pursued and no one knows what new development may completely transform the problem.

Even to those who believe that in the state some value is expressed which transcends the value of all the individuals composing it, the liberty of the individual is essential and it is here that in practice they must agree with those who think that liberty is a value in itself.

II

To say that liberty is profoundly important is not, however, to say that there are no other values or that no limits should be set to the extent to which the individual can do as he likes. There are first of all the limits set by considerations of mere convenience, one man's liberty if too great may endanger that of some other people. This is the old argument for law and order. There are also other values and since the Renaissance politics have chiefly been concerned with the question of how far these other values transcend that of liberty. The debate was at first concerned with how far the state should interfere to ensure that everyone shared the national religion; it was generally held that the interests of "the community as a whole" demanded that individual liberty in this respect should be curtailed. Today the same limitation is demanded in the name of equality.

Equality is a word which is in as much need of definition as liberty. It can mean, as Aristotle pointed out some time ago, either that unequal things are treated as if they were equal, or that different treatment is given to different things according to the extent of their inequality. To the Greeks human beings were unequal, there were men who were slaves by nature and there were barbarians; both these were inferior to Greeks. It was the

Stoics who asserted that there was a sense in which all men are equal, simply because they are men. This is the conception that underlies the Christian idea of equality, but this kind of equality exists in spite of all the outward differences. This idea underlay the conception of natural rights; but it depends on the recognition of some law of nature, of a principle of rationality in the universe which men can recognize and share because they are themselves endowed with reason.

The majority of those who are most concerned with equality today would unhesitatingly reject this whole complex of ideas. Modern equalitarians are not much interested in the qualities that bind all human beings together; their main concern being economic equality, it is more important to them to stress the difference of outward circumstances. It is not easy to say that economic factors are the most important both in history and in individual life and to maintain that they can do nothing to destroy the real equality of men. It is, however, by no means obvious what is meant by the word equality when used in other than the Stoic sense. A right definition is unusually important because according to the meaning which is given, it will produce quite different results. If unequal things are treated as if they were equal, you get for example the rule of law, under which as has often been pointed out, the rich and the poor are equally forbidden to sleep in doorways. If unequal things are to be treated unequally, the standpoint of that psychology, which would like all the experiences of the criminal's life to be taken into account in any criminal case, is reached. There is no doubt that there is a certain kind of equality under the rule of law, because although the rich may not want to sleep in doorways no special consideration is given to any rich man who might wish to do so for a bet, or because he had some sort of nervous complaint. There is also a kind of equality, which may be called the handicap conception of equality, in the psychologist's attitude. If there are two men convicted of the same crime, of whom one is a son of rich parents, the graduate of a university, while another was brought up in an orphanage after seeing his father murder his mother, then the special circumstances of the second should be taken into account. The horse that has already won a race should carry more weight. It is impossible to say which is the 'fairer' of these two concepts, but it is immediately plain that the second introduces another kind of inequality, the inequality of authority. Under the rule of law the Judge himself is bound by the law, he has only a very limited discretion; in the second case the discretion of the Judge or of a panel of psychologists who might replace the Judge would be almost unlimited.

The equality claimed in the French revolutionary slogan was equality before the law; this equality had already been confirmed in England by the Revolution of 1688. There is no doubt that this kind of equality contributed to the great expansion of wealth in the nineteenth century, but also to a growing inequality because, although everyone got richer, some people got much richer than others. It is now contended that inequality of wealth or economic circumstances is as intolerable as any other kind of inequality. The difficulty, however, appears to be that the pursuit of equality leads merely to the substitution of one kind of inequality for another. Every step towards economic equality increases the power of the state and the authorities that control the state; indeed the passion of some politicians for economic equality is partly, even if not consciously, due to resentment that there should be anyone who by their economic independence may escape their control or challenge their importance in the public eye. The existence of such people is peculiarly annoying because the great landowner or industrialist tends to be rather more permanent than even the most successful of politicians.

Policies of economic equality mean, and their advocates do not only admit but boast of it, that most industry would be state-run and the rest so closely supervised that there would be little scope for individual incentive and decision, except in illegal activities. Nearly everyone would be employed by the state, including the managers who, although they might be allowed to earn more than the average, would 'have no opportunity to secure what the nineteenth century so rightly described as an 'independence'. Property owning, except perhaps the ownership of a house or car, would be progressively eliminated. What would any Government be like in these circumstances? How would we fare at the local food office and the local labour exchange? It is of course contended that all this would be without danger to liberty because the Government would be elected by universal suffrage. For example, Mr. Strachey says: "The power of the British House of Commons is, since the latest curtailment of the House of Lords' power of delay to nine months, virtually absolute. But British liberties have in fact never been more real. . . . Every section of the British people has found a way of bringing to bear its influence on the making of the Government's decisions."[3] It is always assumed that no party with totalitarian ambitions will ever gain power in this country; at the moment nothing looks less likely but we cannot count on the indefinite continuance of common sense or apathy, whichever one likes to call it. The Labour party's own policy, even as soon as the next election, if it wins it, is bound to create an atmosphere of crisis. And it can plausibly be argued that if a really Socialist policy was carried out, it would be bound to lead to a much stronger Communist party, for with a Socialist party in office the embittered and aggrieved, finding no redress from their previous leaders, are only too likely to turn to the Communists. Or some other and new issue may rouse us to fanaticism. In considering these questions it is useful to ask oneself not how one would feel if one's own party were in control of such a state, but also how far one would trust the opposing party with it.

Even assuming that the British people have so assimilated the lessons of tolerance that they are immune to the perils that menace less fortunate people, the whole policy of equality is aimed at destroying the 'sections' alluded to by Mr. Strachey, and making the British people into one undifferentiated mass, organized indeed into trade unions; even these, however, would in the equalitarian state be brought under the control of the Government.

No one doubts that the present Labour party is genuinely concerned with liberty; indeed in 1947 they passed an Act extending the power of the subject to sue the Crown and its agents, but although it may be an exaggeration to say that power corrupts, it certainly changes. Two dangers exist: that of the self-righteousness which consumes left-wing parties and which ultimately derives from Marxist psychology, and that of administration becoming an end in itself. Real Socialists must reject in theory the right of an anti-Socialist party to exist. Most members of the Labour party are not of course real Socialists, but when every act or word of the other parties is assumed to be the effect not of intellectual miscalculation but of sinister and selfish motives, an argument to which Socialist parties are only too apt to resort, a dangerous atmosphere is built up. If any attempt to safeguard property or any other kind of right is immediately classed as capitalist self-interest, it is only a short step to all kinds of protest against Government action being regarded as merely another form of capitalist intrigue. The imputation of unconscious motives is very useful; however difficult it may be, on the face of it, to accuse a well-known Socialist or anarchist of wishing to preserve the capitalist system, it can always be said that he is unconsciously reacting against the Socialist state.

III

Even for those who are not Socialists, administration can become an end in itself, as anyone can see who reads the evidence before the Franks Committee on Administrative Tribunals. The Permanent Secretary to the Ministry of Housing, when asked why the Ministry did not publish the inspector's report, in cases of compulsory acquisition, kept on saying that it would embarrass the Minister. The Chairman said: "The first argument on which you rested the case for not publishing the inspector's report was administrative convenience." The Permanent Secretary agreed. The Chairman then said: "Now that, I am sure is there, but it is not a principle. It is simply that it is quicker to work that way, I think?" The Permanent Secretary: "And less embarrassing than for a recommendation to the Minister by one of his officers to be published." And in answer to another question she said: "I think it is the Minister's own feeling that his complete freedom of action in reaching a decision might be somewhat inhibited by the fact that a report and recommendations, which he might wholly disagree with, had to be published."[4]

o

There is, of course, something to be said for the Permanent Secretary's point of view; everyone has an overall interest in good administration. These cases, however, must be of more importance to the individuals concerned than to the Minister or his officials, and there is no doubt that in some cases people have felt aggrieved because they could not see the inspector's report and therefore did not know what case they had to answer.

Those who felt the rule of law to be a limitation on the actions of Governments used to refer to it as a 'Whig' idea, therefore implying that only Dukes benefit by it. Today, however, the powers of Government departments extend to the supervision of private schools, to refusing to allow a doctor to start practising in any given area, to calling up any man for National Service or to exempting him, to dispossessing any farmer, whether tenant or owner of his farm, on the grounds that he is farming badly, to refusing a licence to anyone who wants to run a 'bus or a lorry; and these are merely a few examples taken at random. The pursuit of equality would enormously increase the list. The heavier the burden of administration, the less consideration is likely to be given to the citizen. If Parliament has commanded a Civil Service already overburdened to undertake a great deal of additional work, can they be blamed if they are loath to adopt safeguards which may make their task even longer and more complicated?

It is hard to see how this sort of State could remain a democracy in anything but name. It would have so little in common with what we call democracy that people would probably lose interest in what remained. In a Socialist State all that anyone would care about would be efficient production, because of the immediate and disastrous effects of inefficiency. It is difficult to believe that they would let any antiquated ideas about liberty stand in the way. Nor, even if voluntary associations continued to exist and were really free, is the liberty to join an association adequate compensation for the loss of all other liberties. The relation between the individual and the governing body becomes, just as much as that between the national Government and the individual voter, one of direction and acquiescence. In the large association, no more than in the large town or in the whole country, can the individual member govern. If the associations are not large, they are powerless against the Government anyhow, because they do not represent the majority in the occupation or profession, or if they do the profession itself is too small to be taken into account.

IV

The main danger to democracy is an obsession with equality; but even if this is modified by other tendencies as it is in this country, the modern system carries with it certain weaknesses, among them the overloading of the Government machine by responsibilities which it was not designed to carry, and the position in which it places those citizens who fall outside the organized group. The effect of these operating together may produce policies which will finally lead to such economic deterioration as will threaten the existence of democracy itself.

Neither the Government of this country nor democratic government itself was devised to produce a machine which could operate an overall control of the economic system, administer universal social services or supervise great industrial monopolies. They are tasks which it is a platitude to say are beyond the powers of any legislative assembly. Their effect in weakening the control of the House of Commons over the executive is also a platitude; they have however other effects, not so widely realized, in making modern Governments less suited to their responsibilities than the Governments of other periods. The Parliamentary system produces men trained to take political decisions, to manage the House of Commons and to understand and guide public opinion. Many of the functions of modern government are not concerned with any of these, but demand knowledge sometimes of a highly technical kind, or at least the ability to decide between differing expert opinions, or great administrative experience, or all three. The House of Commons or any other democratic assembly gives no training in such qualities. Nor are the men who possess them necessarily those who are most successful in debate nor in that ill-defined but supremely important quality of being 'good in the House'.

Occasionally, of course, we get a political genius like Sir Winston Churchill who combines all these qualities, but it must be remembered that he was for many years an eminently unsuccessful politician.

The Government's overriding responsibility for the whole economy, the Government's ultimate responsibility for the nationalized industries, even the role of the trade unions in politics, call for qualities which a life spent in politics tends to smother rather than encourage. As the qualities demanded of a successful Minister have changed, so the power of the House to judge his performance has declined. It is immensely impressed by a good speech. In the days of Chatham and Gladstone this was indeed of overwhelming importance, not only because of the lack of party discipline, but also because a good speech displayed many of the qualities most necessary in a statesman. Today these are often irrelevant to the main tasks of government. The whole system tends to push men into posts for which their training and aptitude are inadequate, and to conceal from the House of Commons the qualities of a really capable Minister because he may not be able to read out answers to questions as if he had written them or may incline to a too academic manner. The success or failure of a speech is immediate, the success of administrative measures or even of political decisions may take months or even years to appear. Genius no doubt could overcome even these difficulties, but for any system to require genius to make it work is in itself a sign that it is unfitted to cope with its particular tasks. The inadequacy of the average politician to carry out functions which no one could successfully perform without some experience will either discredit one Government after another and finally the system of·government itself, or more and more will power fall into the hands of the trained administrator, the permanent heads of departments. No political system will last, at least in England, if it is not efficient. One of the authorities on constitutional history has said: "Most historians of British responsible government have attuned their story to the theme of liberty. It might with equal appropriateness be tuned to the theme of efficiency."[5]

It might seem as if the demands of efficiency, welfare and

democracy would all be met if more power did pass to permanent officials, and there have been Ministers who have regarded their function as being that of getting through Parliament measures which their departments advised or wanted. Civil Servants, however, suffer from their ignorance of politics and of political requirements, and where they have been forced by the defects of their Minister to take on much of his proper work, the result has not usually been successful. Even if this were not true, if the permanent officials could do the job better, such an arrangement would transform the system more or less completely. The troubles which delegated legislation have already produced would multiply a hundredfold, and Civil Servants are just as susceptible as Ministers to the other aspects of trying to do too much—the permanent overwork which it entails. Administration is now so heavy that no head of a department, whether he is the political or the permanent head, has time or energy left for the consideration of wider and less immediate problems.

In a period of tranquillity this might not be without its advantages; the adage "Satan finds some mischief still for idle hands to do" is probably as true of rulers as of other people. There is no need to point out that today the world has to deal with problems of unparalleled difficulty and of overwhelming importance, and that it is these that politicians should be trying to solve. Their experience, so hopelessly inadequate for most of the things they now try to do, would give them a background of knowledge which no one else has. It is easy enough for those who have never tried to deal with the Russians nor to negotiate a multi-racial constitution to be ready with facile solutions, but no situation can ever be accurately assessed from the outside. This is not only true of political situations; further knowledge of any subject or event always transforms one's first impressions to a greater or lesser degree.

It is always assumed that the more a government tries to do the more powerful it becomes. It is doubtful how far this is true except in totalitarian States. Not only must the selected government share its power with the permanent administrators, but groups organized to defend themselves may become so powerful as to trench on the government's authority. A great deal of nonsense is talked about these pressure groups, even the most intransigent of trade unions perform many valuable functions besides that of defending the interests of their members. They, no less than local authorities, provide an opportunity for the ordinary person to take some part in public life. It is true that the ordinary person does not at the moment seem anxious to seize these opportunities, but this may be temporary. There is a great deal at the moment to distract people from politics, even trade union politics, and not much to attract them. Even when the ordinary member fails to do his share, these organizations give their officers some training in administration and in negotation, and teach them that the world does not only consist of electrical engineers or teachers. Even Communists have to learn this from their colleagues if not from their opponents. What would a Labour Government be like without its trade union members? There is, of course, always the danger that the people most prepared to take the trouble of attending to the association's affairs are the most extreme, and this does not only apply to Communists in trade unions, but also seems to happen in the Farmers' Union, where the officials appear to make larger claims for agriculture than the average farmer.

But however admirable these institutions may be, they have their dangers; their influence may become too great and they may use it to interfere in matters, such for example as foreign policy, where their knowledge is likely to be least and their prejudice greatest. The most obvious danger at the moment is that those people who are not included in such organizations may feel that their interests are neglected. No form of representative government has prospered in which any important section felt itself to be excluded from all power or influence. There is no doubt that the professional middle class feel this today, as the industrial middle class did in 1832. Many of them think that they are submerged in the mass of working-class votes so that no Government, Conservative or Labour, is prepared to consider their interests, and that in the other aspect of modern government, the group organization, they are also helpless because industry and finance are so much more powerful. Their main complaint, it is hardly necessary to say, is against the trade unions; but they now tend to look with some dislike at the other side of industry, the employers or at least the large employers, or even at anyone fortunate enough to possess an expense account. These ideas are exaggerated; after all any lawyer, doctor, bank manager has individually far more opportunity of exerting influence or of putting forward his own ideas than the ordinary member of the most powerful trade union. It is true that inflation has hit them harder than anyone else, for if their income comes from a salary or from fees although these may have risen, they have risen less since 1945 than prices; if a part comes from investments, they have over the same period risen even less, and if they are living on pensions or interest on Government stock their plight is worse still. The other aspect of inflation, the chances which now exist for sons and the daughters, of middle-class parents, is often neglected. There is no longer, as there was between the wars, any 'public school' or 'gaduate' unemployment. They are not even in quite such a helpless electoral position as might be thought, for there are middle-class constituencies. There is, however, no doubt that their standards have been severely cut by high taxation and by rising prices and that under universal suffrage they are a minority and they are not in a strong position to bring pressure to bear as a group. In any case, these feelings exist, and anything which exists is a political fact. If it is necessary to take into account the mistaken ideas of factory workers about dividends because they are 'psychologically' important, so it is to consider the views of bank clerks, doctors, officers of the Army and Navy and accountants, even though they may attribute to politics what is really due to economic and industrial development. It would be a disaster if these people really decided that there was no place for them in the political structure of the country.

v

These problems, though serious, could clearly be solved without overwhelming difficulty. More menacing to the future of democracy is the gradual disintegration of the British Empire, which may, once it really comes home to people, cause a revulsion against democracy, especially among the young. The great disadvantage of democracy in foreign affairs is that it has no principle which can bind States together unless they are already firmly cemented by race or geography. Hereditary monarchy had this power; it solved the Anglo-Scottish problem, which must have seemed insoluble at the time and which universal suffrage, as Macaulay said, would have made eternal. The spread of democratic ideas has had a disintegrating effect on all empires or associations composed of people of different races because it offers no basis for a common loyalty and can give no answer to the demand for self-determination. It has already destroyed the Ottoman and Austrian Empires and is in process of dismembering the British Empire in Asia.

This seems to most people, whether they applaud or lament it, to be an affirmation of democratic principles, and whatever else it may damage, to offer no threat to democracy. The relations between events are, however, not so simple; if the world was as much of one mind as it was during some part of the nineteenth century, the ebbing of Great Britain's strength would be of little real consequence.

It is important to understand exactly what this loss of strength means; regarded from one point of view, Great Britain is stronger than she was between the wars, when it was obvious to everyone that she could not face Germany alone. Any power which has atomic weapons is stronger than any power that has not got them, and with them Great Britain could probably prevent Russia from attacking any member of the Commonwealth. The risks of such a course, however, are so obvious that a stalemate has, as we all know, been reached. The very fact that Great Britain is still a great power in this sense shows up the decline in other matters. For example, if Great Britain had still had the control of the old Indian army, her position during the Korean war would have been considerably stronger. A different point of view is of course widely held; it is often said that what Great Britain has lost in power she has gained in influence. This is far from evident at the moment; but after such changes a period of readjustment always follows and it is possible that after the tremors of the earthquake have subsided the world will come to recognize the wisdom and patience we have displayed, and the fundamental rightness of our ideas. Possible, but not likely. Ideas are valued according to their association with success or failure. Everyone must have known people who dislike equality, economic or otherwise, who are even opposed to state socialism and yet who feel there must be something in any system which produces anything so powerful as modern Russia. The reputation even of a national literature is enhanced if the country in which it was written can also manage to win a few battles.

This aspect of Great Britain's changed position is not yet realized because it is concealed by the American alliance. English and American ideas are fundamentally the same, liberty and democracy are the foundation of both; it is only in the application of those concepts that differences may arise, as they did in the crisis in the Middle East. If, however, a real conflict of opinion ever occurred, Englishmen would learn that it is not possible both to abdicate and to retain power. This has already been illustrated in Britain's relations with South Africa. Liberals of all creeds find it hard to understand that we cannot both grant a country independence and continue to interfere with its internal affairs. The same lesson may have to be learnt also in Asia.

It is to be hoped that these painful situations will not be multiplied because the victory of nationalism will also be the victory of liberty all over the globe. But it is useless to shut one's eyes to different possibilities and dangerous not to mention them until they happen. Dangerous because it means that the victory of hateful ideas can be seen as the outcome of democracy. If they are, the risk of a violently anti-democratic nationalist reaction is increased. The mood of the country is so completely unlike this at the moment that there may appear to be no such possibility. The anti-American feeling that exists among certain sections shows, however, that the germ of such a feeling exists. The people who originally showed most resentment at the power of the United States were the people who were most anxious to make India and Burma into independent States. When an empire is dissolved it is often forgotten that the change will have repercussions all over the world; it seems always to come as a surprise that when one power is weakened others are strengthened. It is not easy for a country to fall from first to third or fourth place, because its citizens have been used to finding pride and satisfaction in their country's greatness which not all of them could discover in their own lives. The prevailing stress on the group and the community will tend to make a suddenly realized weakness all the more painful. The leaders of public opinion, writers, Members of Parliament, and advanced thinkers in general, do not understand how serious this might become, because when they say that Great Britain is no longer a great power there is still the delicious thrill of shocking respectable opinion. Simpler people, in all classes, do not have these intellectual compensations.

Democracy is on trial in Asia and Africa, and, illogical as it may seem, its success or failure will influence English sentiment about it also. If democracy does not survive, or survives in some degraded or repellent form, opinion in England will certainly move away from democracy. If it seems to have thrown away strength won by the efforts of other centuries, and yet to have gained nothing for itself, there can hardly fail to be a loss of faith in it. One of the main foundations of modern conceptions of democracy was its supposed universality and if it was irrefutably proved that it could not live in all climates, the effect on public opinion would be incalculable.

The disintegrating effect of democratic ideas continues even when the links with Great Britain are broken. In the Gold Coast, for instance, the Ashanti are claiming a substantial degree of self-government on the same grounds as those on which Mr. Nkrumah originally demanded independence. Within the Ashanti country itself another tribe appears to be demanding its own democratic rights. On purely moral or political grounds it is hard to reject these claims or to refuse the similar demands of the Shan tribes in Burma, or of the Nagas in India. The only case that can be made against them is practical or economic, but sentiment and the selfish interests of individual leaders both tend towards the fragmentation of states.

The substitution of small, weak national states for a powerful empire would, in a period of tranquillity, quite likely produce in the end, if not greater happiness, at least a more variegated and interesting world. The policy of the Soviet Union, however, means that independence may be for a few years only and those few years may be bought at a terrible price. India and Pakistan are less able to repel Russian or Chinese aggression than was British India, and independence has left Burma almost defenceless. These powers may be prevailed on by the fear of a general war or by other motives to leave India and Burma alone, but suppose they treat Asiatic nations as they have treated European, and the end of the story is merely the exchange of British paternalism for an alien and inhuman tyranny? Democracy would then lose much of its appeal in other countries, not least in Great Britain.

It is not only in Commonwealth matters that the record of democracy is vulnerable, in foreign policy also it is open to criticism. It is unfortunate that the introduction of universal suffrage coincided with the opening of a period of unparalleled difficulty in international affairs. It may well be that no form of government could have saved Great Britain from the disasters of the twentieth century. But even in theory the argument for democracy is less strong in foreign policy than in any other aspect of government. The fundamental argument for the people's control of their own affairs is summarized in the phrase 'only the wearer knows where the shoe pinches', and in addition in domestic matters universal suffrage may bring to light many things which Governments might wish to ignore and would manage to ignore under any other system. In foreign affairs, however, the ordinary voter can bring nothing to the problem, he has to rely on others for information and there is no certainty that the information provided will be either adequate or accurate. It is now plain that if action had been taken against Hitler when he marched into the Rhineland the Second World War might have been avoided; it is also plain that under universal suffrage it was difficult to take it. It might be thought that Great Britain's difficulties were caused not by any of the complications of democratic government but by the shifting of economic and military power to other countries. That this is not completely true is shown by American experience. Mr. Walter Lippman, certainly no anti-democrat, has analysed the obstacles which democracy in the United States produces to a firm and consistent foreign policy.[6]

VI

This list of the possible dangers to English democracy contains items so diverse that it may seem as if they were merely a random choice from modern developments in general, and it will certainly seem as if each of them would require a separate diagnosis and a separate remedy. In reality one policy would serve to ameliorate them all and this the simple one of admitting that Governments are not omnipotent, that in real life as apart from constitutional theories, checks if not balances exist, if not in the Constitution, then in the organization of groups and interests that have grown up to supplement it. A revolution could no doubt sweep all these away and deliver everyone to the dictatorship of the proletariat, the middle class or, more likely in England, to the rule of 'sensible men of all parties'. But unless we have a revolution, it looks as if the organized interests will continue to act as a check on the authority of the state.

It might, therefore, be a better plan to end the fiction of an omnipotent Government, and in some way incorporate the differing interests in the Constitution, rather than leave them to organize themselves outside it. This would, to some extent at least, mitigate all the dangers. It would make the pursuit of equality more difficult by insisting on it being more gradual. It would go some way to persuade those who fall outside the organized groups that the State still has a place for them. And it would, by giving an example of moderation in practice, lessen the chances that democracy in Asia and Africa will run into insuperable difficulties.

The answer always made to this sort of suggestion is that the real guardians of moderation are not institutions or rules, but the traditions of the country. This is, however, not an answer which applies outside this country. We are teaching people that the majority are omnipotent in countries in which no traditions of tolerance and fair play exist. The other immediate objection to a more balanced Constitution is that it would work entirely to the advantage of the Conservatives, of vested interests, and of property in general. This is perfectly true. But it is not really unfair, whatever it may appear at first sight. It is reasonable to expect revolutionary proposals to undergo a longer probation than those that merely carry on and support the existing state of affairs. If the existing state involved widespread suffering it would be different; Socialists might then have argued that speed was necessary, but even on their own premises there is now no such hurry. If they are right in their view and want those views to prevail, and not merely to exercise power, what does it matter if their programme is slowed up by five years?

Some people will object here and talk about the importance of 'timing' in politics, and point out that if the favourable moment is missed the cause may be put back for years. The political metaphors always employed in such discussion show that this whole complex of ideas is fundamentally undemocratic. It treats the electorate as a flock of sheep which can be driven wherever the shepherds wish if only they know how to handle their dogs. It is Machiavelli edited for the party boss and the party agent, and displays all the Machiavellian contempt for the ordinary person. If Socialism comes in England it will come, as universal suffrage came, with the consent of all parties. *Coups d'état*, even carried through by means of the ballot-box, are dangerous things, and in a civilized country it is not possible to make fundamental changes simply because the officials of one party are better electoral tacticians than the officials of the other.

There are three possible ways of reintroducing a balanced Constitution, there may be others not yet discerned, but the obvious methods are a recognition of fundamental rights which could not be infringed by any Government however large its majority, some system of proportional representation, or a second Chamber with substantial powers.

The first of these alternatives, fundamental rights, would be the best choice if only it was open to us. Surely there is something in Judge Jackson's statement to which everyone would respond. "One's right to life, liberty and prosperity, free speech, a free press, freedom of worship and assembly, and other fundamental rights may not be submitted to the vote, they depend on the outcome of no elections." Unfortunately, however, this way is closed. It is a pity that the eighteenth-century idea that Englishmen had fundamental rights under the old Constitution did not persist into the new age; but its introduction today does not seem to be possible. The only thing that the omnipotent Parliament cannot do is to curtail its own omnipotence. The modern world is unfavourable to permanent solutions; in it no institution can be considered permanent, no form of government as more than temporary. Fundamental rights requires a state of affairs in which people think their political arrangements to be eternal, and it also probably requires some background of belief in natural rights, which no longer exists and would be hard to re-establish.

To most people the introduction of some form of proportional representation will no doubt seem the most possible method because, without outraging democratic convictions, it would allow minorities more representation. Surely under it those who now feel they are disregarded would be able to organize themselves to secure special representation in the House of Commons?

Proportional representation, however, although it might have this merit, if it is a merit, might also have the contrary effect of giving to a few Members, for whom a minority of the electorate happened to have voted, the power of defeating or keeping in office any Government they pleased. There are even more fundamental objections to it than this. It tends not to restrain the power of the state and to keep Governments to their proper functions, but to weaken their performance of these functions themselves. If it allowed the representation of people who now feel that neither of the two parties either fulfils their ideals or looks after their interest, then its natural results must be coalition Governments. Some of the advocates of proportional representation deny that it encourages a multitude of parties, but even these agree that it would tend to establish three instead of two parties in England, indeed this is why they want it. This would have no effect on the relations between the State and the individual or between central and local government or between the various kinds of organized group. But it would make policy on foreign or colonial affairs less firm, thus making Governments weak just where they need to be strong. It would do nothing to reduce the activities of the state, it would merely mean that the decisions would have to be made at the administrative rather than the political level, by Civil Servants rather than by Ministers.

Nor would its effects on the electorate be any happier. The present system with its two giant parties does, most fortunately, mean that most of those voters must have some regard for considerations other than their own immediate advantage, and that no one agrees a hundred per cent. with the party programme. A system in which any group which was seriously dissatisfied could elect a few members pledged to ventilate their grievances and to that alone, would increase and acerbate every division which now exists.

The difficulty, often noticed, that it is only possible to vote for the candidates who stand and that they are put forward by two parties, so that the unfortunate voter who thinks that a capital gains tax should be introduced and comprehensive schools should be prohibited can be truly represented by neither. This may be unfortunate but it does force the voter to consider other items in the party programme. This is particularly important when he is considering his own immediate interests, because he will find he has to take those of others into account as well. Do we really miss much because the electoral system does not allow us an independent co-operative party?

We are thus left with the possibility which to most people seems the most impractical of all, a second Chamber with substantial powers of delay. The argument against this institution which always seems unanswerable is that either it would be in agreement with the majority in the country, when it would be unnecessary, or it would be in disagreement, when it would be swept aside. This argument, besides taking too simple a view of the democratic process, was developed when it was really believed that a majority in the House of Commons could do anything it liked, and at the same time no one thought that any majority would wish to do anything very much.

Of course the idea that Governments would not do anything really revolutionary was not a conscious one. Conservative opinion was outraged by Asquith's Irish Home Rule Bill and by Lloyd George's Budget, but no one conceived of the vast designs which drive modern Governments mad. Even in this comparative tranquillity it was found impossible to force Ulster under the new Irish Government. And if anyone supposes today that any Government, whatever the constitutional theory may be, could denationalize the mines or make Christianity illegal, he must be completely devoid of any sense of reality. It may be argued that, if this is true, there is no need for any further check on the Government's powers, especially when it is remembered that Governments in England are after all elected. As Sir Ivor Jennings says:

> Democracy rests not on any particular form of executive government, nor upon the limitations of the powers of the legislature, nor upon anything implicit in the character of its penal laws, but in the fact that political power rests in the last analysis on free elections, carried on in a state where criticism of the Government is not only permissible but a positive merit, and to have parties based on competing policies and interests are not only allowed but encouraged. When this is so, government must necessarily be carried on in such a manner as to secure the willing and active consent and co-operation of the people; for a Government that fails to persuade public opinion will be overthrown at the next election.[7]

Even the most convinced believer in our present arrangements will agree that this is somewhat naïve. It is true that a Government which has lost its hold on public opinion will fail to be re-elected, but not everything it has done can be undone; having made the omelette you cannot reassemble the eggs. Nor, considering the part which the timing of measures and the presentation of arguments plays in politics, can it be certain that the electorate knew what it was voting for. If a large and permanent majority of the country really want an authoritarian, equalitarian State, modified only by periodical elections, it would be futile to oppose them, but there are powerful arguments for allowing them another chance of deciding when they may be more conscious of the consequences of their choice. Is there any reason why if the House of Lords throws out any piece of legislation it should not be necessary to have an election before it again appears in the House of Commons? Under one-Chamber government serious and irreparable damage could be done to the country, and great injustice to minorities with only a half-conscious acquiescence on the part of the electorate. It is true that there are some things which no Government could do; but they could not do them because they are things which would harm the interests or outrage the sentiments of those who can bring pressure other than political to bear on the Government, as the coal miners would if any proposals for denationalization were made. There are, however, people, and this is the real complaint of some sections of the middle class, who cannot get their views attended to because they are in a minority among the electorate and have no means of taking effective counter measures. It is difficult to argue that a minority is entitled to veto the wishes of a majority for ever, but it is reasonable for the minority to ask for two debates rather than one on their own extinction.

The present House of Lords would be by no means unsuitable to exercise such powers; they contain, as we are constantly reminded, men of great intellectual distinction and wide experience, and some of the less distinguished members belong in reality to that professional middle class now so disillusioned. No one, however, could be expected to believe this and any increase in their powers would undoubtedly involve some reform in the composition of the Upper House.

The composition of a second Chamber ought to depend on what purpose it is designed to serve. It is often supposed that the only purpose a reformed and strengthened House of Lords could fulfil would be that of delay, of giving the country another opportunity for reflection. This is important, but even more important it would give the Constitution an element of stability, which today it sadly needs. We live in fearful times and may at any moment walk into a minefield. No one can say with certainty that any constitutional change can save us from this; but we risk the continual danger of waves of emotion sweeping over the country, and carrying away journalists, editors and Members of Parliament with it, to leave them stranded on some quite unexpected shore. If this emotion is roused by domestic matters, action taken under its influence may do great damage, may ruin individuals and even whole classes. From financial and economic ruin, however, a country can recover, the real danger comes in

P

foreign policy. Members of the House of Commons are even more vulnerable to these waves than others because they have been trained for years to regard 'public opinion' as omniscient, and in politics it is. From an objective standard the electorate may be wrong, but no such standard exists. The people are sovereign and if they reject a party or a policy there is no appeal. And yet in matters outside their own experience the individuals who make up the sovereign people must depend on others for information and even for judgments. The journalist and the broadcaster are, however, no more likely to be right than is unguided opinion. A second Chamber, which was accepted by public opinion, could give invaluable help to the people in making up their minds. The Peers are to some extent isolated from transient changes in opinion; this, which is one of the complaints against them, is in modern conditions, one of their main assets. No second Chamber, we are constantly told, could withstand for long the wishes of the people. But it could withstand momentary gusts of enthusiasm. It could give advice to which people would listen. It could present the permanent rather than the momentary views of Great Britain to the world.

If a second Chamber used powers to delay legislation, it would almost certainly be using them against a progressive rather than a Conservative party, although politics since 1945 have held many surprises and we might get a surprise here too. But in its use of its function of steadying public opinion, there is no reason why it should favour one party rather than another. Conservatives are human beings and therefore no less liable than Socialists to political passions and wrong judgments.

If the House of Lords is to be this element of stability, of balance, then it is clear there must be no popular election of its Members, indeed as little election at all as possible. No one is likely to suggest that Members of the Upper House should be elected either directly or through an electoral college, as some second Chambers are; but it might be proposed they should be representative of the political parties. Proposals for reform are either concerned with making the House of Lords more representative of the large divisions of opinion in the country, of making it indeed a replica of the House of Commons, or of ensuring that all good and great men are nominated to it. Increasing the number of Labour peers would merely be to strengthen those elements in the country which already have most power, both through their voting strength and through the trade unions. No particular proposals have any special validity. The essential is to get away from the clichés and platitudes that have been the basis of political discussion since 1918. Pure democracy was a noble ideal, but it was not an ideal that really suited the British people, as is shown by their return to the older idea of the representation of interests rather than persons. That this return was not consciously planned but was largely an adaptation of Socialist theory to British experience only demonstrates what a powerful hold the idea of a balance between classes and interests has in this country.

A second Chamber would never work in the prevailing state of public opinion, but would it really be impossible to persuade people that it would have its advantages? Everyone, including the industrial workers, who would probably dislike it at first, is accustomed to the balance of power outside Parliament. The most arrogant or independent employer has to negotiate with trade unions, the most Communist shop steward can hardly fail to notice that his employer has certain rights. Public opinion in all classes is persuaded of the necessity of a balance of interests in ordinary life. Why is it impossible to translate these ideas into political terms?

When the democratic idea captured Europe it was believed that the new political system could save mankind, when the Socialist ideal caught the imagination of generous and enlightened spirits it was thought that Governments could do vast good and little harm. Today we know that the evils Governments can produce are without limit and that their powers for good are strictly circumscribed. In a few years they can destroy the civilization accumulated through centuries of effort, they can deprive their subjects of everything which makes them men. Against this background constitutional changes may seem trivial, but the mere fact that one country consciously and deliberately limited the power of temporary majorities would do something to remind the world that Governments need not be omnipotent.

REFERENCES

INTRODUCTION

1. "Utilitarianism is destroyed and no part of it left standing."
   J. Plamenatz, *The English Utilitarians* (1949).
2. See Popper, 'Indeterminism in Quantum Physics and in Classical
   Physics', *British Journal for the Philosophy of Science* (August and
   November, 1950).
3. Letter to Max Born quoted in 'Natural Philosophy of Cause and
   Chance', Waynflete Lectures (1948).

CHAPTER I

All quotations from speeches in this and other chapters are, from the
beginning of the nineteenth century, from *Hansard*, unless otherwise
stated.

1. *The Life of Napoleon.*
2. *Commentaries on the Laws of England* (1765).
3. Ibid.
4. Sir Lewis Namier, *England in the Age of the American Revolution*
   (1937).
   Richard Pares, *George III and the Politicians* (1953).
   D. L. Keir, *The Constitutional History of England* (1946), chapter 6.
   Reference to other modern authorities and to original sources
   will be found in all these works.
   There are also the contemporary Memoirs, among them Horace
   Walpole, Memoirs of the Reigns of George I, George II and
   George III; Memoirs of Rockingham; Memoirs of Hervey and
   many others.
5. *History of English Law*, Vol. X. (1937).
6. A. V. Dicey, 'The Balance of Classes' in *Essays on Reform* (1867).
7. "A land, perhaps the only one in the universe, in which political
   and civil liberty is the very aim and scope of the constitution."
   Blackstone, *Commentaries on the Laws of England* (1765).
8. Speech quoted in Brougham's *Statesmen in the Reign of George III*
   without any date. It will no doubt occur to many people in reading
   these quotations that as the debates were not allowed to be printed
   we have no guarantee of their authenticity. From the point of

view of the present book this does not much matter. Speeches, however, were sometimes published as pamphlets and the general sense of what the more famous speakers said was probably known. The more glittering bits were also probably preserved in something like their original form. The latter speeches of Chatham are considered to be fairly authentic. For details see appendix in Basil Williams' *Life of Chatham* (1913).

9. Edward Porritt, *The Unreformed House of Commons* (1906).

10. T. H. Oldfield, *The Representative History of Great Britain and Ireland* (1816). Oldfield was a solicitor largely engaged in election business; he was, however, a keen Parliamentary reformer and wrote his book in this cause. His bias must therefore be kept in mind.

11. *Observations on Civil Liberty, the Principles of Government and the Policy of the War with America* (1776).

12. S. Heywood, *A Digest of the Laws Respecting County Elections* (1816).

13. Ibid.

14. *The Wealth of Nations.*

15. Walter Bagehot, 'Lord Althorp and the Reform Act of 1832', in *Biographical Studies* (1899).

16. Thomas Day, Speech at the general meeting of the freeholders of the county of Cambridge, March 20th, 1782. Published as a pamphlet by the Society for Constitutional Information.

17. *The Citizen of the World* (1762).

18. Blackstone, *Commentaries.*

19. Compare however Dicey. "In England the so-called principles of the constitution are deductions and generalizations based upon particular discussions pronounced by the courts as to the rights of given individuals." *The Law of the Constitution.*

20. A. Aspinall, *Politics and the Press, 1780-1850* (1949). "During the Napoleonic Wars there was no attempt to censor the Press, the newspapers published unhindered details of the movements of troops, which were said to have been useful to the French."

21. *A Dialogue between a Gentleman and a Farmer* (1782).

22. *State Trials* (1814), Vol. 21

23. *Commentaries.*

24. Thomas Gisborne, *An Enquiry into the Duties of Men in the Higher and Middle Classes of Society in Great Britain* (7th Edition, 1824).

25. *Principles of Moral and Political Philosophy* (1785).

26. J. D. Chambers, *Eighteenth Century Nottingham* (1932).

27. The Political Papers of the Rev. Christopher Wyvil (1795-1806).

28. *Covent Garden Journal*, No. 49. June 20th, 1752.

29. William Ward, 'Letters to Ivy', quoted in Halevy's *History of the English People*, Vol. I.

30. Martin Dunsford, *Historical Memorials of the Town and Parish of Tiverton* (1790).
31. J. D. Chambers, ibid.
32. *Works*, Vol. III.
33. 'The Repeal of the Corn Laws and the Politics of the Forties', in *Economic History Review*, 2nd series, Vol. II.
34. E. Forrester, *Northamptonshire Elections and Electioneering* (1940).
35. *Complete collection of all the Papers which have appeared from the different Parties in the Present Contest for Members for the County of Northumberland* (1774).
36. Memoir of Lord Wharton (1715).
37. William Cowper, Letter to the Reverend John Cowper. March 29th, 1784.
38. Richard Ferguson, *Cumberland and Westmorland M.P.s'*, *from The Restoration to the Reform Bill of 1867* (1871).
39. Edmund Fitzmaurice, *Life of William Fitzmaurice, Earl of Shelburne* (1875).
40. R. H. Webb, *The English Working Class Reader* (1956).
41. Quoted in *History of Local Government*, Sydney and Beatrice Webb.
42. "The century of steady civic and municipal growth which followed the Reform Bill was made possible by the revolutionary events of the century preceding it."
Sir George Newman, 'The Health of the People', in *A Century of Municipal Progress* (Edited by Harold Laski, Ivor Jennings, William Robson).
43. D. L. Keir, *The Constitutional History of Great Britain* (3rd Edition, 1946).
44. *Reflections on the French Revolution.*
45. *The English Utilitarians.*
46. John Selby Watson, *Life of Richard Porson* (1861).
47. *Dictionary of National Biography.*
48. Graham Wallas, *Life of Francis Place* (Revised edition, 1918).
49. Boswell's *Johnson.*
50. *Travels in France.*
51. J. Towill Rutt, *Life of Joseph Priestley* (1832).

CHAPTER II

1. *Essay on the Right of Property in Land* (1782).
2. Joseph Addison, Hymn 662. Hymn A. &. M.
3. Speech to the freeholders of the County of Cambridge, March 25th, 1782.
4. *Ode to Liberty.*

5. Speech.
6. Letters of Horace Walpole.
7. Letters of Lord Chesterfield.
8. Lord John Russell, *Essay on the History of the English Government and Constitution* (1823).
9. *Treatise on Government* (1690).
10. *Correspondence of Horace Walpole and William Mason* (Edited by J. Mitford, 1851).
11. Blackstone, ibid.
12. Martin Dunsford, *Historical Memorials of the Town and Parish of Tiverton* (1790).
13. Chatham Correspondence, edited W. S. Taylor and J. H. Pringle (1838).
14. *Annual Register* (1771).
15. This declaration and many others were published as pamphlets.
16. A letter from the Right Hon. Lord Carysfort to the Huntingdonshire Committee (1780).
17. *Political Papers of the Rev. Christopher Wyvil* (1795–1806).
18. "Whoever is not a Lord of Parliament or of the Lord's House is of the House of Commons either in person or by representation." Sir Edward Coke.
19. F. D. Cartwright, *Life of Major Cartwright* (1826).
20. Wyvil Papers.
21. ibid.
22. *State Trials* (1818), Vol XXIV.
23. *Memoirs. of the life of Sir Samuel Romily written by himself* (1840).
24. *Considerations addressed to the Ruling Classes of Europe.*
25. Quoted in Graham Wallas, *Life of Francis Place.*
26. A great deal of information about the early democratic movement can be found in Butterfield's *George III, Lord North and the People* (1949).
27. S. Tomline, *Memoirs of the Life of the Right Hon. William Pitt*, 2nd edition 1821.

CHAPTER III

1. J. H. Clapham, *An Economic History of Modern Britain* (1930). W. H. Hutt, 'The Factory System in Early Nineteenth Century England'. *Economicon* (March 1926).
2. Thomas Paine, *Letter to the People of England* (1804). Perhaps it is as well to point out here that Paine was a quisling in the Napoleonic Wars and that this pamphlet was issued from Paris as part of Napoleon's propaganda.

3. T. S. Ashton, 'The Standard of Living of Workers in England, 1790-1830', in *Capitalism and the Historians*.
T. S. Ashton, 'The treatment of Capitalism by Historians', in *Capitalism and the Historians*. Edited by F. A. Hayek (The University of Chicago Press, 1954).
T. S. Ashton, *The Industrial Revolution*.
4. Clapham, *An Economic History of Modern Britain*.
5. Ibid.
6. W. R. Brock, 'Lord Liverpool and Liberal Toryism' (1941).
7. A. Aspinall, *Three Early Nineteenth Century Diaries*.
8. 'Lord Althorp and the Reform Bill of 1832', in *Biographical Studies*.

CHAPTER IV

1. Alexander Mackay, *Electoral Districts* (1848).
2. Norman Gash, *Politics in the Age of Peel* (1953).
3. *Essays on Parliamentary Reform* (1850).
4. See Enoch Powell, 'The House of Lords', in *The Listener* (September 8th, 15th and 23rd, 1955).
Mr. Powell has also kindly allowed me to see the MS. of his History of the House of Lords, which he had to lay aside when he joined the Government.
5. *The Quarterly Review*, Vol. LIII.
6. *The Examiner*, July 1st, 1833.
7. Nassau Senior, *Remarks on the opposition to the Poor Law Act* (1841).
8. Archibald Prentice, *History of the Corn Law League* (1853).
9. Nassau Senior, ibid.
10. G. L. Hilton-Clarke, *Peel and the Conservative Party* (1929).
11. J. F. Harrison, *History of the Working-men's College* (1956).
12. George Saintsbury, *Life of Lord Derby* (1892).

CHAPTER V

1. Gash, *Politics in the Age of Peel* (1953).
2. 'Gladstone, the Whips and the General Election, 1868.
3. F. A. Thompson, *English History Review* (1948).
4. See Edward Hughes, *Studies in Finance and Administration* (1938).
E. Cohen, *The Growth of the British Civil Service* (1941).
5. *The Public Career of Sir James Graham*, A. Erickson (1952).

6. Report on the organization of the Permanent Civil Service (1854).
7. Ibid.
8. Although Sir James Stephens, once permanent head of the Colonial Office, attributed it to the system of nomination. "Papers relating to the organization of the Civil Service" (1855).
9. *Quarterly Review* (1864).
10. *Unemployment. A Problem of Industry* (1906).
11. *An Economic History of Modern England* (1930).
12. *The Radical Programme*. With a preface by the Right Honourable Joseph Chamberlain (1885).
13. *Return from Utopia* (1951)
14. *In Place of Fear* (1952).
15. Rostow. *The British Economy in the Ninteenth Century* (1948).
16. *The Clever Woman of the Family* (1886).
17. *Cambridge Modern History*, Vol. XII, chapter 23.
18. Arthur Balfour, *Chapters of Autobiography* (1930).
19. Garvin, *Life of Joseph Chamberlain* (1932).
20. Bernard Holland, *Life of Devonshire* (1911).

CHAPTER VI

1. Quoted in Henry Pelling, *Origins of the Labour Party* (1954).
2. "In the neighbourhood of Oldham, there are weavers, common hand weavers, who throw the shuttle with unceasing sound, though Newton's *Principia* lies open on the loom." Mrs. Gaskell, *Mary Barton*.
3. Ernest Hutten, Review of several books on psychoanalysis in 'The British Journal for the Philosophy of Science' (May, 1956).
4. *The Principles of Political Economy* (1848).
5. Sir William Graham-Harrison, Memorandum submitted to the Committee on Ministers' Powers, 1932. Quoted in S.H.L. le May, *Select Documents: British Government, 1914-1953* (1955).
6. Le May, ibid.
7. Colonel Ashley. *Hansard*, February 18th, 1930.
8. Herbert Morrison, *Government and Parliament* (1954).
9. D. N. Chester, *Central and Local Government* (1951).
10. Letter in the *New Statesman and Nation* (Oct. 29th, 1955).
11. F. A. Hayek. *The Rule of Law*.
12. Paley, *Principles of Moral and Political Philosophy*.
13. Minutes of evidence before the Committee on Administration Tribunals and Inquiries (1956).
14. William Robson, *Justice and Administrative Law* (1951).

CHAPTER VII

1. T. D. Weldon, *The Vocabulary of Politics*, Penguin Books (1952).
2. "Foundations of Academic Freedom" in *The Logic of Liberty* (1951).
3. *Contemporary Capitalism* (1956).
4. Minutes of Evidence before the Franks Committee on Administrative Tribunals and Enquiries (1956).
5. Sir Keith Hancock, *British War Economy* (1949).
6. *The Public Philosophy* (1955).
7. *The Law and the Constitution* (1938).

INDEX